THE ALTITUDES OF ACCEPTANCE

FROM MY *Lifescape* TO YOURS

DEANNA KULBETH

The Altitudes of Acceptance © Copyright <<2025>> Deanna Kulbeth

All rights reserved. No part of this publication may be reproduced, distributed or transmitted in any form or by any means, including photocopying, recording, or other electronic or mechanical methods, without the prior written permission of the publisher, except in the case of brief quotations embodied in critical reviews and certain other noncommercial uses permitted by copyright law.

Although the author and publisher have made every effort to ensure that the information in this book was correct at press time, the author and publisher do not assume and hereby disclaim any liability to any party for any loss, damage, or disruption caused by errors or omissions, whether such errors or omissions result from negligence, accident, or any other cause.

Adherence to all applicable laws and regulations, including international, federal, state, and local governing professional licensing, business practices, advertising, and all other aspects of doing business in the US, Canada, or any other jurisdiction, is the sole responsibility of the reader and consumer.

Neither the author nor the publisher assumes any responsibility or liability whatsoever on behalf of the consumer or reader of this material. Any perceived slight of any individual or organization is purely unintentional.

The resources in this book are provided for informational purposes only and should not be used to replace the specialized training and professional judgment of a health care or mental health care professional.

Neither the author nor the publisher can be held responsible for the use of the information provided within this book. Please always consult a trained professional before making any decision regarding treatment of yourself or others.

For more information, email **altitudesofacceptance@gmail.com**

ISBN: 979-8-89694-549-9 - Ebook
ISBN: 979-8-89694-550-5 - Paperback

This book is dedicated to every teacher, student, family member, and friend whose individual realities and experiences have added color to my lifescape, and to all those who have guided me in my pursuit of life's adventure and understandings of who God is and who he wants me to become.

DISCLAIMER

Each story in this book was inspired by real events and experiences. To protect the people and places who are represented in my stories, I've changed individual names and have used the names of real locations sparingly.

Although my stories are true to the best of my recollection, the reader must remember that they were written from the perspective of a personal narrative. Since many of you may see yourselves in these pages, please know I have done my best to portray all major events and interactions as accurately as possible. However, I cannot guarantee complete accuracy, given the limits of my own memories and understanding.

TABLE OF CONTENTS

Chapter 1: Life's Adventure of Change	9
Chapter 2: Best Laid Plans	42
Chapter 3: The Purpose of Pain	66
Chapter 4: Building Connections	79
Chapter 5: Awesome Adventures	101
Chapter 6: "Training" Ground	116
Chapter 7: The Adventure of Laughter	155
Chapter 8: The Magic of Dance and Good Health	193
Chapter 9: God's Adventure is Us	227
Chapter 10: The Adventure of Perspective and Reality	249
Chapter 11: Trust the Path	273
Chapter 12: Loving Who You Are Now	301
Chapter 13: The Adventure of People	327
Chapter 14: Take the Ride	358
Acknowledgements	384
Citations	390

Chapter 1

Life's Adventure of Change

Home was not home anymore. It hit me hard as I stood there watching my mother start to pack the cups, plates, and cookie sheets in the kitchen. Normally I would have reached out to see if I could help—always proud of being Mommy's little helper: a kid who could handle anything! But not today. Today I felt—small, powerless, and only eight years old.

I could feel my mother's eyes follow me as I turned around and dragged my feet to my bedroom where a different box waited for me to pack my favorite belongings. I felt as jumbled as my pile of stuff, with my heart as empty as the box itself. A few days ago, my parents announced that we were moving to Colorado to follow my dad's new job. Since then, tears seemed to stain my cheeks—all the time.

They said we would leave Oklahoma, the only home I had ever known. I had to leave behind my friends, my school, our tree forts, and all the rest of my favorite places. Every time I thought about it, my head seemed stuck in agony. How could I possibly enjoy adventures without our big backyard, the fields and forests, or our gardens—where a little imagination made magical things happen?

Normal, cheerful, resourceful little me had disappeared.

Apparently, change was not good for me. Or was it? ...

As I sat in the gloom of my dark, disheveled room, Mom walked in and turned on the light. I looked up and noticed a book in her hands. Tilting my head sideways, I read the title, "Mm-you-ur … *of the Mountains*…?"

"I picked this book out for you from your Dad's library, Deanna. It's about a man named Muir who loved nature and went to Colorado."

Nature? Me too!

But I raised my eyebrows and narrowed my eyes at the word, "Colorado." I had heard about that place. It was about to swallow me whole and leave nothing behind.

However, Mom knew about my love of books since age three, so I imagine my response of inviting her to sit with me and read was of no surprise.

As I listened to her voice detailing Muir's observations about nature, I stared at the colorful pictures of the mountains on the cover. The soft purple and evergreen colors against a deep blue sky brought a flash of memory from when I first felt what it was like to be surrounded by and in awe of mountains. My family drove through the Grand Tetons when I was very young on our way to Idaho. As I looked out the window, completely mesmerized, the feeling of wonder shifted into pure reverence. In that moment, I became convinced that no matter how big a mountain was, it was the one place I would probably never feel small or alone. After all, if I took enough steps, I would eventually reach the top, taller than everything else around me.

Looking back, this moment could have been the first instance I sensed a closeness to God in the mountains. I may have been too young to recognize that feeling for what it was, but now I was older, and *that* moment helped me find a new way to think about *this* moment.

I took a deep breath as I realized two things. One, it wasn't that I didn't want the adventure, but my future seemed to be spiraling out of control into the dark unknown. Two, I had felt drawn to the mountains for a long time, and now, a place that had mountains was going to be my new home. I looked a little more closely at the book's cover and as I kept my attention on the story, the mountains on the cover beckoned me with various hues of hope.

THE ALTITUDES OF ACCEPTANCE

After Mom finished reading, she said, "In Colorado, you will be in the mountains. I think you will grow to love and experience them the way John Muir did."

She reached down for a hug as I beamed up at her, a sign that I agreed.

We chatted for a minute as she helped me pull my clothes out of the closet; then she left me on my own to think and pack.

How did Mom do that?

She knew things about me before I knew them. She knew I needed something to look forward to. She knew if I could be convinced that our new home would contribute to my happiness, I would be able to handle it better.

Even though I was still eight years old, with her parental wisdom, I no longer felt helpless. I felt peaceful knowing Mom had a way of finding the right tools to set me straight, even when my world was in turmoil because of change.

Somehow, in that instance, my emotions transformed into energy. I bounced into the box to flatten down the flaps, then jumped back out to pack my books on the bottom. It was like a game to see how much I could fit into one box. On top of the books went my stuffed animals, crafts, and trinkets; then, I snatched a suitcase for clothing and shoes from the storage shelves in my room.

Those shelves were covered simply by a yellow curtain, and when I moved it aside, out from behind it walked my marmalade orange-and-white cat, Tommy. He sat down, watching me as I finished packing. Then he started mewing for lunch, so I followed him to the kitchen and fed him, stroking his back and thinking while he purred. Then, I realized Tommy needed a travel bag too.

Hmm …

I found a gallon Ziploc and poured A LOT of cat food into it before placing it in a grocery bag with a little plastic bowl. Then I found an old towel to make the perfect little sleeping pad inside his cage and put everything near my box in the living room.

Anything else?

I couldn't think of anything else to do, so I found my brothers and sister who seemed to be moving too slow, and I told them, "Please hurry—the mountains are waiting!"

And they would continue to wait.

Finally, two days later, we started the nine-hour drive to Colorado. The other job had a tight timeline, and for some reason the adults wanted to travel at night, so we left after dinner. Our family split between the four vehicles in the caravan: our big blue seven-seater van, a long U-Haul towing an old Toyota with a camper shell that a family friend drove, our green Chevy truck pulling a U-Haul trailer, and then an old blue Ford truck towing another long trailer—all heavily loaded, strapped down, and quite the sight to see. Granddad controlled the wheel of the Ford with the company of one of my brothers, while the other rode with my dad in the Chevy. I chose to ride in the big blue van with my mom, baby brother, little sister—and cat.

I had settled into the seat above my poor, pathetic feline, who seemed determined to annoy everyone. He had begun yowling to get out of his cage, so I tried to reassure him.

"Tommy, stop crying. You're okay!" I tried poking a piece of jerky through the door.

His noise continued. I sighed. Who was I to be upset with his groans about this trip?

I shifted my weight to a more comfortable position. My cat's cage took up all my leg space, and I couldn't lay down. Every single seat was surrounded by boxes or blankets.

This trip was not going to be comfortable for anyone.

"Tommy, you're lucky to have your own space in the cage," I reminded him with a frown.

My words didn't seem to make a difference, but eventually, either exhausted or finally accepting the fact he couldn't change his circumstances, the poor cat stopped yowling. Then, as darkness fell, he curled up and closed his eyes. He was followed into sleep by my siblings.

I, on the other hand, was wide awake!

THE ALTITUDES OF ACCEPTANCE

As I stared at the lights rushing by outside the window, I started asking my mom all kinds of questions. "What is our new home like? ... Are there any kids close by? ... How far away is the school? ... Are the mountains close?"

I liked making plans, and details were required to make plans for my new home. Mom didn't seem to mind the questions—at first—and with all my plan-making I stayed awake a long while into the night. However, the chattier I became, the more nonsense came out of my mouth. The next thing I knew, Mom sent me to ride with Granddad who, knowing how late it was, invited me to lie down on the blankets covering the suitcases in the truck's back seat.

They were right: I was sleepy, and the blankets were a welcome sight.

As I slid between them, my last thought was of Tommy finally calming down. Now it was my turn to sleep away some of that endless road. I remember very little after that ... although I vaguely recall a bit of trouble when the green truck with my dad and brother veered dangerously off the road. The incident scared everyone, especially me who lacked a seatbelt while lying down. Shaken, the incident convinced my family to stop and rest for a couple of hours. Finally, we arrived at our destination around noon the next day—where the mountains were waiting!

Bolting like horses from a barn on fire, my younger siblings and I scattered, finally free to run. We charged through the empty house and yard; exploring the new home was *our* job while the adults figured out how to handle the unloading. After ducking in and out of rooms, we gathered in the living room to share our excitement and observations.

"Our new house is a little bigger than our old one, but the yard is a little smaller!"

"We're going to need to plant more trees, and the yard is kind of weedy!"

"There's a little forest down the road; I didn't see a fence, so maybe we can play there."

"Did you see that playground across the street? How did we get so lucky?"

Eager to share our observations with our parents, we headed as a group for the front door, but that's when it dawned on me—we had the biggest living room window I had ever seen!

It faced northwest and showed a school playground across the street, but that's not what caught my eye. Beyond the playground, our living room window perfectly framed the sheer mass, grandeur, and majesty of Pikes Peak standing regal and high above all the other purple mountains in the distance. Against the brightest blue sky I had ever seen, the view brought back certain feelings of reverence. The mountain was gigantic! Extraordinary! So far, to me this view was the best quality of the house.

Evidently my observation had nothing to do with how small I was, and everything to do with how big and close those mountains really were. As I let that view sink in before heading back outside with my family, the awe I felt was overtaken by a powerful sense of peace. One thing I knew: I did not have to worry about where I belonged. God had brought me home.

That's one thing I love about God: he is a master of helping me feel peace when I am where I belong. For the first time I knew that God found joy in leaving little memorable landmarks for us when we have literally landed where he wants us to be after an experience. That view of Pikes Peak marked a memorable milestone for me as well as a divinely communicated "welcome home."

To this day, amazing mountain views continue to bring that feeling, though strangely enough, that incomparable view of Pikes Peak only existed from that window while I was living in that home as a child. As the years passed, the community grew, and so the school across the street added classrooms and a tall gym that blocked the view.

Since then, God has often used symbols and moments to build connections with me. This is his way of giving me hope in a complicated world. Without God, I think I would feel like a stranger all the time. With God, I know eventually all my square pegs will find their square holes or finally be whittled into round pegs that fit more fully and easily into the plans he has for me.

THE ALTITUDES OF ACCEPTANCE

Or if not, there will surely be a reason. My life is a masterpiece in God's grand design.

Though today I am an avid hiker and mountain explorer, partly inspired by John Muir, I was initially a walking contradiction when it came to loving mountains and enjoying hiking.

At first, hiking up and down felt like a slow roller coaster—lots of anticipation on the uphill, usually very little climax, and sufficient pain to make me wonder if it was at all worth it—especially the way my family hiked. We would start out in low impact/free camping zones and charge up any mountain that beckoned to us—usually without well-developed trails.

At that early age, I knew most people hiked on trails, but not my dad. His motto seemed to be "No trail, no problem." He had lived, hunted, and worked frequently in mountainous areas before my family came into his life, so hiking through cascades of large boulders, fields of nettles, thick bushes, and steep hillsides was totally normal for him.

Truth be told, many people come to far worse ends when they go off trail, but somehow, on our family adventures, we never did. Instead, something incredible and uncanny would happen to my family at the tops of mountains or between peaks in the saddles—or really, when exploring any untamed mountainous territory. When we were nearly ready to turn around and head home, we would discover a real trail, a deer trail, or an old mining road. All too often, it would be working its way downhill in the desired direction.

How we never found these trails on our way *up* the mountain, I will never know.

We generally used compasses and landmarks to help us confirm directional accuracy while adventuring, so when we found a trail, we could tell if it might help us get within yards of our car or at least onto a familiar road. We might have been a little scratched and bruised, but we always made it home. And though we often teased him about having planned it that way, Dad always seemed surprised as well as grateful for how frequently this happened.

As a result, spontaneous trail-finding became known as our family's gift. It has also continued into the next generations, almost like a genetic trait, evolving as we all continue nomadically traversing throughout the wilderness. We have found that lessons learned from navigating unfamiliar environments are applicable beyond the outdoor wilderness, making this a pretty good and valuable gift from our father. Furthermore, doing hard things together as a family rewarded us with shared appreciation of the outdoor world and each other.

For us kids, our family's hiking habits also delivered a stimulating crash course in adventuring. We learned to research for ourselves and rely on experienced wisdom for each trek. We loaded our backpacks with practical resources, like food, first aid, rope, and even water purification, and we never let the fact that we always found our way back home prevent us from being ready for any possible adventure mishap.

I remember throughout our adventures there were moments when I breathed so hard that I thought I would never catch my breath. Sometimes, I had to pull myself around a tight spot using only my grip on the edge of a boulder, while other times, I had to stop myself from sliding down a steep embankment by grabbing hold of a firm rock or a stiff branch of Gambel oak. Another time, I had detoured so far from everyone else that I needed to be extremely silent to hear their location and redirect my course. To be sure, at times it was a very real relief to get back to safety.

In the earlier years, I often found myself envying my brothers. With their longer legs and stamina, they often took independent, high-energy charges up the mountains and left me behind.

Why does it seem so much easier for them? I know I am in love with the mountains, so why do I struggle and worry? One brother is even younger than me, so why don't I make more sense?

Eventually I realized they were just more used to it than I was, due to Boy Scout campouts. I also accepted the fact that I kept up with everyone else well enough, for an eleven-year-old. I didn't like feeling inadequate or frustrated with my success but feeling that way did not mean I loved the mountains any less. Besides, Dad was patient when I struggled, and because I wasn't always bounding ahead of him like my brothers, I could enjoy Dad's lessons about interesting rock features or plants along the way. Someday, I would do the things my brothers did, but for now, I could follow my dad's lead and connect with the natural world.

On a personal level, I eventually came to know for myself that I could get a little lost in the wilderness and face mountainous territory with courage, bravery, and directional confidence. I was able to navigate the ups and downs with competence and peace, and I knew for myself that the best paths were not always the most obvious or easy ones.

When I look back at how I began my relationship with the mountains, I realize how it aligns with what God, our Heavenly Father, intended life's journey to be. There are uphill climbs and opportunities amid downhill plunges and adversity, with many chances to get lost—and then found. The "ranges and basins," or "mountains and valleys," of life provide features as intriguing as geographical landscapes and dynamic experiences as beautiful and diverse as mountain scenery.

If you're anything like me, these landscapes of life—what I call lifescapes—call upon us to explore them. Lifescapes are markers that mix and shift with our choices and circumstances along life's trajectory to create the unique and individual phenomenon of who we are. Multiple lifescapes are connected through intersections and memories, making up the layers of experience that inform and improve us throughout our lives.

We have lifescapes of childhood and adulthood, and everything in between. Lifescapes represent learning curves, seasons of life where we navigate toward our dreams and are influenced by our upbringings and expanding mentalities.

Every lifescape holds stories, and every story shapes us—especially the ones that teach us meaningful truths, make us laugh, and connect us to God and other people. We develop perspectives, try to understand reality, and pursue transformative experiences. We *need* the will and discipline to do the hard work God asks of us along the way, and pure-hearted dedication to know God can lead to more fulfilling and successful progress through each lifescape.

Who we are in each new lifescape might feel a little different than who we were in the last, but each one plays a part in who and what we ultimately become. The best part is, God as a loving Father is right there with us, hiking up and down, teaching us, and providing opportunities for us to come face-to-face with him through challenges—challenges that not only enhance our ability to comprehend him and ourselves, but also help us understand that God is always greater and more in charge than we know.

One of the first lifescapes that transitioned me into adulthood involved many of the same things I loved as a child, including family and mountains. It started as I took my first full-time summer job as a hiking ranger in New Mexico and worked to teach young people how to do hard things. I had been away from Colorado for some time, for the first two years of college in the neighboring mountainous state of Utah, so I was able to use my personal mountain experiences and passions to help several teens improve their life perspectives and physical abilities.

In turn, their experiences influenced how I valued mine and wanted more. As I honed my perspectives and physical conditioning, my parents planned a surprise for me after the summer ended. When I visited Colorado for a week, they took me on a trip to climb one of Colorado's fifty-eight mountaintops that rise above 14,000 feet in elevation. They called it Mount Democrat.

This adventure began with a night under the stars in a tent, with Mom, Dad, and I enjoying a meal beneath the trees at the base of the mountains. We awoke to eat a quick breakfast made mostly of oatmeal and protein at a "dark-and-early" hour, then hit the trail before sunrise—yes, a genuine, man-made trail. It was about four miles long, and although we could have taken the boulder route, we preferred the three miles of trail as our assurance for a successful ascent.

After about an hour, shafts of light began to reach out of the horizon and creep across the cloudless blue sky. Soon, peaks, saddles, and valleys in all directions traded their shadows for layers of light. I breathed in the warmer air but dared not close my eyes. I was fascinated by the slow reveal of our stunning surroundings, with the ever-widening stage covering miles of glowing rocky terrain. A few mountain goats and marmots even posed like award-winning actors for photos.

The higher we climbed, the harder the terrain, but childhood frustrations about hiking were buried deep in the past beneath years of hiking experience. I felt nothing but anticipation!

Burning muscles got me to about eight hundred feet from the top, so I breathed a bit, noted I was not too far ahead of Mom and Dad, and then pushed through the burn to reach my destination. When I finally reached the top, the first view of the basins and ranges from the highest peak reminded me how worthwhile that climb had been.

Instead of looking up at a fourteener for inspiration, now I was standing on top of one.

While keeping an eye on my parents below, I wandered around, absorbing that feeling of awe and taking in the view. It was hard to mentally capture the countless magnificent landscapes within the wide expanse below me in every direction. As I explored, I noticed some rocks near the peak were about the same size as me, while others were smaller and comparatively insignificant. Most rocks seemed super stable, although a few seemed ready to topple off the mountain. Fourteeners get their name from their height, and I was not inclined to make this mountain a thirteener, so I steered clear of those loose rocks.

Then it hit me.

No, not a rock. A realization!

God sees us the way I'm looking at rocks on this mountain. He is already aware of our size, shape, strength, and stability; we are wanted and needed. Our individual and collective qualities may differentiate the terrain, and sometimes, we might try to topple off our foundation, but every single rock matters.

Still lingering from a recent autumn storm, I came across a patch of pure white snow and collected a small handful to rub on my forehead and cheeks to cool off and wash away the perspiration on my face. It melted against my warm skin, then drips of water trailed to the tip of my chin, cascaded off, and disappeared into the rocks below.

I imagined the water cycle at work—if the water did not evaporate or meet the roots of a plant first, it would eventually drain or filter through the earth to the rocks at the bottom. Water was clearly not meant to stay in the mountains forever but rather to flow away from the mountains and serve the earth around it, and to one day return to the mountains after exploring the world.

It sounded like an adventure to me!

As I explored the top of the mountain, I decided there's no real competition between water or even rocks. All water could nourish thirsty plants and communities, and the rocks that form the top of a mountain weren't more or less important than those at the bottom, or those that carry runoff from melting snowpack through watersheds to lower elevations.

So there I was, finally higher than I had ever been on foot. As the body is lifted, so is the mind! Even though I wasn't in Idaho, this immersive experience recalled another memory from my childhood—a road trip with my family through the Tetons on our way back to Oklahoma. I reflected on how I gazed up at the tall mountains and knew at age three that I would one day immerse myself in those canyons and peaks. Those thoughts graduated into musings about how prophets of old had sought spiritual and physical refuge in the tops of the mountains. That is where they met God and came face to face with his reality and majesty. Along with these thoughts came a feeling of deep awe. There was something else too. A sacred, new feeling of *belonging*. It was connected to that earlier feeling of "welcome home" from that first day in the Colorado house. It was like hearing and feeling God's voice tell me I was welcome, wanted, and could always come back.

Finally, Mom and Dad arrived at the top, so we celebrated the victory, took pictures, and absorbed the beauty in every direction. I wanted to stay up there all day, but a storm was coming, so we headed down quickly.

A few days after this trip ended, I returned to Utah to complete my third and final year of college. Brigham Young University was a school in the mountains, but not having a car, I tended to remain tied to campus. Schoolwork was demanding, so I didn't do much hiking that year. I had to content myself with simply looking up at them. I knew then that I would always be hungry for the mountains, but at times I needed to be "water in the valley" and focus on working for my future.

As a young adult, preparing for a career had its own mountains anyway. There was still homesickness to mitigate and courses to handle; tests to take and relationships to navigate; extracurricular activities to pursue and values to determine; new friendships to discover and new places to see. With so many life-things to handle, I could not help but trust and reflect on lessons learned from all my previous ups and downs, including the guidance and support from my parents. As I adjusted and learned to manage this new life experience, I felt stronger as a person.

Along the way, with every decision, another increasingly unmistakable truth came to light.

It was that only one other individual really knew the extent of my personal chaos and circumstances. That individual wasn't my parents, leaders, or teachers, although I knew they were interested and eager to help. Despite best efforts to plan and prepare, I had no idea what I was doing, or where I was really going—but God did. And God cared. He cared a lot about little *me*.

I knew God cared because each time I experienced a colossal collision with another person's worldview or with a schoolwork situation that seemed irreconcilable, he showed me what I needed to know, do, and feel. For example, once it angered me to discover it took me two hours longer on average to study for accounting tests than other students, including my own brother! It became clear that if I wanted to prioritize good grades, I would have to limit social experiences. After thinking about it and talking with a few friends, I chose to keep one day a week for socializing and not studying. On Sundays I was able to focus on God and others, and I even hosted low-scale service opportunities where I discovered great friendships and actively learned from different opinions and perspectives. Instead of seeking out people in fun places, God sent people to me.

Being a more experienced student, I also decided to lead study groups, which proved to be another way to meet interesting people. Sometimes I had to deal with hard situations. For example, usually we studied well and performed well, but occasionally I led my classmates astray with a test question or two. It hurts to live with the consequences of personal mistakes that affect others.

All this work with people sometimes created situations where problems had to be solved. Sometimes I would say things I didn't mean, which led to hard conversations with people I liked. It reminded me of a question I had had since childhood. *What age or maturity would I have to reach in life before I could govern myself better, and with all the wisdom that seems to arrive too late?*

It was a question without an answer. At least for now.

Sometimes, when answers don't come and our circumstances feel like torrential currents during catastrophic weather events, all we can do is flow—like water. I've learned clean water is the true center of the human struggle for survival. How we control it by redirection, storage, or diversion is so different than how God nourishes and operates with us! God's world centers around us for sure, and while I'd say he is in control, I believe he doesn't see the need to control us. Instead, he encourages our decisions and integrates our experiences into the network and flow of surrounding circumstances. He encourages us to do all we can with what we know, turn to him for help, and then allow him to take care of everything else. In fact, I believe God is always looking out for our best interests through spiritual comfort and inspiration as well as occasional redirection.

At least that's how it's been for me.

College was when I recognized two things about anxiety.

First, that it wasn't going away, and second, it triggers feelings that are hard to process.

The more I learned about anxiety, the more ways I discovered to manage it. In my case, I chose to seek training and solutions in self-esteem practices, exercise, mental health counseling, interpersonal communication styles, personal work ethic, and so on, until I found out how to transform those anxious feelings into persistence and resilience. This focus got me through to graduation, but even as I earned my scholastic degree of choice, I understood I would always be learning how to deal with anxiety. It seemed inescapable, as though it was a necessary part of earning an individually tailored PhD from the "University of Hard Knocks."

God was in all those lessons during college, but living and dealing with constant hard knocks convinced me of a few things about adult life. For one thing, believing in God, walking with him, and letting him in without hesitation were all different spiritual behaviors.

But knowing is different than doing.

I believed in God, and I believed him when he said he loved me. I even tried to think about him wherever I went. But in college, I became certain of one thing—really letting God in was the hardest behavior of them all. I knew it was up to me to open the door, but when I felt anxious, I really struggled to stay open to God and his guidance. This left me with one conclusion—that the package I entered life with, including what I loved about myself as well as the characteristics I couldn't change or remove easily, would always impact my progression, and might even affect my ability to get where I wanted to be and become the person I planned to be. Sometimes, genuine personal change seemed beyond impossible.

What I didn't know then was that God meets us where we are, and loves us as we are, and has customized methods and plans for teaching us how to work *with* our entire package, if we are willing.

In my case, God had a few places for me to go and lessons for me to learn about changing, being taught, and letting him in.

Near the end of college, I turned twenty-one. In my faith, women of this age could make a choice whether to serve a mission. I knew what I wanted, so I prayed and asked God if my choice to be a missionary for the Church of Jesus Christ of Latter-Day Saints was right. In time, I sensed a firm and clear, "I trust you to make this decision," so I chose to trust him at his word.

I wanted to teach and testify of Christ. It was what I had wanted to do all my life, and I felt it was time to go. However, I also wanted to travel, so I applied for two things: a mission and a study abroad to New Zealand for my last semester of school.

I didn't expect the two opportunities to collide, but when my mission assignment arrived, the date of departure was in February—exactly in the middle of when I would have been in New Zealand. I was crushed! Why did it feel like I had to go one way or the other? When I realized I didn't have enough money for both opportunities, I didn't bother to ask if delaying the assignment was an option, but I should have! Now, there will always be a part of me that wonders how my life would have changed if I had gone to New Zealand and found out how to do both things. In the end, I left Colorado and my family to make Ontario, Canada my temporary home for the next year and a half.

I had this idea of myself, based on what I felt capable of, and imagined myself as an outstanding teacher—a perfect servant of God. God had given me so much and prepared me so well. I really wanted to give back, to really ace the tasks God set before me, so this attitude didn't seem prideful—it seemed natural. I had met a lot of missionaries, and they all seemed amazing to me. I figured that even if I lacked anything up front, it would be in God's best interest to make me the best version of myself pretty much overnight, and I was ready.

What I didn't realize was that my anxiety and the complexities I experienced when dealing with other people were not going away. They were still a part of me. Believing my "University of Hard Knocks" would take a vacation while I worked for God proved to be a narrow viewpoint. Instead, it was the other way around. Why? Because hard knocks seemed to multiply for missionaries, and only God decides when you get that PhD.

I don't know why I didn't see this before my mission, but now I know the truth. All throughout history, servants of God have never been placed in any kind of preserving, protective bubble wrap. He helps them accomplish his work, and he makes miracles happen through them, but they aren't immune from relationship struggles, soul-searching, darkness, or hard choices.

Anyway, I knew within the first three weeks of training that I would have to resign myself to forging ahead and facing the facts: where there are people, there are problems. And of course I brought problems into the mix. But such problems didn't have to stop anyone including myself from connecting with God. Deep down, I knew God trusted me, and I knew I wasn't alone in the challenges of navigating people problems.

God did it all the time. No wonder he was so good at helping me.

However, it was still near the beginning of this story, and I still thought I was the main character. It took me a while to realize my character wouldn't be complete, and it wouldn't be much of a story, until I got better at sharing the missionary stage with God.

Which is probably why a thunderous hailstorm of anxiety blew in, roaring so loudly to get my attention that I became deaf to my strengths and could only see the strengths of other people. I would see that a companion had strength in an area, and then conclude that because I didn't, I was automatically less than her as a person. I believed I was a mess and was convinced it was my fault, that my weakness was creating my hardships. I asked God a lot of questions as the storm settled in, but this was a storm I had no control over—and one he didn't want to calm right away.

All day long, almost without realizing it, my brain would translate every situation into a reason to be harder on myself. For at least the first nine months, I was stuck. I felt blind, lost in my swirling, emotional storm. My jokes and joy were limited. I couldn't take compliments graciously. Thinking I was being humble, I continuously shot down well-intended praises from friends and then felt miserable because I knew they meant well and deserved better.

That's when I discovered how to be a real expert at self-sabotage.

Internally, I began to criticize myself, succumb to fear, and then hesitated too long to do the right thing. I even pushed away opportunities for personal enjoyment and became more disconnected with my whole self than I have ever been, before or since then. If it didn't matter to the mission goals, it didn't matter to me, and I had to walk that line.

I became a skilled and dedicated missionary but after teaching great lessons, I could always find something that had not gone well. Self-improvement is important, and no one is perfect at teaching, but I kept over-analyzing things I hadn't said, instead of recognizing the value in what had been said. It seemed like I couldn't stop throwing good things away and keeping the bad things.

Amidst all the confusion, I strove to connect with missionaries and people of my mission. I fell in love with everyone and all the mini adventures we pursued together, including several hikes and delicious holiday meals. I participated in laughter and good conversations. However, deep inside,

THE ALTITUDES OF ACCEPTANCE

I couldn't help but feel like no one else was struggling the way I was. I genuinely believed that everybody had graduated from the "University of Hard Knocks" except *me*.

Even my happier days were imbued with the grayness of confusing internal conflicts, sprinkled with an exhausting mix of blame, pride, criticism, failure, tears, humility, and prayer. But there were enough days with sunshine and inspiration to help me have the tiniest hope. On those days, an enlightened, hidden part of me still glowed with enough self-confidence. I would make it.

Make it where?

To the end? To the next day? To the day when I would finally not feel so empty?

I couldn't believe it was so easy for someone like me, who had once been so happy with life, to feel so utterly miserable. I wanted to believe solutions would come, but I couldn't stop thinking about things that went wrong. I kept measuring my value and my contributions based on what I had failed to do each day. Constantly comparing my imperfections to what I admired in others made me feel out of control. Being out of control rubbed me raw. I had always been the girl who had it together, and now I was falling apart.

Finally, it was autumn, and I was dragging myself along our walking route. I had my head down, deep in thought about an appointment that day, when I trudged right into the post of a tall white sign with black letters. I had to pause abruptly in my tracks, and my poor companion nearly tripped over me. The sign appeared to be in the middle of the sidewalk.

I raised my head slowly and read, "End of Sidewalk."

Well, duh. I can see the gray concrete stop, like, right here. I'm not blind.

We turned around and found another way to our destination. There were too many tall weeds past that sign. Besides, I didn't need any more uneven, unstable ground in my life.

A few days later, my mission president asked me at the end of an appointment if I might be focusing on my inadequacies because of my pride. At first, I wasn't sure how to answer.

That couldn't be right. Me, suffering from pride? I was nothing to be proud of!

But in my mind came a whisper, *I am proud of you, but you don't see yourself like I do.*

That felt like one of God's hints, so that night, I prayed for help to start seeing me the way God saw me, but the answer didn't come right away.

In fact, not until months later, when winter was in full swing. My new mission companion and I were out walking in knee-deep snow. We didn't have much to say to each other, so I was left to think about how weary I felt. I had been sick at heart and hungry in spirit for so long, and I was so worn out from feeling like I couldn't escape my weakness and personal failings. I decided to pray in my heart:

God, a fourteener is like a foothill compared to this mission mountain. College is like a stroll through the park compared to this trek. I thought I was prepared for this, but honestly ...

Who threw out all the supplies in my backpack and replaced them with bricks?

How could I have believed I had so much to give, show up, and then mess up, so badly?

I'm closer to the end than the beginning now. Why couldn't I be who I was supposed to be?

Seriously, God, where's all the abundant joy that comes from serving you? I don't want to feel broken anymore. I don't want to carry the weight around forever, and I don't want to build a wall. I am throwing those bricks at my failures and struggles, but—

Okay, okay—I know I'd never throw anything at another person who was struggling. And if throwing bricks at my own brokenness would fix me, it would have already worked by now.

Sigh.

Maybe you have some kind of purpose with this, but I don't see it.

Bonk!

This time, I really did hit the post. Eye to eye with white paint, I tipped my head up to see a familiar sign. It looked just like the one I had seen in the spring before the snowfall.

"End of Sidewalk."

Beyond it, a deep, potentially weedy embankment was completely invisible. It was covered with snow up to the level of the sidewalk. In a blizzard, if the sign were not there, a person might keep walking, only to sink into a deep hole they couldn't escape on their own. If no one walked by, there was no hope of being rescued until spring. And by then it would be too late.

Signs were important. Wouldn't want to miss a sign like this.

No matter how insignificant and redundant the sign looked in all the other seasons of the year, the value of it made me shudder inside.

Then I turned around and smacked my mission companion's shoulder with my gloved palm. She had been walking through the deep snow a few footsteps behind me. Her eyes went wide and she jumped out of the way in concern, luckily missing the edge of the embankment.

"That's it! I have been missing the signs. There are some things I need to know and learn while I'm here so that I don't end up in a place I don't want to be."

Still stunned, she raised her eyebrows and glared at me with disapproval. "Okay, you're nuts." Then, thinking again, she leaned forward slightly, trying to catch sight of what I was seeing. As she recognized the sign above our heads, her eyes twinkled as she met my excited expression with a nod. "Oh, now I get it—you saw the sign, and it opened up your eyes."

Of course, she kept humming the old song as we turned around to find another way to get to where we were going. I laughed aloud at the strange certainty of the moment, and then with a skip in my step and a celebratory mood, I joined her for a verse of the song.

She didn't mind that I wasn't ready to explain myself fully, and when she went on to another song, I sank into silence. While my heart felt relief, my mind raced to keep connecting the dots.

All I could do was try to accept what I brought to the table, failings and all, and learn to love the package of me. As hard as it was, my mission was just a long lesson through which God was showing me something, or some things, over—and over—and over.

For one thing, when a path was too rough or going in the wrong direction, it was usually time to turn around and try a new approach. I hadn't yet tried counseling, but acquiring some tools for healing and understanding whatever was going on inside of me sounded like a great strategy.

Second, as usual, God had given me many good friends in a new place. Most of them possessed gifts and ideas that could help, if I let them. If I could rethink my hardship, I might find that I had a great capacity for being able to see the goodness in others.

Third, many missionaries around me had experienced terrible hardships. They'd lost family members and loved ones or were struggling with health concerns or injuries. When I struggled to love myself, it was harder for me to love others. But when I intentionally loved them and did things for them, it was easier to love myself more.

I grimaced, just a little bit. The solution was clear. I had been doing all the right things, I just needed a new approach, a new perspective. Reaching outward and getting help with the hard stuff was a new way that could change how I saw the world and my struggles in it. Life didn't have to be the way I was perceiving it. Loving other people with real intent was more than a key to freedom from sorrow. It was a sign that pointed to further hope and healing.

The scriptures say that what we give to the world comes back to us one way or another. If I could give something of myself or of God to another in need, then out would come the new perspective I so deeply needed. Throwing those bricks around wasn't the answer, so maybe I could be more organized about using them for my good. And even when I didn't feel like doing the work, I knew I had to try. God would help me stack those bricks and their associated perspectives into a far more informed and secure defense against the darkness that seemed to surround and seep into me.

THE ALTITUDES OF ACCEPTANCE

Apparently, I used to think God wanted me to live through the storms, be grateful when the storms were gone, absorb their effects, and just keep going. He does want that—but that's not all. God wants us to do much more with our lives than just simply live through the storms. His deeper purpose is to use our stormy circumstances to help us focus on him. His plan? To prepare us for future storms by strengthening our trust in him.

That's why he builds the signs.

That's why we need to see them.

He knows what's on the other side.

We don't.

So, we have a choice—to lose ourselves to God or lose ourselves in a snow drift.

Or something equally as deep, cold, and overwhelming.

The truth was, I had only started to accept that I had some level of anxiety in college, so I was still new at understanding its effects. Before entering the mission field, I had no idea that my active lifestyle had helped me deal with it adequately and in ways I couldn't easily implement as a missionary. But after three sessions of counseling, I learned several tools for recognizing and reducing the signs of deep anxious distress. Now I could stop them before the storm intensified.

I also learned I could stop doing and start doing certain things to more effectively refrain from comparative thinking and anxious feelings that magnified my perception of personal flaws. For one thing, comparing my weaknesses against others' strengths had to be replaced with appreciating others' strengths without comparison. I also had to stop believing all imperfections were weaknesses and sins. Some things just made me different, and that was more than okay.

Somehow, I had gotten stuck in a cycle of confusion about what goodness was. I expected myself to be a perfect missionary, so I held myself to that standard and used other people's strengths to fill in the gaps. I didn't understand that no one does God's work perfectly. I couldn't comprehend that it had never been about doing God's work perfectly. I had let my personal expectations for what I was supposed to do override God's expectations. I had been proud of my own expectations for myself, and then I was too proud to admit I had missed the truth.

The truth was God could do his work perfectly through me, as I was and as I would become.

He expects us to grow, but he's not trying to make us exactly like him, or like another person, or even into the best versions of ourselves overnight. He's not in that kind of a rush. With God, it's always about the growth involved, and rarely about the time it takes.

In my case, the whole time God wanted me to treat myself a little more like he treated me, with love and patience. I resisted, thinking I couldn't do that until I got missionary work right. But once I accepted that missionary work was all about loving others and myself and recognizing God's lessons, I was more effective at sharing love and patience with others. Becoming this version of myself was more important than not becoming the perfect version I had originally envisioned.

In choosing to serve, God had given me an incomparable opportunity to grow. He needed me to understand how imperfection was an intentional part of life. God wanted me to see how focusing on failure in life is a problem and learning from failure is the solution, and that he doesn't see failure the way we do. He wanted me to understand I didn't need to compare myself to others but rather do my best and find open spaces in my heart for other people.

It was an enabling truth.

With less than nine months to go, I did what I had to do to keep that truth alive in my heart. Soon several Post-It notes filled with quotes and ideas for treating myself and others better appeared on my wall and mirror.

Some of them were scriptures, and they acted like trail markers to reference if I strayed from what I now understood about God's expectations. Others were questions I could ask myself at night to keep my journal entries positive and reflective of the good things I had done each day, even while I admired what others had done.

All these personal endeavors tipped the precarious scale of my anxiety in a more favorable direction, but the last thing I did was the hardest. I shared with a few others why I had seen myself as so broken, and why that wasn't the truth.

The truth was, I had come to teach, but God wanted me to learn.

To learn so that I could teach from a deeper yet higher place.

A place from which I could learn even more.

At about month thirteen, I stood silently with my missionary companion on the grassy slope just above one of the many bays in Ontario. We watched the waves rise into white crests, which seemed to be glowing as the sun set across the water. As the waves moved towards me, I was thinking about how far I had come and the lessons I had learned. The waves grew huge and then crashed on the banks, only to be replaced with more rising swells.

Those waves ... they reminded me of—mountains of water?

I was taken aback by how much they looked like miniature versions of the snow-capped ranges back home. They were mountains, that weren't really mountains.

Just like my mission experience.

In this lifescape, the mountains I had to climb were pressing out like the water in the bay. The mission was like the banks of this bay, holding me in, safe but far from the mountains I knew and loved as a child. Here, God had allowed me to rise, then crash down against my limits, surging forward, again and again, until his work to calm and steady those mountainous waves was done.

If I hadn't always known it, now I knew I could crash down against God's love and patience any time I needed to. It also seemed that even though God preferred me to be an eternal student in the "University of Hard Knocks," maybe I wasn't the only one. I could see how no one was allowed to through life without ups and downs, and no one actually "figures it all out" in this life.

In fact, God knows we will get the most growth out of life that way.

I used to think life was about finding out what we wanted and asking God for help along the way, and I still think that is true. God wants us to tell him what we want, so that he knows, and we know we're ready to receive it. I also believe God can give us what we want, but sometimes he doesn't, especially when it doesn't align with his will or his wisdom. In fact, he seems to have an agenda beyond just granting our desires—if I had gotten my desires as a missionary, I would have missed out on learning things that have changed the rest of my life.

I believe God gives us much more than what we want. He gives us what we need exactly when we need it. He can do that because he is right there with us, and because he wants us to have everything we need so that we can someday return home to him at the end of our adventure of life.

Speaking of coming home, the closer I got to my year-and-a half mark, the more frequently I spent my evenings on my bed, desperately pressing pen to paper. There was so much to remember and never forget, so I endeavored to record every precious lesson and every meaningful moment. However, I was always in a battle with the clock! I felt constantly caught between recording memories and making memories.

One day I heard a man I admired humbly say he was praying for the gift of memory and the ability to ponder. That thought stuck with me until I realized how pondering and writing were permanent partners in preserving memories. Pondering was essential because it could inspire greater conciseness and attention to detail, and even greater accuracy regarding memories.

I was never going to be able to write everything down, so I took his example and began to pray for the gifts of memory and the ability to ponder.

Soon, the gifts began to show in the little moments; those we taught would ask a question, and even though we hadn't prepared an answer, I would recall information from previous studies. My memory had gained power. I had been diligent in studying throughout my entire mission, and now that I desired to remember things and no longer fear my mistakes, I was able to reflect on quotes and scripture passages without hesitation. I felt like I had finally figured out how to be what I had always hoped to be as a missionary—a conduit through which God reached others.

Sometimes, when rides in the car drifted to silence, I started to sing, and my missionary companion would turn on a music CD. Not because I had a bad voice—I hope! It seemed she thought I wanted music. I would usually start to listen and then think more than sing. I often became overcome by awe and peace over something God had done for us that day, like keeping us safe when we came across people who had the power to hurt us or helping us find a safe meal when we needed one. Moments like this added value to my mission experience, and these moments helped me realize music was distinctly connected to my ability to ponder.

As I learned the lessons of memory and contemplation, I felt like I had more time to write after I took time to quietly ponder, as though I could record the most important things more efficiently. I decided the ability to ponder was a great gift, and the silence to do it in was an even greater luxury.

Recording my stories was one thing I would never tire of doing after my mission, I hoped.

Another key thing I wanted to do often was to seek and find quiet places, particularly in the majesty of mountains where I believed I would hear God better after my mission. Mountains were a big part of my life before my mission, so making time for mountain excursions seemed like a good tool for dealing with anxiety after my mission. Or, for simply dealing with trials of life in general.

By the end of my mission, I felt I had learned how to take God's route more willingly out of my anxious messes. I still felt very anxious too often, but the self-assurance I gained from navigating through the experience helped me not only withstand the nine-month storm but also refill my toolbox with things the Lord wanted me to use in the future. For example, the lessons of self-compassion and self-acceptance changed my outlook on the world. Also, now it did not matter when or whether I got that PhD. The hard knocks were God's way of equipping me to take on life's adventures with a better version of myself.

It was a gift I would be striving to understand and apply for the rest of my life.

The time came to conclude my mission, get packed up, and go to the airport. Those last few days were not my favorite, but then, I had never been great at saying goodbye.

A serious, pensive mood fell over me as I gave hugs to my companions and mission president. I slipped through airport security, then turned and waved goodbye one last time. They were all gone by then, but I waved anyway. This time, I was waving to Canada.

Once I reached the gate, I began pondering everything that had got me to this point. Here I was, sitting alone in the Canada Toronto Airport with a ticket to Colorado in my hand, looking back on my life and mission. From moving to Colorado, going to college, and completing a mission, it all felt so right—yet so strange. It felt like so many lifetimes, and yet it was just one life.

Now it was time to think of my future. Unlike many missionaries, I was already done with college. What were my next steps anyway?

Okay—baby steps! First, I'll fly home, rejoin my family, and share all my stories with them about the people I'm going to miss. If possible, I will somehow convey all the feelings about how I have been transformed into this new me with God's help.

THE ALTITUDES OF ACCEPTANCE

A mission had been a good decision for me—I learned to trust God to make more out of me than I could make of myself. But could I trust myself to make another good decision, about a good job, or a good man? If he could trust me, I could too. Right?

Of one thing I was certain. The old me, the missionary me, and the new me had something in common. They had all had a role in creating "Deanna of the Mountains," and I didn't wish to wander too far from the mountains for any reason. If I did, though, I trusted it would all work out.

Now, what do I think about my mission? People are going to ask me that.

I loved everyone I met. They loved me. Especially after that nine-month mark.

Nine months! Why had it taken me that long to get out of my own way?

Had my mission been more about me than the people I served? That wasn't how it was supposed to be; that wasn't how I intended it to be.

The echoes repeated in my mind as I kept wondering if I had been emotionally selfish with my time serving God. I wasn't sure if I could trust my judgment. But what did it matter anyway? Even if I had been the only one who I had helped to come closer to God, that was still someone.

And I counted for something!

I knew better than to retroactively suspect that my life going forward would be messed up because of how I had handled my mission, but it was a tempting thought. My reflections told me God could use imperfect people, but I had met wonderful, imperfect women everywhere who had not served missions. It seemed they already knew things I was learning.

Apparently, there were other ways to learn what I was learning.

Ugh! I needed to find a way to boost my mind past these doubts and concerns.

But what if I hadn't served? Would I have still learned?

Likely, but God had used my mission to teach me. It had been quite the opportunity for God to prove how well he knew me. But still I wondered if a mission had been right for someone like me, someone who had needed so much tender loving care.

This begged the question—no, never mind. Did the answer even matter at this point?

But still, I had never asked God to tell me that before—if I had been where he wanted me to be. I had just assumed I was, no matter how hard things got. He had trusted my decision, after all.

A spiritual alert flag waved to me from the depth of my thoughts, signaling that there was something right about asking God such a question. I looked at my watch—ten minutes had passed!

Silence filled the air as I looked around. Strange. The busy airport seemed a lot less busy than it should have been. The black faux-leather chairs were empty for two rows in every direction.

With so few distractions, no wonder I had pondered so much in so little time.

I guess not many people fly to the United States from Canada! At least not today.

Window seat!

I refocused—there was less than an hour until departure, so I spent the next half hour thinking about my mission. I kept my mind positive. My missionary work had not been perfect, but my whole heart had been in it. When I had just a few minutes left, my heart was ready to urgently whisper a quiet heartfelt prayer.

God, was I where you wanted me to be for a year and a half of my life?

But a moment later, my thoughts scattered as I nearly fell out of the chair! The intercom static startled me when the attendant's voice called my flight to Colorado.

I stood to gather my things. In the process, I noticed one other man heading toward the gate. I thought it was strange how he took the long way around all the chairs to get to the gate. There was a much more direct route, so I started going that way, but a certain feeling stopped me.

I turned around.

I'm supposed to follow that man.

Weird, but stranger things had happened to me in my life.

THE ALTITUDES OF ACCEPTANCE

Redirections and indirect paths like this were nothing new. As a missionary, such feelings had usually led me to interesting people, but it was not great timing to talk with him.

Then I noticed a coin on the floor just ahead of the man. He didn't bend over, but the image of someone picking it up came to mind. That someone was me.

So that was what I needed to do.

Picking up lost coins was not a new thing to me. It was an old habit of mine, but I had not done so in a year and a half. I had seen plenty of currency scattered along Canadian streets, but I hadn't ever felt the urge to pick up such coins the way I did now.

When I reached the coin, I quickly picked it up, placed it in my pocket, and continued onto the plane. In my seat, I dug out my journal to write a few thoughts. About thirty minutes into the flight, I realized I hadn't even looked at the coin. By its weight and size, I assumed it was a Canadian Loonie (a dollar coin), but I reached for the coin anyway.

Holding the coin up to the window, I drew in a deep breath as an overwhelming feeling of God's love washed over me. My thumb brushed across a mountain view that looked so much like the one that had graced my family's wide living room window every day for my entire childhood.

How did God do that?

In a way that only God can do, with a feeling only God can give, I was being welcomed home. His assurance that I had done well was more than I had ever felt before.

If I cried, I don't remember. I probably did.

What I do remember was settling into the feeling. It brought deep peace, an internal knowing that I had been right where I needed to be: a whole nation and fifteen hundred miles away from Colorado, learning what God wanted to make of me. Nine months or eighteen months of time didn't matter. God likes prioritizing comparatively short segments of time to influence and enhance entire lifetimes. After all, a lifescape of time is a good trade—our time is not ours after all.

Time is God's, and we have merely borrowed it in exchange to learn his greatest lessons.

As I marveled over getting all of that from simply looking at a tiny image of a Colorado fourteener on the back of a Colorado state quarter, I realized this was the first time I had ever seen one of these coins. I had left on my mission only about two years after this coin had been minted and hadn't managed to find one in circulation before leaving the United States. So, I had had no idea the image of an iconic fourteener, Longs Peak—which looked very much like Pikes Peak—was on the Colorado quarter.

To anyone who noticed me, I was just a girl holding a quarter, crying for no apparent reason. But to God, I was precious. I was someone who he cared so much about that he would arrange this extraordinary moment to rescue my anxious mind with a personal, tangible symbol of hope, comfort, and belonging.

As the plane continued, I hardly noticed the leather of the seat and the way the neck rest cocked my head forward. I kept my head forward anyway, leaning against the window, absorbing the view without really seeing. It didn't take long for the anxiety to dissipate, and be replaced by a sense of calm self-assurance. It seemed like God had welcomed me home—before I even got there—and saw fit to send a clear message of what I needed to know, when I needed to know it. God had reminded me in another amazing way that he knew my needs and that I could trust him.

For the record, I preserved these stories for so long as precious personal reminders, and this book is the first place I'm telling these stories. I hope those who read them might be inspired to recognize their own moments where God has stepped into their lives—and lifescapes—whether it's a window-framed view, or something as collectible and concrete as a coin.

THE ALTITUDES OF ACCEPTANCE

Whether we believe in God or not, life is not only about human reason and experience alone. It's about leaning into the bigger truth that is better and more complete than our own truth.

Once a wise friend shared with me how faith can be defined simply as a matter of starting out on a path or in a certain direction before we know how it will all turn out. And you know those moments when you know you've *made it*? Those are moments when you have collected a piece of your best self for the puzzle you are diligently trying to make sense of. For me, such moments represent something I can move forward with, something that tells me a little bit about how things will turn out *if* I continue to let God contribute to my life through small, precious moments.

I believe there are times God uses a chain of events to inspire knowledge and action. He often moves our lives along in the desired direction without fanfare or larger-than-life exhibitions. It's amazing and awesome how God sets it up so we cannot doubt he had a hand in it. It is hard to be clear on how he does it, but God is masterful at reassuring us in completely individual ways. He helps us navigate our personal seen and unseen weaknesses while simultaneously guiding us. All he asks in exchange for making our lives more full and complete is our time, effort, and trust.

All the experiences in this chapter set the stage for how getting closer to God through my life's adventure involved both self-acceptance and a growth mindset. The next several chapters are based on true stories as well. What I learned from these stories reinforces several truths about accepting your whole self that deserve to be passed along—from my lifescape to yours.

CHAPTER 2

BEST LAID PLANS

*A*fter returning from Canada, I was immediately offered my first full-time job at the same place I had completed my last college internship in Texas. It allowed me to use my skills, and I enjoyed competitive pay with a full benefits package. The job deserved my best work, which is what I was prepared to give, but in truth I went there having one foot already out the door. For some reason, I maintained doubts about how I could possibly thrive if I stayed there permanently.

Looking back with fifteen-plus years of wisdom and working experience, I am glad I had the experience if only to learn from it, but I can hardly believe how willing I was to give up that solid start on my retirement savings and the ability to save or invest over $3,000 a year. I also paid less than $500 for my own single bedroom apartment, an unheard-of amount just ten years later. Honestly, I wish I had more fully prized and respected the stability and resources of the job and how it might have helped me achieve a bigger dream: to travel and see mountains all over the world.

But that brings us right to the issue.

The longer I was in Texas, the more I ached for higher altitudes, access to wild areas, and hiking for cardio and strength training. I truly enjoyed the people and my new friends in Texas, saw beauty in the gorgeous wide landscapes and sunsets, and sang my way through cavalcades in the canyon country. However, in Texas, most of the land is private property or has

THE ALTITUDES OF ACCEPTANCE

limited public access, so my only recourse other than walking or running for exercise at local parks or in town was seeking the tallest buildings and climbing the stairs to the top floor.

I kept trying to find a view that would connect me to something mountainous or be reminiscent of my mountains, like those I had witnessed in Colorado, New Mexico, and Canada. I even tried sharing my efforts to find higher altitudes with others as I had the mountains.

On one middle-of-the-workday break, I took my mentor to the tallest building. The elevator was not functioning, so he had to climb the twenty-four flights of stairs like I did. I did not mean to giggle at how the climb completely wore him out, but I had to laugh or else I would cry. I did not like what I saw. His enervation triggered my imagination, and I predicted that if nothing about my life in Texas changed, I wouldn't be happy with my physical condition ten years down the road.

Maybe there was a reason I came to Texas, but there was also at least one clear reason to leave. How could I thrive if I became unable to climb a mountain? For me, staying in shape meant I could hike whenever I visited the mountains. In Texas, fitness gyms were an option but not preferrable. Even though I knew how to use them, I loved being outside. I could run, but in the flats, I would get weary. Clearly, there was a tugging at my heart.

I had a decision to make. Did I stick it out with this job, or should I consider what other interests and dreams I had that could become new career paths?

All I knew then was that dreams were shiny, new, and inviting, and that my current path seemed honorable and safe, but rather dull. Going with what I knew about myself, I decided to chase a dream and become a religious educator instead of a scouting program administrator.

When I discovered the only place to train was in Utah, where I had my college adventure, I felt compelled. The Utah package came with regular access to rugged mountains and old friends. I had my own car this time, so the potential for new friends and more adventures was real!

The move seemed like the recipe for my happiness. It seemed like there was no way this plan could fail. I had made the best decision I could with what I knew and comprehended about life at the time, so why wouldn't God bless this plan and continue to help the pieces fall into place?

It was December 2010 when my dad and I arrived to unload my U-Haul into the largest room of a duplex. I wasn't so excited about having two roommates, but I figured I would make it work. Been there, done that! Besides, giving up a little of my independence to make my dream more affordable was the right thing to do since I didn't have a paycheck on the horizon.

I started training to be a religious educator in early January 2011. Soon, I began to understand how to bundle and layer concepts in scriptural passages into interactive lessons. I also tweaked a few of my tricks of the missionary trade, such as extracting doctrine and recognizing connections, to meet the needs of teenagers. However, because the program required two months of training before I could work full-time, I found a part-time job at a bakery to help me make it financially. Despite that extra pressure, everything seemed to be going well.

Until it wasn't.

I had been in a relationship when I moved to Utah. I thought I could marry him but then discovered he had been hiding a destructive addiction that was morally troubling to me. As our connection crumbled, I felt betrayed and confused. I prayed for weeks and counseled with God, friends, and family. In the end, the breakup proved to be a catalyst for change. I found out I didn't love him the way I wanted to love someone someday. I realized I had been hesitant and felt confined and unhappy all along, and that I needed to be honest with myself and with him.

It turns out the truth really does set you free.

Although I dreaded having to tell the story of a failed engagement, this was a hard decision I couldn't regret. It felt like I had simply turned away from a mountain or path that threatened imminent danger. I knew from experience that there was sorrow but no shame in that.

A wise aunt taught me that a broken engagement is still a successful one, and I knew she was right. Mentally, I understood that this was one lesson in life I was grateful to learn. However, emotionally, I still needed time to recover from the betrayal and learn from my choices.

Anxiety over my future set in as my self-confidence took a huge hit.

To help with the heartbreak and find focus, I pursued my teacher training with greater dedication until March 2011, when the chance to prove myself as a teacher arrived. I was asked to substitute in an early morning class for three whole weeks, which was the final test of consistent leadership in a high school classroom. As I got to know the students, I truly enjoyed learning from how the teens thought about life and God. As they shared things with me, I discovered that although they were so young, many were experiencing huge family or personal challenges.

I loved them, yet I occasionally felt overwhelmed by their trials. I hadn't experienced such tragedies myself. Dealing with anxiety was one thing, but traumatic family deaths or foster home situations were on another level. I had already learned the lessons of comparative thinking, so I tried not to absorb their sorrow or compare it to my own. Instead, I listened. I shared meaningful music, stories, and life lessons with them. I encouraged them to develop their own faith and connection to God, the way I had through my personalized trials. By the end of those three weeks, I learned the youth needed empathy, compassion, and truth more than anything else.

Later, I sat in the room full of other teachers-in-training waiting to hear my name read with a full-time job offer and an assignment for the following winter semester. The words never came, and I was taken aback. I thought things had gone well. I hadn't expected to fail. No one ever does.

But God, you brought me here. What do I need to learn this time, and why?

As I considered the time and emotions I had devoted to these kids and to this dream, I could only conclude that God sometimes leads us to fail—not my favorite lesson.

I didn't enjoy feeling deprived as I silently watched my fellow teachers celebrate. After congratulating them for their achievements and trying to feel happy for them rather than deprived, I realized there were just some words in this world I would never get to hear, no matter how hard I worked for and wanted to hear them.

But why did the administrators not choose me? What did the others have that I didn't have?

In an exit interview, I came to understand there were things missing in my teaching style that could not be taught. Choosing people for this job was their sacred responsibility, and all I could do was accept their decision as graciously as possible, with a strange certainty that I was not right for this dream I thought I wanted. I knew I had given 110 percent effort, but I was still not hitting their marks, so I began to accept that this professional path was now behind one of life's closing doors, at least for me, and at least for now.

As my head swirled and churned, the dull ache growing in my heart tempted me to think comparatively about the other teachers. I thought about trying to reopen this door later in life; I had the skills just as they did. However, now I lacked the courage because I had been told I lacked that certain "it" factor they sought. My previously clear path had become so muddy that this time, sticking through it might not be worth the effort. I had no choice but to return to the trailhead.

For several weeks, I struggled through the gloom of a wet, early spring to make sense of my situation and to make ends meet. My poor bakery coworkers felt the burden of my search for answers as I kept asking questions; I felt more lost than a traveler on a road with no signposts.

THE ALTITUDES OF ACCEPTANCE

How could I have been so wrong? God wants us to succeed at things that matter to us. Why not this thing for me?

A few of Mom's words seeped into my mind, "No education is ever wasted." I now had a unique set of skills, but where would I ever use them, if not in the field where I had learned them?

Next, my grade-school teachers' words rattled around in my mind. How often had I heard them say I was the kind of student who could do whatever I set my mind to?

I kept working and pondering. There was a certain lesson from my mission about how dedication didn't mean you knew exactly how things would turn out, and I had to accept how life could be mismanaged. Even carefully envisioned career decisions might not work out as planned, for any number of reasons. Other people, God's mysterious plans, personal mistakes, and unexpected circumstances tended to have a say in what people ended up doing in life.

Yet, some limits could only be found by trying. I had done a lot of things in life I had never done before. I didn't generally fear the unknown, but this was the first time I literally had no direction, and now—I was afraid. So far, this year was a downhill plunge I hadn't expected.

My timeline said I was supposed to be in a great full-time job and married at this point, not starting over—again. Others in my age range were traveling the world and preparing to buy houses, but this turn of events had set me back, making investments like that far beyond my reach.

Amidst all this failure, I started pondering about two things: why God would not change the person to match the needs of the dream, and why a person could work so hard and follow so many signs toward a something good and desirable only to lose it in the end, even for the right reasons?

While I waited and searched for answers, I decided that pursuing dreams was a little like trying to ride a balloon over the mountains. It could be done, and it would be exciting, but also fraught with danger and potential mistakes. It was too easy to poke holes in a dream balloon.

Not feeling happy about my dream balloon ride so far, I decided resiliency was more the direction to go. Eventually, I could dream again, but only after I survived the fall and found energy for climbing another mountain. But even then, I figured I would rather keep my feet firmly planted on the ground. Or find another dream ride where less risk was involved.

Earlier that year, as the gloomy months gave way to spring, I had discovered I could use a tall iron post just outside my bedroom window to pull myself onto the flat part of my roof. There, I often laid out a blanket and claimed the warmest spot in the sunlight. It was a magical spot where I could pray, write, and think without any distractions. It became my place to escape to on Sunday afternoons that didn't involve muddy trails or wet tree stumps from the spring snowmelt.

After a few sunny occasions of reflection, it occurred to me how the mountains rose above me to the right while the valley sank lower on my left—much like my life's current crossroads. I was in a precarious situation in more ways than one. I was not yet ready to climb out of the valley of freedom, and not yet ready to decide what mountain to scale next.

As I struggled to process my feelings and ponder any options I could think of, I returned to my thinking spot often. I had to work through the effects of being stuck in some kind of fog, as though I had tried to climb a certain peak from where I wanted to view the world, only to realize there was a glass wall four hundred feet from the top, blocking me out—letting others in. I was just a small person in a big world—a world that stifled me while liberating others. It didn't seem fair, and I didn't know why. All I knew how to do was keep going and ask the right questions.

Why was I allowed to make it so far only to find myself so low, far below the clouds with no clear rewarding view? Was my direction of choice so wrong?

THE ALTITUDES OF ACCEPTANCE

Why wasn't my life getting less complicated with experience?
Why couldn't that lingering dull ache go away?
Ugh ...

Then loyalty to myself and frustration with my lackluster thinking surfaced.

Grr ... So what if I had not made it to the top? It was just one mountain. I'm allowed to hurt from the exertion, to rest and recover before taking on the next one.

After I decided to be my own best friend and stick up for myself, I found that I would spend less daily time navigating through all the self-shaming and more time focusing on doing all the things that made me feel good. Eventually, I realized I had unknowingly done some things that were hard for even the best of people. I had given up a good and solid job for something I thought might be more fulfilling—although it had been riskier. Then I moved, gave up a job, then a relationship, and lost a future. All in less than a year.

Higher risk can lead to higher reward—but when it doesn't, the alternative is failure. But failure wasn't the end. It was just a new beginning. In failing, I resisted the temptation to blame God when things did not work out the way I had planned. I was not bitter, and I felt willing to believe, even if it was not obvious, that I might become better for it, though not right away.

There were spiritual and emotional muscles to gain from this experience, and they would likely show up more fully as I moved forward. That was enough for a while.

Just like education is not wasted, faith is not wasted either—someday, I'd understand.

That I did not need to question. In my heart I knew it to be true.

As the summer of 2011 loomed ahead, it seemed I was going nowhere in some ways, and everywhere in others. With so much unexpected free time,

I joined groups of singles on several inexpensive trips in the search for fun, joy, and star-filled skies at Utah's national parks. As my social circle opened, I stayed busy and active but hoped and expected my situation to be temporary. I believed with the rest of the world that happiness and fulfillment required successful money management, good work-life balance, and a career—I was back to square one, and I hated not knowing my next steps.

Meanwhile, I worked less than thirty hours a week at the bakery, so I found an additional summer job at a camp at the University of Utah. With jobs like this, I was able to spend more time outside and have a lot of free time in the mountains to think and try to navigate the combination of loss, hurt, confusion, and concerns with inadequacy.

I found it easy to talk to God in the mountains about my situation. I could trust God's view of my life. However, I didn't want to add stress to my family or ask for help from my parents.

A sense of shame creeped in whenever I thought about talking to my family because I had so little to show for years of effort and the choices I had made. Explaining how I had no money and no future in a way they would understand felt daunting, and I had no answers for the hard questions. So, when we talked, I kept the details about finances quiet. I had been taught to handle life independently, and for better or worse, this was me handling it. I had something to prove.

This won't last forever, and I'll tell them all about this experience when things get better.

But as usually happens, things got worse before they got better.

Shards of something surrounded my tongue. Judging by how sore my jaw was, it felt like I had done more than bitten into a Wint-o-green mint.

The vague awareness that I had been nowhere near a bowl of mints that day seeped through the fog that was my brain. As my tongue skimmed

THE ALTITUDES OF ACCEPTANCE

through the shards into the forward parts of my mouth, I cringed. I could taste sticky, liquid iron and my left lower lip had the texture of hamburger meat. I felt a gap where before I had two teeth—and then I put two and two together.

Apparently, I had taken a hit. A severe smack to my now-disfigured face.

Only moments ago, I had been riding a wave runner through the rippled lake surface under the bright blue sky, enjoying the sunlight and the cool mountain breeze.

Now, the wave runner drifted not far away while I bobbed on the water's surface.

I leaned onto my back to rest and float, sputtering and spitting as I tried to recollect my scattered thoughts.

My church group had been invited for a beach day at a reservoir in the mountains, and I had been flying around the lake for a half hour with one of the guys in our group. He had taught me things I needed to know for my first solo run, and within minutes I was flying by myself over the waves, having the time of my life!

Why hadn't I seen the writing on the wall?

I should have known my one-hundred pound lightweight frame was no match for the wave runner's five hundred pounds of horsepower. Now something was terribly wrong.

Calm down! Breathe in, breathe out. Don't suck in wave water! Water is my friend. Isn't it?

I shuddered, vaguely aware that my face had smacked into the handlebars after riding a towering wave behind a small speedboat. I had flailed forward, both arms giving way as I slammed hard into the seat after the huge jump. The chance to ride a big wave alone had appealed to the adventurer in me, but I might as well have landed on concrete! Under certain high-impact conditions, water's surface tension could make a landing much harder on the body than usual.

A mental red alert had seeped in, accompanying an image that flashed through my mind. The Velcro strap around my wrist was attached to the key, which was in the machine just under the wheel. Then came the words, like whispers and light through the fog.

Turn off the machine, now!

But how? I seemed unable to command my hand to pull out the key. Fear had gripped me as hard as I was gripping the handlebars at that moment.

I couldn't let go.

Jump, and you'll pull the power switch off.

The realization illuminated the cloud darkening my mind like lightning as I realized I had to jump off into the water. That meant letting go of both handlebars at the same time. And facing the fear head-on. A fear of not being able to survive a swim through murky bottomless water.

But in my situation, I didn't have another choice.

Five, four, three, two, one—jump!

I had begun to tread water, knowing I had jumped from a perfectly good wave runner into a lake. I couldn't see through to the bottom, and that meant I had been motivated to ignore the fear and escape a more threatening situation. Having the skills to swim and the encouragement from a quiet voice in my mind had helped me supersede that fear.

I shook my head at the memories, feeling very grateful to be wearing a life jacket, but also aware of a rising terror. I had no history of encounters with this kind of situation.

Oh God, what is going on? Should I scream for help?

I began grasping for context from all the stories I had heard about boating accidents. Soon, I started assessing my resources.

I floated fifty or so yards away from the bank, bobbing up and down. I eyed the shoreline, moving my arms and legs. They were all okay. I even noted that the key was still on my wrist.

Good. I can swim or ride the wave runner out of here as soon as I'm ready. This damsel could rescue herself!

Or not.

My wet hand touched my face, exploring the injuries my tongue had discovered. I instantly winced, and only then did I realize two things. One, that I had lost my favorite Ray-Ban sunglasses. Two, that my head was starting to throb, and the source of the throbbing was whatever injuries were in my face. And, that there was more to be concerned about than just shredded lips and lost teeth.

Panicking, I felt around for embedded glass or plastic shards. Finding none, I was relieved to know both of my blue eyes were unharmed and intact.

If those sunglasses had had any role in protecting my eyes, they would never be forgotten.

I made a move in the direction of climbing onto the wave runner but stopped cold just short of pulling myself up. The pounding in my head increased, and I realized vertical lifts would not be possible without assistance. As a screaming pain took over, I was no longer certain I could even swim to the bank.

I was helpless and out of control.

I became more and more desperate to find relief from the growing pain, and less and less able to think clearly. However, through my weary haze, and as clear as if it had come from someone right next to me, I heard a certain familiar voice whispering that my reality was going to change. It told me this new reality would last a very long time, but that I would be okay.

Sigh, I relaxed. *What did God have in mind for me to learn this time?*

It had only been a few minutes since I had jumped into the water, but it felt like a lifetime.

Ahead of me, I could see the boat I had been following. It was turning around! Passengers were cheering and shouting how awesome the jump had been, but I hadn't waved or climbed back on. As they came closer, my garbled and barely comprehensible "thank you" must have made my injuries more obvious, so that they knew along with me that my situation was so—*not*—awesome.

The driver circled around so that his riders could pull me out of the water promptly. Then someone gave me a shirt to stop the blood and a shoulder for comfort. I sensed more than saw how the shirt and the shoulder did not belong to the same person, and that someone else handed me a cup of water to swish out what was left of the blood and tooth shards so that I would not swallow them and choke. The driver asked where to find the beach and my friends, while an older youth drove the wave runner along behind the boat to make sure it arrived back to the beach with me.

Miserable in my seat, every movement seemed to be in slow motion. As the boat approached the beach where my friends were gathering, I saw them watching—whispering.

Many hands reached up to help me down out of the boat—but their compassionate stares brought tears I didn't know I was holding back. Their efforts to help made me conscious of my wounds and suffering.

Eeek—what was I going to see and feel when I looked in a mirror?

Feeling apprehensive, I stumbled toward one of the older women who wrapped her arm around me and set us on a path up the hill toward the house. I laid my head on her shoulder.

"That must really hurt, dear, but you'll be okay. We'll get you some help."

She spoke so fondly and confidently that her words reminded me of the earlier whisper.

"It doth-n't hurt—tho bad! One minute I wath fine, and the nec-tht—"

"You poor thing. Don't talk, just walk. Look who's coming!"

My mom has often said to me, "Bad things happen to good people in good places with good help." My rescue had so far been very timely and welcome, and now, evidently, one of the leaders coming toward us must have felt the call of duty—after all, he was a dentist by profession!

Doctor Perry took one glance and then, like a man on a mission, took me softly by the elbow. As he guided me toward the house, we passed the owner and host of our event, to whom he directed a question I didn't expect but deeply appreciated.

"Do you have connections to the local dentist? I saw his office when we came through town. It's not open on Saturdays, but maybe he would let me use it to give her an anesthetic?"

"Yes, of course! I have keys to it, too—I do paperwork for him a few times a week."

Without any difficulty, she gained permission to open the office for the emergency. In no time, I was lying back in the dentist's chair, blood congealed and barely trickling at this point. Doctor Perry used a saline solution to rinse out my mouth, then took a few long looks from various angles. Several group leaders stood by—curious and concerned—discussing who would drive me to the nearest hospital. Meanwhile, Doctor Perry administered shots and anesthetic to give me relief for the two-hour trip and then shared his observations.

"As you know, Deanna, you're missing teeth—one lateral incisor and one central incisor. The lateral was already an implant, as you probably know. I mean, it looks recently placed to me. Anyway, it fractured through to the metal bar, which then bent and tore your lower lip. I can't see any other injuries, but given the mechanism, you may have bone breaks too."

Only two teeth damaged? Well, I expected more from those wave runner handlebars!

"Am I going to need stith-hes?" I queried as the numbing agent began to kick in.

"Yes, unfortunately. Stitches for your lips, cheek, and chin. It won't be too bad."

"Not too bad" sounded droll but decent. I already knew this could have been worse.

Then I saw the faces around me exchange concerned glances. I could sense they perceived a very serious situation, so maybe "not too bad" was just Doctor Perry's way of easing the nature of such troubling news. After he finished his work, I took a deep breath and asked him about using the bathroom, knowing there would be a mirror. It was my turn to see what they all saw.

When I did, I stared for at least a minute. The skin below my eyes was starting to show purple, including my nose and lips. My face had already begun to swell. I found a paper towel and cleaned off the rest of the dried blood, feeling the tenderness, looking for further or more severe injuries. The pain was everywhere, and I realized my task was futile. So, I breathed in again, turned the handle, and opened the door to move forward into my new reality.

Immediately, I was ushered back to the house to grab my things. I found my keys and gave them to friends who could drive my car back, and then I was directed to the bishop's car for the imminent drive to the hospital. Some of the young men stood around gawking a bit, which made me feel uncomfortable again, but then one murmured some kind words, so I looked him in the eyes and promised I would be back cracking jokes again in no time.

As the drive began, I started out energized, trying to make plans, but the bishop reminded me that it was best to take one step at a time with these kinds of things. He was right, and eventually it felt hard to talk and focus on a conversation, so I just sat and thought while he put on some soft rock music. It helped me feel calm, to be doing something so normal like a car ride. Even though the numbing pain reliever helped me feel less pain now, all the sub-surface concerns from this terrible yet (I hoped) tolerable twist in my lifescape came rushing in like the flow of a waterfall.

Eventually the flow would slow, right?

I didn't want to feel so overwhelmed. I wanted to handle this extreme situation from a calm place—after all, I had been told I would be okay. But first, I needed to get to that place. This was a catastrophe, a major dilemma, and I needed to come to terms with and grieve for my losses.

So far, I have been watched over well enough, but what would tomorrow bring?

My thoughts shifted and I wondered about what I had said to my friend as I departed.

"Cracking jokes" was just a phrase, just a way to take the gravity of the situation lightly. But then again, we had all been camping out on the lawn the night before, and I had been sharing funny stories with my imitation Southern belle accent with that young man. It was interesting that I wanted him to remember the last time I was laughing super hard.

Ah, so I wanted people to remember me at my best, in case something worse came of this.

And then it hit me.

I wanted to remember myself like that too.

My new reality was not going to be an awesome experience, but I could think of worse things. It was not like I had suffered a near-death experience in a World War II concentration camp. I had clearly understood this would be hard, but I had always been incredibly motivated to get through hard things. This was just an accident, another hard thing. I could handle it, find a calm place every day. Somehow.

Yep. I'll feel tired and upset but freaking out is not an option. I just need more information.

Wilderness medicine training had taught me that the intense pain and bleeding of a head wound made the injury seem more severe than it really was. I also knew some of my pain and fear were related to the involuntary, temporary fight-or-flight responses in the human systems.

As I reflected, I felt effects of shock wearing me down and knew I needed to conserve my energy now, so that it would be easily directed toward a more informed and intentional action plan later. Then it occurred to me—I had so far been protected from experiencing a worse injury. I could have lost my eyesight, or I could have drowned! Instead, I was in one piece, and I felt like I still had command over all my senses and faculties. Then there was the way I had been literally snatched out of the water and brought to shore so quickly! And I had had a dentist right there to help.

This is what God promises us—that he'll send protection to the faithful amid the chaos.

The thought made me feel safe and secure. Something about the moment felt like home.

As the car slowly rose and fell over the mountainous curves in the road, I started to feel tired too. My folded jacket made a handy pillow, so I gingerly laid on the right side of my head.

In my drained state, I had no problem drifting off to sleep.

Next thing I knew, I was walking into the emergency room of the hospital. The bishop stayed by my side as we learned the waiting time was forty-five minutes, so we aimed for some seats. The bishop was a wise man—he gave me a side hug, pulled out a book, and handed me his iPad. He knew I needed someone there, and that talking was simply out of the question.

I welcomed the distraction from the pain and was amazed at how quickly the time flew as I played game after game of Bejeweled. When we finally went into the room, the doctor arranged for X-rays very quickly, but it still took a few hours before I received the rundown of the full extent of my injuries. As I laid in a bed, I tried to make plans for my immediate future with the bishop. If I couldn't take care of myself, what would I do? Could I go home? Could my roommates help?

At some point, I used the hospital bedside phone to call my parents and tell them what had happened and how I was handling the situation. I could barely talk, so the bishop shared most of the details. They were so grateful for the bishop who cared and stepped in as a parent would have.

Finally, the doctor came in with the images, and I learned that in addition to the two shattered teeth and smashed lower lip, I had three facial fractures. One angled from below my left ear through my left cheek. Another was situated within my upper jaw, just under my nose and above the gap in my teeth. The last lay along the left side of the bridge of my nose.

Somehow, it made a strange sort of sense. *All* the injuries in my past were on the left side.

Why was it always my right side that was saved?

With all the facts in the open, the doctor expressed an optimistic take on the bad situation. He said that all the breaks were localized, so I did not require surgery. All I needed to do was go home, rest, take antibiotics and pain medication, and meet with my dentist.

His recipe for healing was familiar, and he made it sound so simple. Yet even with his optimism, I knew it wouldn't be quite that simple. Nothing ever was. My injuries were intense, and even if they didn't require surgery, there could still be surprises. Still, the doctor's words were illuminating—ahead of me were tasks that needed time and energy.

With everything else going on, how was I ever going to manage this?

I took a deep breath and gave myself a brief but honest pep-talk.

I will be able to bounce back from this—misadventure. But there will be scars.

An hour later, we left the hospital. On the way out, I thanked the nurses, feeling giddy to the point of gushing compliments. I had always been kind-natured, but I didn't know when to stop! They went along with me, all grins and amusement, probably knowing that while I was genuine, I was also on a lot of medication! One of them advised me that this level of adrenaline would wear off and would be followed soon by a psychological drain and a lot of pain, so I should get the prescribed medication immediately.

They also told me I wouldn't be able to drive for as long as I was on the medications.

Along the way to Walgreens, the bishop and I discussed how not being able to drive would affect me. I wouldn't be able to work, and I wouldn't be able to go shopping. He also expressed concerns about how drained I would be and how emotions attached to such experiences could be complicated by loneliness. Staying at my apartment meant I would be surrounded by stress and burdens of life. Also, my roommates had lives and varied schedules of their own, and what I needed now was a quiet place to heal and recover with people close by.

As he helped me see my situation clearly, he was leading up to a point. With foresight, he had called his wife earlier and arranged for me to stay at their home for a few days—if I believed that was what I needed. When I heard his solution, I understood his wisdom and kindness. It was like someone was showing me true north after I'd been lost for hours. The relief of having people watching over me and ensuring I would not bear the burden of healing alone was nearly tangible.

Before I could rest at their home, however, there were still a few things only I could do.

First, the bishop dropped me off at my apartment so that I could take thirty minutes to pack my suitcase for a week and claim some pudding and soup from my pantry. Meanwhile, I think he must have gone to the store to get food that didn't require chewing. I was never hungry at their house. Plus, they took me out for soup and bread a couple of times, which was much appreciated.

Over the next few days, I evaluated my physical condition and energy level. I found I could take short walks to the pharmacy or along trails with friends without triggering a headache. However, keeping up with children at the summer camp would be too much, even if I could drive.

When I was around other people at church, I saw how my new appearance affected them. Some friends treated me the same way they always had, with lots of love and encouragement. However, it was bittersweet to realize some people—particularly my male friends—were deterred or made uncomfortable. I couldn't blame them—the gaps in my front teeth were hard even for me to look at. It hurt a little, but I could only respect them, their feelings, and even their actions when they refrained from spending any time around me.

It was interesting when people I hardly knew came forward with stories that really helped me gain perspective. For example, I was not the only person in my ward who had experienced facial trauma in a boating accident that summer, but he had broken his nose and needed surgery. I counted my blessings—his nasal surgery distressed me more than my upcoming tooth implants.

I also discovered new friends in random places while doing normal life activities. At one point, I met a cashier who only needed to see the grocery items on the checkout conveyor belt (e.g. pineapple juice, applesauce, canned soup—nothing crunchy or hard to chew, etc.) to guess my injury right away. After a brief conversation full of kindness and sympathetic words between us, the calm place in my heart was reinforced because her face appeared healthy, healed, and rather lovely after her own similar experience several years ago.

Never had I ever found the gift of hope in a face before, but it was there, and it was precious.

I don't know how it works, but that's another thing God does for us. He might use our closest friends for some things, but he often sends specific hope to our souls through strangers.

Some days my feelings all got jumbled and frustrated as I dealt with a load of adult decisions. Hope gave way to stress as dentist bills and insurance issues loomed in the distance. I worried about how long I wouldn't be able to exercise. I had good friends, but I was far from the comforts of family. My employer had expressed an understanding of my situation, but being unable to work for several days meant a cut in my wages.

And so, the *why* questions began.

Why did this have to happen now?

Why had I not been blessed with the full-time job and benefits I had missed out on earlier that year? Sick leave would have been nice right now.

My overall health and safety were more important than missed opportunities and empty bank accounts, but I couldn't help myself. I kept praying and hoping, but the worries lingered.

Just when my doubts and anxiety were about to drown me deeper than I had ever been in the lake, solutions I had not expected were laid before me, one after another. It turned out that God had done greater things behind the scenes than I could have ever asked for.

First, my bishop came forward to let me know our church's insurance would cover all or part of the expenses because the accident had occurred at a church activity.

Second, my father's government job insurance would help cover the costs as well. In fact, the timing of this accident made it possible for all expenses to be paid by insurance rather than by me. If it had happened even seven days later, they wouldn't have covered it because I would have no longer been twenty-six years old. Even the copays were covered, or at least I don't recall having to pay very much out of pocket.

Third, when I started looking for ways to heal my mouth and obtain dental procedures, I loyally went to the dentist I had been seeing before the accident, but issues with them pointed me to a far better path. Their emergency response style focused on maintaining that space for future implants while my face was healing, so they fitted two fake teeth to fill the space. It sounded reasonable to me, but as I stared in the mirror at the miniature opaque white Chiclet gum pieces nestled in between my naturally colored teeth, my thoughts were filled with disgust—which I hid well at first. I had never seen such teeth before.

My smile was stolen and then replaced with a coarse substitute! It looks like I just shrunk and got a French manicure on two of my front teeth. They make my mouth look worse than it did without teeth. No pictures, puh-lease! How will I face others if I can't even look at myself? I want—no, I need—another way!

I wanted to believe this dentist's office had done their best in an emergency, but to me it looked like they had added cheap insult to injury. A day or two later, I did what should have been obvious to me from the start: I arranged to get a second opinion from Doctor Perry, the same dentist who had helped me at the lake. At church he would say, "If you're happy and you know it, tell your face!" I usually smiled broadly at his joke, but this time, as I walked toward his dentist office, I whispered what I hoped would come true: "I'll be happy and I'll know it when he's done with my face."

Then I prayed and stepped inside.

The first words Doctor Perry said brightened my day with relief.

"Deanna, I'm so happy you're here! I wanted to help you, but I didn't want to come across as soliciting your insurance money." There was his caring nature again. What a guy!

"I get that, thank you. I know it had to be my choice!"

I expressed how much I hoped he could do better than what was in my mouth. Then Doctor Perry took a close look at those ugly teeth from the other dentist. After frowning a bit, he muttered with disdain, "Well, not all dentists are created equal."

I had never heard considered such a statement before—but I believed him. Sometimes differences between people were a good thing!

As he began to describe what he could do, I learned his training in family dentistry included a high level of orthodontics and aesthetics. He even had friends who built good-looking artificial teeth for a living. Not only was this appointment filled with assurance, but I also discovered his office took both insurance companies that were supporting me through this nightmare.

Doctor Perry's plan for treatment was so different than the previous dentist's. I relaxed when he said the first order of business was to take out those two ugly teeth. In their place, he planned to introduce a professional-style denture-flipper, complete with remarkably real-looking teeth that matched the nuances in my own teeth. I would have to take it out for eating, but during the day, the gap in my mouth would stay filled with teeth that felt and looked more real. I knew this would save me mental and emotional stress while my face healed and became ready for drilling and installation of two implants. Bones grew quickly, so I would only have to deal with the flipper until September. A few months felt like no time at all!

After the appointment, I sat in my car offering a prayer of gratitude. I repented of certain *why* questions as I realized God's plans and blueprints had again been far more reliable than my expectations. I don't know how he does it, but he works within our choices to turn the most unlikely and potentially life-changing situations into things that work out for our best good.

Many people struggle to see God's miracles within the mayhem of life, but I am a witness to say that they are always there. In fact, the more I continued to see how good God was to me, the more I discovered ways he'd been looking out for me all along. For instance, I learned that the full-time religious educator job did not have insurance benefits equal to those

I had currently. Being on my father's insurance was a real asset to the costs of the situation, and the claim was completely covered as an emergency. If I had gotten the job I wanted, I would have taken my job's offered insurance because it was the adult thing to do. It would have felt natural to do so without comparing insurance benefits. So, in a way, my expenses were reduced because I didn't get that job.

With great divine foresight and wisdom, *God had given me a loss I didn't want, to ensure a gain I didn't know I needed.* Which brought me to another *why* question.

Why was I worthy of the way things worked out?

All I truly know is that somehow things work out for those who God loves and who love God. When he sees fit to bless us, we receive in abundance. Blessings like this aren't about being superior or special, but rather being rescued or snatched away from potential or harmful realities. Blessings like this come to the faithful for reasons only God knows, until—or unless—he sees fit to share them with us.

Once I obtained the flipper, things felt normal. I started smiling again and quickly learned how to talk clearly around the flipper. It felt easy to implement daily extra dental hygiene practices, such as brushing my teeth and using salt water in my mouth after every meal to encourage healing. Gradually, it was harder and harder to feel like I was still climbing a major life mountain. It felt more like I had finally reached the summit, and it was all downhill from here.

Seeing and hearing about similar accidents helped me realize my experience was not normal for this type of incident and trial. Time and time again, a certain thought resurfaced—if God had wanted permanent physical deformity and financial discomfort to happen for me, he easily could have allowed it. Those life-changing conditions could have been my story—they would have taught me a lot, and I would have been a good student. But it appeared I had gained more spiritually than I had lost physically, so it seemed safe to conclude God had other lessons for me to learn through the hardships in this lifescape.

On the other hand, in less than a year, I had relocated, lost a career path and endured a broken engagement, so perhaps in God's plan, I had already met the quota for trials this year. At the very least, all the issues I did *not* have to deal with—loneliness, financial compromise, loss of life, appendage, or eyes, and so forth—seemed to make the ones I *was* dealing with seem small, even if they were still significant.

Looking back, I remember thinking if I had truly lost anything, it was time. My twenties were supposed to be full of dating and marriage and starting a family, but love—real attraction versus compassion—might prove to be hard to find or trust while I healed. It was like God put me in a holding pattern, where amid the craving for that kind of happiness, I'd have to accept the possibility of living without it for a time.

I didn't know what it would be like to return to normal daily activities, but I felt determined. If I had to learn about returning to life from a place of pain, I also needed to understand healing. And if I was going to heal from one thing, I might as well try to heal from them all.

CHAPTER 3

THE PURPOSE OF PAIN

Would it surprise anyone to know that my first day back at work was the day the whole summer camp was trekking up a steep mountain hillside to tour a cave?

This was nothing like a walk in the park with kids. It was serious, strenuous hiking. The trail started at the visitor's center and ended at the cave entrance just a mile and a half away, but it rose 1,092 feet. For comparison's sake, the average fourteener rises 4,000 feet while covering about 10 miles roundtrip. So, you can see why I just couldn't miss it.

It was only a week and a half after the incident, but this was the first hike I wanted to go on after my accident. I honestly wanted to see what I could handle, but my supervisor was worried.

"Deanna, changes in altitude are not recommended for head injuries. Don't you think you need more time to heal?"

I appreciated his concern, but I sensed only certainty, confidence, and determination. I was already accustomed to altitude from all my previous mountain adventures. My physical healing was going well, and something inside me said I needed to make an honest assessment of my mental and emotional stamina. Having a group of kids to motivate me would bring out the best in me and help me endure. I felt I needed to be with them, and that they also needed me!

"Sure, I could take more time off work, but who and what would that serve? I don't know what future treatment will be like, and I'll probably need the money later. I promise I'll be careful! I have been recovering well, and if I can prove to both of us that I can handle a mountain day with my injury as-is, neither of us will need to worry whether I'll be able to work the rest of summer, right?"

A short silence followed, indicating that my words had an impact.

Then he said, "I'm still a little concerned, but I can't deny that. I'll approve a group for you."

Victory!

Although this hiking adventure became a test, I handled it with caution. I made sure I had my pain medication and avoided running or exerting myself into a headache, but I let my motivation to do hard things carry me step by step.

Mountains had always put such motivations into perspective for me.

The day went exactly as proposed. I stopped and rested when my group of kids did. I drank water when the kids drank water. I led them up the mountain with all the determination of a person on a mission, and then they got me down the mountain with their stories and giggles to distract me from the minor aches and pains. Nothing terrible happened, and a wordless nod from my boss indicated I had passed our mutually determined assessment of my ability to work.

Somehow, I think it was meant to be.

Throughout the summer, the kids became part of my healing process.

They reminded me how healing comes with service and purpose, and as I taught them things, they taught me things. Once, a clever ten-year-old camper was leading my group while I was giving instructions and walking backwards right up to a crosswalk. Seeing something he didn't like, he rushed to stand behind me, barely fitting in the inches between my body and where the first white strip started. As I spun around to stop him, he raised his arms in a "T" shape and said, "The last thing you need right now is getting hit by a car, Miss D." He was right!

It was easy to appreciate where this young man was coming from, and to see where he was going with his thoughts on this occasion. He was the kind of kid who was often getting injured when he wasn't looking in the direction he was going, so in addition to reminding me to focus and live in the moment, he showed me he really did know when enough was enough and that safety mattered.

Sometimes, younger campers asked me when I would grow new teeth. It brought a smile every time, and even though I tried to help them understand the difference between adult and baby teeth, they just couldn't comprehend it. I reconciled to let them figure it out later!

When it came to the older campers, especially the new ones, my teeth issues proved to be a tool for gaining rapport. At lunchtime I would get into a mischievous mood, look the new campers in the eyes, and smile directly at them while taking out my teeth. It was delightful to see them gasp and elbow their nearest friend in shock—who was usually someone I had played this trick on a few weeks prior. That friend and I would grin at our silent inside joke.

Such moments proved to be one of the best pranks ever! Experienced campers looked forward to it from week to week, and so did I. Laughter like this helped me control the subsurface turbulence of life and the emotions that these days always seemed to threaten my peace.

In a few weeks, most of my bruises healed. All that was left to see from my accident were my missing teeth. Under these circumstances, I felt like I had returned to normal.

THE ALTITUDES OF ACCEPTANCE

Almost.

There were still hidden scars and sadness over my losses, but at least I was in a good place.

Each week I became the leader of a new group of kids. My group usually aged from nine to eleven, and they were old enough to monitor themselves with minimal direction and enjoy conversations with each other and with me. Many kids participated every week, while others attended alternating weeks. Some were brand new, and one of them, Tanner, joined my group near the end of July. The minute we met, I observed and valued his thoughtful and bright disposition.

For the first couple of days, he stuck close to me. He was quick to find ways to help, and based on interaction with his peers, I believed he had figured out how to balance leading and following. He seemed to know how to act mature when he was with adults but still had loads of fun with other kids. One day, our group was trekking across the university campus to an activity, so I started a casual conversation with Tanner, who was assigned to be group leader for the day.

"Hey, Tanner, what awesome things have you been up to this summer?"

"Well, I did a lot of biking with my family. We had a family reunion too, and we went boating on a reservoir in the mountains. We had a lot of fun! Oh, and something scary happened."

"Something scary? Uh oh, what happened?"

"Well, we were on the boat and this girl was riding a wave runner behind our boat. When she took a high wave, it was fun to watch her. But then she slowed down, and Dad turned the boat around. We found out she got into an accident. We got her out of the water and took her back to the beach. It was bad. There was a lot of blood. I've never seen anything like that before."

A cold shiver ran up my spine as I listened to someone else telling me *my* story. My steps slowed, and I looked at him. *Was he teasing me? Did he hear something from the other kids?*

But all I saw on his face was solemn concern. In his mind, this was *his* story. The event he had witnessed deeply distressed him—plus, he never gave me any signs that he recognized me.

"Tanner, did someone give that girl a gray shirt to soak up the blood on her face?"

"Uh, ye-es. I gave her my shirt. How did you know?"

"And what lake were you in and when were you there?"

"Pineview Reservoir. It was in June—I think it was almost the end of the month."

He was giving me a quizzical once-over now, so I took a deep breath.

"Tanner, that was me. I was that girl. *You* helped *me*."

The other kids were now gathering, curiously appraising our stillness as they realized all the urgency to reach our destination had been replaced by whatever exchange had absorbed our attention. Tanner was staring at me with those blue eyes, mouth wide open. He shook that light-colored hair a few times, trying to make sense of what he was hearing.

Meanwhile, I was about to cry. The shiver was gone, replaced by gratitude and awe.

What did this mean? Why him? Why me?

"That was you? But you were so … injured. Your face was so messed up!"

I could have made light of the moment and said, "Well, thank you very much!" but I didn't.

"Well, the breaks in the bone didn't need surgery, and now I wear a flipper to cover the gaps in my teeth." I realized he hadn't seen me eating the day before, so I showed him. "I also have a bumpy lip now, over here on the left side. That's where it was torn."

I pointed as Tanner looked closely at my face, then he took a step back.

"Wow. You look so much … better. Miss D, how did I … I can't believe I'm in your group!"

"Me neither! I feel really lucky, and I don't know why we have met this week, Tanner, but it's really awesome to know you."

THE ALTITUDES OF ACCEPTANCE

Tanner was resisting tears as most young men do—caught in that space between shock and awe as he said, "This is so crazy, but I'm really glad you are here."

"As am I!" Then we talked more about the incident and swapped our observations. As Tanner's emotions barely reached the surface, I couldn't help but notice he felt spiritual feelings like concern for others very deeply.

Maybe God knew he needed to see me again, to know I was okay.

Our amazement about this incredible revelation stayed with us, and by the end of the week, Tanner and I held a special bond. When the time came to say goodbye, it was hard to let him go, knowing I wouldn't see him again since he had other adventures to pursue that summer. There was never time for a discussion about the boating accident with Tanner's parents, so I was left to wonder if Tanner ever told them or kept his feelings about how he experienced my pain to himself.

At some point, I found out Tanner was a member of my church, but we didn't discuss our faith. I have often wondered what lessons Tanner learned from God, although I believe God's purpose was more for Tanner than for me. Maybe someday I'll find out why when I meet Tanner for the third time, but if that never happens, it's okay.

I think when God's working to bring lives together, to make lifescapes intersect or collide, we can sometimes *sense* meaning, but we often don't get to *know* God's full purpose. In time, we may get to know why most of these connections are made. But when we don't get to know why a connection occurs, I like to think we are being blessed by something so mysterious it is sacred.

When things like this happen, maybe it's enough to know God has his reasons.

Maybe God is simply showing us he is in charge.

As the end of the summer of 2012 approached, I had gotten used to the simple operations of managing my teeth issues at camp, and I loved my young support group, but I still had no future plan and two jobs. One of them ended with the season, and the other couldn't be full-time.

I hoped God still had a good view of my life, because I certainly couldn't see what was next. In this lifescape, I was in between peaks or in a deep valley, and the view from such places tends to be far less scenic and inspiring than from the top. I also hoped I could get to the top my next mountain in life without it taking forever.

But which mountain would that be?

Between work hours and dental appointments, I had applied for several jobs but was considered for none. I contemplated a few training courses in fields related to my undergraduate degree, but I came up empty because each one cost money I didn't have.

In the end, I did the last best thing I could do: seize an opportunity and make the best of it.

A few camp coworkers told me about a charter school that was hiring. Some of my coworkers had worked there for a couple of years, while others had been newly hired. Like them, I had done well with camp kids, and children were a favorite part of my previous job environments, so I didn't hesitate to think, why not me?

I gave the school my resume, and the school requested an interview a week before school began. In a flash, I was hired. It seemed too easy because the hardest thing was figuring out a carpool to manage the seventeen-mile commute, but with so many friends making the same trip, I could only appreciate the gift of a job.

Meanwhile, I was indisputably ready to be rid of the flipper in exchange for—well, more fake teeth in the form of implants. When the long-awaited appointment arrived in September, the first implant went in easily, like the right light bulb fitting into its base. The aesthetic of the tooth was pleasing, so they moved forward with the installation of the second implant.

THE ALTITUDES OF ACCEPTANCE

As they screwed the base into my upper jaw, a thousand tiny fiery javelins shot out from my jaw and into my entire head. I began to squirm and shift slightly, not sure what to do, but felt certain that something had gone unexpectedly wrong.

Had I been kicked in the head by a horse? Maybe a load of bricks had been swung at my face. Nope. There were no horses or backpacks. Just a dentist's drill ...

In despair, I pulled at the dentist's arm and squealed at him until he came to an abrupt stop. Once everything was clear of my mouth, words spilled out as clearly as I could manage.

His assistant took a speedy X-ray, and then we all saw what had been hidden in previous X-rays. A hairline fracture in my upper jaw very near to the roots of my upper front teeth had not healed completely and was now expanded by the pressure of the implant base in a dangerous way.

We were all confused. Enough time had passed for my jawbone to heal, but it was obvious to the dentist that the intensity of my pain, the evidence in the X-ray, and the rate of my healing demanded six to eight more months for adequate bone structure to be in place before both implants could be completed. I needed to wait for both implants and keep wearing the flipper.

What?

There it was, a dreaded false summit in my current lifescape's fourteener. I knew how these things go; I should have expected it. I'd have to reassess my position on this mountain, though of course I would keep climbing. I wanted to reach the summit and have a mouth full of teeth again.

Still, this shift in issues was really messing with my head—pun intended!

As I left the appointment, I cried hard. I kept reminding myself that things could be so much worse—that I already knew things would work out. The evidence so far was in that direction. My teeth were in a good head, being handled by skilled hands, and I finally had a job. I was used to things as they were, so an extended healing timeframe did not change anything worth worrying over. Yet even after all this time and effort to have patience with healing, my emotions from all that I was enduring were still getting the better of me.

Ironically, around this time, someone asked me what was harder about my year of pain—the physical struggle with my teeth, or the emotional struggle involving my recovery after my lost career and relationship. Without hesitating, I responded that the emotional challenges were far harder to navigate than this physical one. They always had been. My physical circumstances seemed to evolve with surprises, but God had made it clear despite it all that he already had that healing in his control.

It made sense that God would have me learn another layer of the lesson I needed most.

Healing was important, but so was the purpose of pain.

At the time, I bought (or someone bought me) the complete treasury of the Christian works of Clive Staples Lewis, better known as C.S. Lewis. I started reading it often in my thinking spot on the roof. There, under the blue sky on as many autumn evenings as I could, I learned this man started life out as an atheist but was renowned as one of the greatest intellectual geniuses and spiritual giants of the twentieth century by the end of his life. Now—that was an admirable switch! Here was a man who, not liking the name Clive, had also nicknamed himself Jackie at age four. A bold move for one so young, but certainly an interesting concept that activated my mind.

I like my name, but in high school I was nicknamed Little One. I was not really bothered by it at first because it was true and made me feel noticed and accepted. But as I got older, I noticed people found it hard to not let my youthful size be a determining factor of my age or competence. So, I hadn't encouraged that nickname after high school. Maybe that was why C.S. Lewis had changed his name? He didn't want to be wrongly defined or risk that others might be distracted by his name. He was so much more than his name, just as I'm so much more than my height.

THE ALTITUDES OF ACCEPTANCE

The man was also well associated with and inspired by scientists and writers at the university where he worked. I loved that about him because that was what I had loved most about university life—being inspired by those I admired and changing how I thought because of powerful conversations. It was awesome to me how, after discussing and examining at length all the other plausible cases for life on earth, C.S. Lewis concluded for himself that God existed and was good. Not to mention, he stayed faithful even after he later experienced immense pain from tragically losing the love of his life to cancer.

It seemed unlikely that things worked out the way he had planned them from the very beginning. As I became more and more familiar with C.S. Lewis's life story, I realized his dreams must have changed a lot throughout his life. He had likely experienced severe deflations and gained new motivations for living as well. After all, what atheist ever dreams of believing in God and reasoning in favor of God? It had to happen slowly over time. Such dreaming is a bit like writing a book with stories that don't seem united at first, but eventually weave together into one great whole.

I noticed how when he was asked to write his book titled *The Problem of Pain*, he believed he was no expert on pain and simply wanted to offer ideas for solving the problem raised by suffering. He warned he was not a trained scientist and did not himself adhere perfectly to the principles in the book but instead shared his "conviction that when pain is to be borne, a little courage helps more than much knowledge, a little human sympathy more than much courage, and the least tincture of the love of God more than all." [1]

Courage, sympathy, and love of God. I've needed that before, and that's what I need now.

Something about C.S. Lewis's thoughts reminded me of lessons from my mission. I knew my life's pain was individual, unique, and purposeful, leading me to discover a little more about the love of God. I also needed to remember God didn't just listen to me; he also understood and helped me handle pain. God's great love—would no doubt be my rescue this time. And likely every—single—time. I needed his love more than anything; I was still just a kid missing her childhood.

THE PURPOSE OF PAIN

Why was dealing with pain, especially my emotional pain, so much harder as an adult? Why did the answers not feel as clear, simple, or straightforward as they did when I was a kid?

A chill in the air picked up as a thought settled into my mind.

Apparently, I was still learning to recognize God's way of speaking to me, and it usually wasn't what I expected. But why wouldn't I expect a book to make a difference? It had before.

As a kid, my positive response to my mother's love and the book about Muir had been almost immediate. Now, finding an affinity for and answers in the works of C.S. Lewis seemed to indicate relief was coming. Hope's reward was finding purpose in the pain after months of recovering from the effects of unforeseen circumstances on my carefully laid plans.

Whispers in my mind said that we were meant to know so very little about the world at first. We needed to know what it was like to be a child for a divine reason. Then we begin to grow, understand complexities, manage our own problems, and process our own pain and joy. First, we are allowed to ask a lot of questions, and eventually the biggest question of all becomes—

Will life get better, or will we just get better at life—or in the end, will we just have to trust that there is something better than this life?

It seemed to me then that God would never hide two facts from us as adults: one, pain is a very real, intentional part of life, and two, he has ways of helping us manage our pain so that we can do hard things, gain character, and still smile. I think he makes it very clear how his love for us—and what pain can do for us—is weaved into the details of life.

From the beginning of creation, pain has been purposefully incorporated into life's experience as an intrinsic and indispensable part of life's adventures. Pain and discomfort are the risks of making a hard choice, yet if we believe the scriptures and prophets through the ages who have preached about the promises of God, we can deal with hard things and find that growth. We can hope God will consecrate our struggles to our gain, even when we suspect God has set us up for a great deal of pain because of what he gives us to carry through life.

In my case, anxiety and perfectionism.

My experiences have taught me to believe that any pain resulting from what God gave me is part of his plan to help me gain and give the most I can in life. If I believe anxiety and perfectionism will forever taint or obstruct my potential or inhibit my growth, I'm setting myself up for regret and disappointment because of the pain I cannot escape. But if I believe I have been given gifts that make my individuality complete, then the way I operate in life because of them matters to me, to God, and to others. In fact, I'm setting myself up to love better and to feel loved despite the pain.

And there will always be pain.

But if we turn toward God, reach for his love, and let it in, there will also be joy and healing.

We don't have to understand our pain to recognize the power of God's love. His love is never out of reach. Ever. We don't have to appreciate what God gives us in life for God to love us. He just does. God loves everyone, but the thing is, *how much we feel that love* is determined by *how we choose to get through life*, and how close we get to God.

In the story of my life, and in what I have seen of the world so far, it seems like the love and power of God can make everything, even entire seasons of pain, turn into growth and spiritual formation. Of course, when we are in the thick of hard things, we feel tempted to do anything other than appreciate pain. We don't always see God's divine interventions on our behalf. It's also hard to acknowledge how what we are going through might actually be good for us. That's because those are the moments when the purpose of the pain is not obvious.

I recently heard someone say that in seasons of pain, we have three options—we can turn against God, turn away from God, or turn toward God. But God has just one plan, one eternal purpose—to get himself closer to us and us closer to him. And he will do whatever it takes to accomplish that sacred effort.

The lesson from my mission was that how we respond when life is hard is reflected in how we cultivate peace and learn to accept God as the leading hero of our story. Additionally, regardless of where purpose and pain take us, we are not supposed to get everything we *want*, but if we focus on getting closer to God, we get everything we *need*. Then, when we have completed our mission, we come home, and we can rest assured that when God says well done, he means it. He means that he's done his job and we've done ours.

As life continued, these past lessons resurfaced as new ones, letting me know I still had a lot more to learn about the purpose of pain and assuring me that I could get through it all because I had done it before. The conditions for this life are already set, but God is on our side. He wants us to individually experience whatever is necessary for us to learn, and he wants us to make hard choices—but not without him or his love.

This makes God the humble yet glorious hero of our collective human story too. I believe the depth to which we individually choose to recognize the inklings and etchings of God's love throughout the pain of every lifescape can and does have impact on how many others are able to see and feel the same along their life's trail.

It is my hope that each of my stories will share that message—that our lives can fill with color and beauty as we allow pain to be guided and softened by the power of God's love.

CHAPTER 4

BUILDING CONNECTIONS

There were two things I knew for sure after working at the school for just one month.

One, it wasn't my perfect job, but it was good enough for now.

Two, I was surrounded by plenty of good people I wanted to know better.

A paraprofessional was needed in the classroom, but since the role was not considered full-time, it came with no benefits. The hourly wages were not reflective of my bachelor's degree, but even so, I was grateful to at least have enough income to leave behind all my other jobs.

The teachers were intelligent and delightful to talk to. After meeting them during my school tour, I could see they were devoted to doing excellent work despite having few resources. Such was the case at most schools, I gathered, but one teacher said, "It's worth it to be able to work with kids." I believed him and agreed—but little did I know how that idea would be tested.

All my life, prior to landing the job at the school, I had worked with mostly neurotypical children, and I had met a few autistic individuals. But having next to no experience working with autistic children, I felt apprehension. At times, I even wondered why I was being hired to do a job I didn't know how to do. My fellow camp staff reassured me that they knew I could do the work, and I believed them, but after the first few training days, I couldn't help feeling like I might never adjust to a school *full* of neurodivergent children. It would be nothing less than an alarming experience.

The first few days of transition into the school schedule were super hard on these kids—and for me. Most days were normal school days, with consistent education and activities, but in class, sometimes I would need to repeat my instructions or give students a modified assignment. Some of the students could advocate for themselves, others soothed themselves with fidgets or blankets, and still others would not be pacified when they were stimulated. In fact, many of the students experienced major behavioral extremes daily: one boy needed to be held down to prevent injury, and one girl would hurt herself if she couldn't de-escalate fast enough.

As the days went on like this, never quite knowing what would happen seemed intriguing, yet I felt frustrated by chaos I could not control, both internally and externally. I was also terrified of my mistakes and aware of the risk of triggering behaviors. Worst of all, because I didn't understand them, I wasn't sure if I could like these kids, no matter how much I tried to love them.

I understood major behaviors were delicate situations requiring careful attention, but it seemed like everyone else knew what to do—except me. Even with my training, I struggled to determine the right responses. Comprehending and even memorizing each kid's needs well enough to know what the preferred response needed to be was a huge ask, and sometimes what I saw triggered my own anxiety.

I often had to get control of myself before I could figure out how to handle the students.

Over time, I began to accept how the right responses seemed counterintuitive, but they were based on rules that kept teachers and students safe and professional. For example, sometimes punishments for certain behaviors were dissuaded because it was more important to teach them a better form of communication—this made sense to me. Too often what appeared to be insolence, anger, or some other brazen behavior was, in reality, an inability to communicate a personal need with words and social skills.

I also started to understand why I felt like a severely underinformed outsider among the more experienced teachers. A few teachers were simply trained in certain ways that made them the best ones to approach certain kids. However, in some cases, the limited interactions they allowed me to have—often only one tiny minute's worth of attempts at understanding and compassion in an undistracted environment (such as the hallway)—made me feel like I would never truly learn. This time, the swirling storm was not only in me, but around me. It felt like, no matter how much the administrators tried to teach me about how neurodivergent brains worked, I couldn't pour their knowledge into my brain fast enough.

"I feel so guilty and confused!" I said one particularly challenging day after about a month to the friends with whom I had carpooled. "I thought I was good with kids and understood them, but I've been so discouraged by making the wrong calls all the time.

"I have one student who has spent some portion of every day this week in the hall. Today he fell asleep on his desk, so I tapped it with my pencil to wake him up. I took extra time to re-explain the assignment again to him; he said he would do it, but when I went away, he put his head down again and went back to sleep.

"I tried to connect with him a bit later and woke him up, chatted for a minute, then asked, 'What do you like to do?'

"He replied, 'I like to do—nothing!'

"I thought he was being facetious or mocking me about the unfinished assignment on his desk, so I narrowed my eyes at him and said, 'Not today!' And then I shoved the paper toward him.

"I thought he needed a firm hand, but the look on his face sent a knife to my heart as I backed away. His face and eyes had a haunting and forlorn look, as if he was giving up being understood. He said nothing, but what I saw in his face was followed by a glint of steel resolve that made me nervous. He picked up his pencil, took up his assignment, and set to work.

"Meanwhile, instead of feeling like I had just done my duty as a teacher with a tough student, I felt like I had just thrown this student's arm under the bus along with his backpack. Somehow, I destroyed a piece of him that mattered. I did something terribly wrong and knew it but wasn't sure what to do about it. When the class was over, he handed me a half-completed assignment, hung his head, refused to look at me, and went to his next class without saying a word.

"I didn't know what to do. I was crushed. He was crushed. I wanted to be the adult who fixed whatever this was, but I had no clue what to do.

"Later, another teacher told me this student spends his time at home after school cleaning and cooking dinner for his parents. They both work. Then he does homework until late—if he even has energy to do it."

During the storytelling to my friends, tears welled in my eyes. "How could I do that to a kid? He did not deserve how I treated him. Being tired was a fact of his life, a behavior I needed to understand, not a behavior I needed to punish. I need to apologize, and I will, but if I keep making major blunders like that—ugh! It hurts, and every day I go home and cry about what I did wrong.

"These students don't deserve my mistakes. They have enough to worry about in their lives. Also, they don't want to talk to me, and why should they? It's obvious they need so much more than I can give them.

"Feeling this overwhelmed terrifies me.

"What am I supposed to do? I need the job and I want to love the kids, but I—just—can't!"

My friends had heard me express frustrations before, but nothing like this. They had started out being actively engaged in helping me practice conversations and adjust my approaches to the behaviors in the classroom, but now they just looked at me and listened, speaking only at random.

The changes in their behavior were evident, and I knew they had tired of my drama.

As soon as I could, I found an exit from the conversation and started to think about ways to get a little less emotionally frustrated or to know the kids better. It was clear how complaining about my sorrows and challenges seemed to only lead me to temporary solutions, not a complete resolution. My friends were great, but they couldn't resolve the pain for me. This was my burden to bear, to act on, to engage with, to change if I could. Sure, I needed others' insights, but I was starting to sense that I was not yet asking the right questions. Or the right people.

I began cautiously evaluating myself and my options. First, I tried to find a graceful way out by reaching out to other people for greater empathy or wisdom. Then, I realized I was plastering my weaknesses onto the wall of public opinion. I didn't like how that triggered me. As anxiety climbed sharply, fight-or-flight mode took over.

It took me awhile to see it, but I was acting selfish. Compared to many of these kids, I had been blessed with a relatively problem-free life. When I finally started to see my mistake, I knew how I responded to the needs of the students and teachers mattered, but so far, my emotional attention had been on myself, my discomfort, my mistakes, my anxiety, and my powerlessness.

I had not realized when that pesky comparative thinking habit was triggered because it was affecting my thoughts in a new way. Like the students, I was used to a life of hard knocks and dealing with personal imperfections, but I wasn't relating to them. In my mind, I didn't belong with them. I had been privileged to live largely without tragedy, exclusion, persecution, and misery, so it was easy for me to recognize and sympathize with their pain but hard for me to empathize and know what to do with what they were going through.

Finally, I concluded these kids were just people dealing with life amidst personal struggles.

Not having similar life experiences was not just a simple limitation; it was also an arrow, a sign pointing to the one thing I could do for them, and for myself.

That week I started to pray for myself and for the students.

As the months wore on, I spread out my conversations so that I could speak with other teachers about my perceptions and attempts to learn from my experiences involving the students. These conversations were different, not just seeking wisdom or empathy, but to truly understand what their experience had entailed. Eventually, it occurred to me I might be unknowingly setting unnecessary limits in my relationships with the children because of my own discomforts.

While taking refuge on my rooftop and pondering hard in my thinking spot, I concluded that it was time to face the facts, and given my past experiences, the facts were:

One, I genuinely desired to do right by and love the children.

Two, I was utterly dissatisfied with my misunderstandings, incapacities, and blunders.

Three, I was again doing my best but not hitting the mark.

Four, I felt tremendously tired of feeling like I did not measure up to the paths I chose for myself. It was like I was constantly conscious of how my plans and God's plans were not aligning.

Five, my expenses were not going to change or go away. There was no guarantee of finding another job quickly. My degree boasted of a competitive job market and career field, but I was not the ideal candidate due to having so few years in a full-time work environment.

Six, I could not dare to leave this job on the grounds that I was defeated. That would be a huge hit on my confidence and self-esteem, and I had already endured a serious game of whac-a-mole. If defeat was not the way to go, I would need to somehow beat the hard mallet of opposition.

Around that point, a confirming memory flashed through my mind—a pair of purple and white Colorado columbines growing along a backcountry trail, in a crack, on top of a rock covered in accumulated detritus, moss, and lichen. In the mid-morning sunlight, they were completely gorgeous, and no one could tell from the quality of their blooms if growing there had been as rough as it seemed, compared to the more common locations beneath aspen trees. But one could tell they were there to stay.

I too could bloom where I was planted, if I wanted to—rocky foundation or not.

After all, some mountains in life seemed to be more about the choice to stick to the task, especially if it helped a person escape spiraling into a pit of hopelessness. That had to be what the pursuit of purpose felt like.

I was not a quitter, and I knew if I left this job, I would have to find another one. Given my sensitive condition, it seemed God agreed that my mouth and mind could use the stability of having enough of a job even if it wasn't perfect. Also, I was willing to believe this job might be better than the job I didn't have. And I was growing tired of job applications!

But if I was to move forward and stick with my task, how was it to be done?

The following week, the classroom I worked in was rewarding the kids with a movie that also had ties to the lesson. It was the movie *The Princess Bride*. A childhood memory told me I never liked the movie due to a certain torture scene, and I had come home from my mission thinking movies were thieves of time and silence, so I figured my time would be better spent grading papers. However, the stack of papers lay untouched on my desk as I felt myself drawn into the movie.

I felt fascinated by the main female character, Buttercup. She experienced grave heartache upon the alleged loss of her beloved Wesley, and as the drama unfolded, she was transferred beyond her control from one unexpected situation into more disastrous situations, one after another. At first, she seemed to accept everything, even though she didn't like it. Then I realized she was simply willing to make the best of things and live with a broken heart. However, in the end, I appreciated how she learned valuable lessons, gained friendships, and began to trust in love again.

As the movie went on, I related to Buttercup as she learned that pain was a part of the plan for growth and personal development. The movie offered the idea that pain is simply a part of life that comes with or without love, but at times it might also be remedied by the right kind of love.

Then there was the analogy of the fire swamp.

It wasn't hard to compare the maniacal Rodents of Unusual Size (R.O.U.S.s) to the way emotions seemed to charge at me from all directions. The accompanying comparative thoughts were like the never-ending quicksand, making it difficult to move forward or upward. Then there were little fires of frustration that unrelentingly came alive one after another and interrupted my progress. I imagined how the popping noises that indicated "trouble coming" were like the anxious warning signs and patterns that appeared initially when I dealt with challenges.

To recognize and get past those anxious feelings, the movie reminded me that I needed the love and wisdom of someone who knew and understood the adventure of life. God was that for me. In the movie, Buttercup had Wesley, and throughout the story, they relied on the handsome male character's wisdom and experiences to develop strategies and endure every unfamiliar danger.

Watching their strategies unfold, I reflected about how every hero story has a main character who endures suffering, doubt, self-discovery, trust, and even repeated drawbacks before understanding a larger purpose, finding success, or fulfilling the vision of a guide or mentor. Even though I now looked on God as the hero of my story, it was more like he was the writer, the designer, and I was still his main character. To be able to help me, he needed me to change and adjust to meet the odds. As he always had, he would help me develop strategies I could use to figure things out, to reduce errors and find a solution to my current problems and situation. After all, any new environment required a new outlook or awareness of what made it special.

Soon after that, I noticed a trend in how my surroundings—and the people in them—were affected by entertainment media.

THE ALTITUDES OF ACCEPTANCE

Maybe it was just me, but it seemed like teachers couldn't say certain words without sparking an explosion. For example, the Disney movie *Frozen* had just come out, and any time I said, "Please just let it go …", or any other spoken phrase that sounded like song lyrics, I triggered an eruption of noisy musical outbursts that completely derailed the lesson.

In fact, students occasionally insisted on adding a theatrical flair to everyday moments by singing a line or two of incidental music. There were times I felt like I was surrounded by creative talent, and that it was a crime to have a stage on campus and no performing arts club!

Generally, I approve of people singing their way through life—I like to sing too. In fact, from another perspective, working at the school might be the most movie-like, musical life experience I have ever had with people outside my family. But as a teacher, it was hard not to be irritated by what appeared to be a powerful weapon (or at least, distraction) against learning.

For example, when a student needed to go to the bathroom, out came a bold rendition of:

> *Let it go, let it go,*
> *Can't hold it back anymore …*

Or when they were irritated with a teacher's methods, they'd oppose with:

> *I don't care what they're going to say …*

Or when they wanted to emphasize that the rules were not to their liking, they'd sing:

> *No right, no wrong, no rules for me! I'm free …*

"Really, guys?" I'd say, feeling exasperated as well as amused. Then I would try to think of a way to meet the students' needs and return to the lesson.

Even though I tried to be good-natured about these outbursts, they too often fell like bombs dropping on a forest or city landscape. Like the acres of trees and homes, my lesson plans and sanity seemed at risk of being severely decimated without apology. Plus, it was annoying to feel the important elements of our learning environments skittering away into oblivion, leaving us teachers to pick up the pieces—if there were any left.

Several of my fellow teachers and paraprofessionals joined me in encouraging students to eschew this very infuriating habit, but to no avail. Each outburst seemed to fuel the addiction. In the end, all I could do was pay closer attention to the trigger situations.

A few months after I started working at the school, I was convinced the kids had been tricking me into letting them give in to their musical inclinations, so I decided to try a new approach. At the next opportunity, rather than act annoyed, I simply rolled my eyes, then tapped my foot and smiled patiently. Then an idea arrived with interesting clarity—"prevent rather than repent."

Ah ha! The musical explosions were time-stealers, but the students used them as a fun-bringer, and I was simply not able to keep up. They hungered for fun, and with a little research, I could give it to them on their own terms.

So, I started to track popular movie songs or tunes from the newest Disney movie or the newest musical celebrity. My first task was to learn what *not* to say around student ears. My second task was to set the game up against them. I started rephrasing any song's words using a teacher's point of view, then turning it back at them. For example, when it was time, I was ready to say, "*I don't care what you're going to say, let your tune rage on—I'm going to teach you anyway.*"

I didn't always sing my response, but sometimes I did. This was a game, but the students seemed happier because they knew I was playing with them, not against them. When the students were expertly thwarted by my methods, they would simply smile and quiet down. Eventually, they seemed willing to be more selective with their melodious moments. Soon, not only was I able to catch myself before saying certain phrases, but I also gained deeper respect.

That's when I knew I was able to understand these kids. I loved that music had helped me earn real results. Finding a way to relate with the students through music felt like a remarkable beginning of growth and understanding. More importantly, I felt poised for more! I not only wanted to magnify the efforts, but I knew I could. In the words of the students, *it was time to see what I could do, test my limits and break through ...*

I was willing to blossom where I had been planted, or at least, to enjoy the experience. Anxiety still creeped in at the wrong times, such as when I was leading an entire class on my own, but soon I realized I was more aware of and uncomfortable with my inadequacy than the students. In fact, every success and mistake pushed me to understand a little more about what the children needed from me. It seemed I had a lot to give after all, and as the motivation to work anywhere else drifted away, I concluded I had more to learn as an educator. I had made my decision.

After making the choice to stay, I started to feel more awesome than I had felt in years. The feeling washed over me like a waterfall and was no doubt connected to the relief I was feeling, but looking back, I believe God was simply letting me study it out for myself before bringing me peace.

I began to like the word *awesome* a lot. This may have been rooted in the feelings of awe from my past experiences, but the students didn't know that. They thought I sounded a bit like a stuck key on a keyboard because I said things were "awesome" far too many times every day.

I used it to describe something students were doing that wowed me and seemed hilarious.

I used it when I saw them do something nice for someone else in the hallway.

I used it while monitoring activities at the prom to describe a student's skillful dance move.

I used it to describe art projects, chalk drawings, and evidence of student leadership traits.

I even used it in my phone greeting, "Hi, this is Deanna's phone. I'm not available now, but if you'd like to leave a message, I'll do the awesome thing and call you back as soon as I can. Thanks!"

After all, responsive behaviors really are awesome. They matter to other people.

In time, the word became my personal catch phrase. I finally felt happy enough about life that it seemed natural, normal, and even vital to enjoy an overflow of awesomeness. But after the Legos movie came out in 2014, in the second year of working at the school, I was in serious trouble!

In true musical outburst fashion, the students made the song *Everything is Awesome* into my theme music. At first, it was like the students delighted in every opportunity to tease me and take advantage of how much I used the word "awesome." After about three months, students would hum or sing it at the earliest opportunity, almost as soon as I walked into the room.

I never sang it with them, but I laughed with them because I had inadvertently put the song on repeat throughout school. I laughed even harder though when at one point, the students were so intent on singing *Everything is Awesome* that they forgot to sing their other favorite song at least once when I said, "let it go."

As that second year progressed into spring, I became acquainted with two of the high-functioning students who had graduated and occasionally visited the school to follow up with their old teachers. In conversations, I got the feeling that they knew—and had known before graduation—that they had entered a world that did not understand autism.

Near the front office one day, I overheard an animated conversation. These boys were visiting the school that day and sharing with a few friends how their bosses had no idea how autism affected workplace contributions, for better or worse. After realizing they'd employed someone with autism, the bosses established unfair limits over what the boys were allowed to do at work.

To me, it sounded like some employer perspectives on autism were simply undereducated, protective, and a little presuming. The world often

THE ALTITUDES OF ACCEPTANCE

viewed autism through distorted and untrained lenses, and wherever workplace leaders were influenced by these views, our students and their employers would have a hard time.

Given my recent experience of being hired to work with a population of children I knew nothing about, I understood how easy it might be for a good boss to hire someone for their immediately perceived talents without knowing the full array of their abilities. If they were calling the shots differently after finding out about an employee's autism, that would be so frustrating, yet I felt more understanding than critical. After all, I had been afraid of autism too!

Hard work and time had made me less likely to get stuck in the differences I saw, and more likely to handle myself constructively and correctly. However, I knew employers didn't have the same relationship with these kids. They weren't motivated the same way. They had businesses and livelihoods to look after and protect.

As if the boys could read my thoughts, their conversation transitioned to discussing how other people's views might affect what opportunities they could pursue in life. Then one student shared how he had courageously advocated for himself. He had requested a meeting with his employer, expressed his concerns and desires to contribute and do more for the company instead of less, and then shared a few facts about autism with his boss. In that way, he had overcome his employer's beliefs about what he could not do and established mutually agreeable expectations.

I chuckled quietly to myself over how awesome it was that he'd done the work to open that bothersome glass ceiling. It also felt great to know this school was teaching our students the skills they needed to deal with and navigate such life challenges! The young man had boldly given his boss the gift of education and something to think about—an unspoken plea. He wanted to be understood on his own merits as an individual with gifts and skills—just like any other person.

It occurred to me that if they wanted this, they weren't all that different from me after all.

As a person, I wanted to be valued for who I was, for people to take the time to know me, assume less, and inquire more. In fact, all people need the joy of connecting with and being recognized by other awesome people for who they are, rather than who those people expect them to be. But this isn't always going to happen. In a world where decisions are not always black and white, and answers are often complicated to say the least, some circumstances can be so unfair.

So why do they exist?

In my past lifescapes, God had not taken unfair circumstances away; in most cases, God had used them to teach me something. To do that, he had had to meet me where I was.

As a missionary, I had been convinced that others had more and better things to give than I did. Consequently, I suffered social and spiritual harm as I accepted my limitations without hope for growth. But I soon realized how that kind of acceptance didn't make me the better person I wanted to become, that comparing and contrasting what we find in the world can help us gain information for making decisions, and doing so in a manner that creates constant self-critique is not the way to live one's best life. In fact, focusing too hard on human differences, or the effects of being different, can restrict the interactive experiences that bring joy. Real power to change and achieve self-assurance and personal acceptance can come only when we realize how differences and sameness might be at war in the world, but we don't have to be.

Finding peace in the face of my personal challenges was a connection to the lived experiences of these students. I doubted these kids liked how long it was taking them to figure things out, or the fact that the world wasn't going to give them a break. But they'd already learned so much, and they needed to hear how well they were doing, if they didn't already know.

It was a small moment, but somehow, I knew I had met these kids where they were, in my own way. Like them, I had learned to live life with a challenge I hadn't chosen.

It was time to join the conversation and share my thoughts.

"Hey guys! I couldn't help overhearing your conversation. I agree, you have it hard, but you know what else? You are doing a good job of evaluating and seeing the whole picture, and that's important. Speaking of pictures, you know that theme song from the Lego movie?"

They nodded, so I continued. "There's more to it than meets the eye, and it's a bit backwards. The truth is—*everyone* is awesome. Even the boss that doesn't understand you.

"However, some things are *not* so awesome, like the way you've been treated. All those things you fear, especially in the workplace, are not awesome. You didn't choose to have autism, but the circumstances you live with are less important than how you choose to handle them. They aren't going to go away, but as you stand up for yourself and your awesomeness and realize the world is not your enemy but just doesn't understand you yet, things will work out for you."

As this point hit home, I felt like I had crossed a threshold. This was not the mentality I had come to the school with, but somehow, I had arrived! I almost laughed out loud in joy as their faces recognized and accepted my expressions of sincere hope for their futures.

I still had much to learn about neurodivergent circumstances, but now I knew that from battling with anxiety, I had learned things that would matter to others. In retrospect, when I first saw anxiety as something I'd have to navigate for the rest of my life, it felt like a trait that set me apart from others in a solitary way. But that was a somewhat self-centered approach, leading to a separation mentality. Now, this battle was connecting me to something bigger than myself. By learning to reduce the negative ways anxiety affected me, I had somehow gained an encyclopedia of positive, empathetic views that could be opened and shared with others.

Even though my circumstances weren't the same, I appreciated having a lens through which to understand autism. In my story, this was a win that couldn't go unnoticed.

In all honesty, coming into an all-new environment at the school had at first challenged my learned resistance against comparative thinking. Knowing nearly nothing about autism before being thrown into an active school environment had also forced me to face my limitations again and learn to reconcile with them. Experiences with the students helped, and over time, I stopped comparing my weaknesses to the strengths of others, including experienced teachers. I am grateful to report that in this case, escaping the clutches of anxiety took only a few months, as opposed to about a year as a missionary. I couldn't escape it entirely, but it was enough to finally be in control.

When I began to comprehend the connections between educational approaches and several key elements of behavioral science, I became aware that no two neurodivergent children were affected by autism in the same way, yet some children had similar challenges or could benefit from similar treatments. That led to gleaning and creating new ideas for helping students learn social skills. Soon, I learned I could help students adjust their behaviors to function more fully in what is believed to be the normal world by working within their realities instead of against them. I learned to focus my statements on what they could do or do differently to reach the goal, instead of just on what they needed to stop doing.

I think one of the most interesting points I came across was that science has brought forth lots to say about autism as an abnormal psychological issue. The neurodivergent brain structure is completely different from a neurotypical brain structure, making abnormalities an issue of function. However, at the time, I couldn't help thinking about how my neurotypical brain was different from my neurotypical neighbor's brain, which led to considerations for the diversity between people in general and the rise of the number of autism cases. Was it truly fair to call autism abnormal outside of discussions about brain structure? Who decided that anyway?

As far as the rise in cases is concerned, I learned it is generally believed that this might be due to better and earlier diagnoses through increasing research data and improved technology. Others say autism is rooted in vaccines or environmental exposures. As for me, I sit in the camp that says a combination of these things is possible, including the circumstantial evidence related to genetics. It seems reasonable that people with autism are drawn to certain job environments in specific locations, such as cities. Then, they are then drawn to each other through proximity and likeness of life experiences. However, to the rest of the world, they are simply different.

Lastly, out of my own experience, I can share the insight that how we deal with what we call differences between others and ourselves are deeply influenced by personal beliefs and how we value other people in our lives. There are all kinds of ideas and scientific endeavors supporting this perspective, and some people are far greater masters of it than I am, but no matter who is using the word, "different" is not a viable descriptor of a human being. If you've ever tried describing someone as "different," people usually want more information, or they try to fill in the cracks with their own creations rather than searching for true answers beyond their own understanding.

The truth is we are all the same in that we are different, and that concept deserves deeper consideration by all of us. This concept applies not only to me and to the children I worked with, but also to pretty much everyone in the world.

No two people are the same.

Differences will always exist.

It is okay to be different. It is also normal to be different from every single person you meet.

Considering genetics, life experiences, and educational history, how people adapt and conform, how they deal with the unknown, or whether they learn to deal with themselves wisely and with countless personalities—what if the answer for dealing with differences is not meant to be based on how we scientifically manage an understanding of differences, but rather how we culturally, emotionally, intellectually, socially, and physically value a grand array of these things in the overall scope of the human experience?

Unfortunately, this is not how the world works.

Children might not deserve to live in a world where division is created by inability or lack of willingness to understand them, but they do. Young people are often mirror reflections of the real or perceived walls that society builds and uses to influence how we experience ourselves or others.

It turns out demographics or differences alone are not what creates division or difficulty between people.

People do.

Historically speaking, people build walls, and these walls look like war, social squabbles, political debates, or other social conflicts centered around dealing with differences of opinion or operation. Unfortunately, perception on either side of a wall can be so blind.

Such walls can fall, but history illustrates how differences in views, beliefs, or behaviors are often reasons people fight or flee rather than face walls and the reasons they exist. Handling differences as normal and valuable may be challenging, yet when someone chooses decisiveness over divisiveness, or chooses the hard right thing over the easier wrong, we have a chance of tearing down the wall. We risk seeing ourselves and each other as people who are worth being treated well or opening the door to unexpected understanding and solution-oriented approaches.

If we don't take this risk, we halt our forward flow, deny unity, and engage in fear behavior.

It is easy to reflect on how often fear has interrupted my flow through life. It was fear that sparked comparative thinking and disengagement, so comparative thinking was my fear behavior. It was a double-edged sword—with it, I brandished my motivation and courage to admire or desire greater things while slashing into my self-assurance, inhibiting my confidence, and negatively influencing how I dealt with expectations and limitations.

My problem was that I couldn't see the walls I had created and was defending. These walls were based on what was happening, but my thoughts blocked my mind against what was otherwise possible. For that reason, I think we are blind to our fear-related behavior until something happens to help us see it. Or, as I did with comparative thinking, we must accept the soul-searching task of letting fear go. Take it from me:

THE ALTITUDES OF ACCEPTANCE

Letting it go was the only way to make space for peace when moving to Colorado.

Letting it go helped me transition from new hiker to skilled mountain climber.

Letting it go helped me gain knowledge and understanding as a missionary, particularly the knowledge and awareness that God was, in fact, pleased with me.

Letting it go also enabled me to deal with pain after discovering dreams were not reality.

Letting it go helped me accept that life does not usually go as planned.

When it comes to God's design, I believe the plan is for us to learn to let things go, especially behaviors of fear, and even some things that we think make us happy but are actually rooted in our fear, in how we protect ourselves from the things we fear in life's adventure. Sometimes we do actually want what's best for us, but other times, we latch onto unnecessary things or underdeveloped perspectives. Letting things go means paying attention to God, making space for new lessons, and allowing ourselves to realize that we can be awesome and need to grow at the same time. And the sooner we let go of those fear-related behaviors, the sooner we move forward.

As I look back, I realize I might be building meaning into some of my stories with hindsight and wisdom I didn't have at the time the experiences occurred. However, using stories the way I do in this book has served to simplify the truths I learned in my twenties, and to filter out the less important things from that time in my life. I believe my decision to stay at the school was cemented as soon as I became aware of how the lessons I was learning would be significant in my life and that things I had already learned were applicable to the students too.

Many lessons for neurotypicals like me and neurodivergents are the same. For example, how we deal with differences matters, and finding similarities in our experiences contributes to feelings of unity. This is why we tell stories when we communicate!

Also, when we allow differences to complement each other rather than create opposition, they bring us joy, and seeing ourselves a little more fully through the eyes of heaven helps the world's perception to matter a little less.

The scriptures tell us those who receive help from God should expect to pay it forward. It wasn't hard to see how these kids had particularly challenging lives, but it was much harder to know how to help them. However, once I realized that the students had socially and mentally constructed walls to navigate, and that I had experience with climbing those walls and sometimes breaking those walls down, I could only conclude that I had been training to help these students for a long time.

All my life, in fact.

After all, mountains are just walls designed by God and built by nature. Climbing them is all about when (not if) the going gets tough. Such walls must be faced rather than feared. Some mountains hold grander views or are more treacherous than others, just like so many challenges in life. But each climb leads to a feeling of awe, wonder, and empowerment as we better understand our individual worth in the sight of God.

With that new approach literally set in stone, I realized how deeply I believed that God seeks to help us love him, love ourselves, and achieve our full potential, the most complete version of ourselves. God already thinks we are awesome yet does not let us stop there. Along the way, he wants us to learn to identify what is and is not awesome—that is, what is and is not right or good. He wants us to know for ourselves what will bring us the greatest happiness. For example:

It is NOT awesome to hold ourselves or others back because of what we know or do not know.

It is NOT awesome to view or treat ourselves or others as problems without solutions.

It IS awesome to be introspective and work toward change with the right tools.

THE ALTITUDES OF ACCEPTANCE

It IS awesome to seek and find joy and meaning in our life experiences.

Considering life experiences, when things look terribly bleak and beyond our control, don't be surprised when God steps in and does something awesome and unexpected, or helps such things work out in a way that is for the best. As my sister and I continually tell each other, "It all works out in the end. If it hasn't worked out yet, then it's not the end."

There's a point in the process where we might need a little more faith in the moment before God steps in. It's the point where we feel clueless but have the option to choose courage or despair. When we choose courage in that moment, we step forward with the most awesome parts of ourselves, willing to take on a darkened path in life without knowing how things will turn out. It's also the point where we can wisely trust that God is in control and will send his light as needed, that he will work it all out. We believe him even though we see the storms, steep inclines, or the dangers of a flash flood (or anticipate no water anywhere for miles). It's that point where we choose to be awesome, no matter what.

God's timing, responses, and answers tend to surpass the ways of the world. Even when his timelines do not make sense right away, or if any answer from God seems repeated, all God wants is to show us just how we get in our own way and how to get out of our way—and how his way is really the best way to go, and to become what we need to become through the gift of his love.

I used to think God valued my life at the level of hard work, that where my life went and what it became was completely up to me. But now I know God values all our lives at the level of love.

Make no mistake—God expects us to work hard, but life is more about feeling his love and becoming our best self than taking the most direct path or only the one we can see clearly. Even though we can't plan for everything and not *everything* in life is awesome, we can learn from our past experiences, notice God's love in our lives, and build connections with other people.

BUILDING CONNECTIONS

If we do these things, we will find that we have all experienced some truly awesome adventures and beautiful connections throughout every lifescape.

CHAPTER 5

AWESOME ADVENTURES

November arrived quickly that year.

While I had made my choice to stay at the school and felt as awesome as I had ever felt, I had to accept that there was at least a year of regular dental checkups ahead of me. That was far from normal for me, but now that I had a sense of stability, I started to sense that something was missing. I was hungry to find a *new* normal.

Prior to my accident, my normal was a lot of things, but one thing that had been important for how I managed anxiety was maintaining good physical fitness. I utilized a variety of outdoor physical exercises to take care of myself, but for most of the months since the accident, sinus infections and headaches related to my facial injuries were triggered by hard cardio. That included running outside, so I had done little more than walking, hiking, or biking for quite some time.

The deficiency in physical activity took a toll on my muscles, mental health, and resilience. Winter was coming, and it seemed like biking would not be suitable exercise after snowfall and freezing temperatures began. Luckily, I had snowshoes, so I could still hike. Also, there was a gym not far from my home—however, monthly fees at gyms and gas prices were skyrocketing and that was a huge deterrent for my current financial situation.

At this point, I felt understandably desperate for options.

When I heard about the school's big Turkey Trot fundraiser, and that they needed a volunteer to stand sentry at the turnaround point during the 5K, I recalled how I had tested myself by hiking to the cave with the students over the summer. This volunteer opportunity sounded like the perfect test by which I could determine if I could run again—other people would be around and available to help in the unlikely event of an extreme physical response.

I prepared for my first exercise run since the accident, and on the day of the event, the early morning chill gave way to the warm sun just in time. As a volunteer aiming to get to the turnaround point before the runners, I moved out ahead of the milling crowd that was gathering in anticipation. As I ran, I noticed someone had been out before me that morning, drawing arrows in chalk and marking distances along the way. That was so helpful—I had not been out on these trails before.

The path itself smoothly snaked through an open space, west of the school toward another trail that meandered north and south along the Jordan River in the Salt Lake Valley. The pavement was mostly flat, and I thought there were too few trees—if it had been an afternoon in the summer, I would have overheated in mere minutes, but in winter the open sky and sunlight were welcome.

As it was, my heartbeat felt a bit too high and I was breathing hard, having run at least a mile with maybe two walking stops, but I experienced no headaches or throbbing. Ahead of me, I could see the trail junction not far away around a bend, while arrows at my feet led me over a bridge in a northern direction. About a quarter of a mile down, next to a tall wooden fence covered in flaking white paint, I found the promised stash of water bottles and the 1.6-mile marker.

That fence may have been the only guard against people taking a misstep into the steep rocky embankment of the Jordan River, but it was also the only seating I could use and was obviously a great vantage point. So, I climbed up to sit on the top rail where I could more easily spot 5K participants with paper numbers pinned onto their shirts.

THE ALTITUDES OF ACCEPTANCE

First five minutes … then ten minutes went by.

Apparently, the race had started late. I grimaced and shifted my position along the top board of the fence. If I sat aloft much longer, the fence rail was going to leave a permanent impression! Restless, and not feeling too comfortable, I hopped down and began doing jumping jacks and stretches.

Finally, about five minutes later, the first competitors arrived, most of them running with delight and enthusiasm. Matching their energy, I switched into cheerleading mode and distributed words of encouragement, high-fives, and water to the students, siblings, and parents as they crossed the chalk line.

Most wheeled around fast with a smile and hardly a word, but everyone's eyes gleamed with determination and perseverance. I admired what they had done—and then remembered I had done it too, and for the first time in forever! Knowing my head injury could now handle running, I resolved to choose this kind of awesome activity again and again in the days to come.

Along the lines of that same exercise agenda, another curious thought began to seep through. I had heard this trail was the same trail that passed through a park near my house, situated about nineteen miles and in several cities south of the school's location. Some said it was feasible to bike this trail through the entire length of the Salt Lake Valley.

It sounded good to me—for someday. I had the bike, a helmet, leg power, and experience with biking long distances because of a childhood paper route, and the more I healed, the hungrier I became for a more excellent physical exercise repertoire. Why not have a goal of some intensity to work toward? Also, if biking to or from work on this trail was possible, I could make that an interim goal. Combined with transportation by train, biking long distances could become an excellent partial solution to financial concerns as well as increasing exercise on warmer winter days.

But wait! Nineteen miles would be quite a commitment. A thousand things could happen to anyone when biking long distances. Bike commuters got into accidents; others reported unfortunate incidents with strangers or inclement weather. Also, some have simply disappeared. But I have skill, energy, and speed on my side, all of which helps with safety. Right?

I could tell it was going to take some courage to go through with this idea.

I shook my head and climbed back on the fence. I had not seen any runners in quite some time. If they were few and far between, or done with the race, I needed to pay attention and not get so lost in thought.

Just as I acquired the elevated point of view, several bikers passed by. I watched them roll past, one by one. Envy came first, then awe—and then I gasped. As a familiar face rode past, worlds collided! I couldn't believe how in this inconspicuous location I had seen the face of one of the most athletic men I knew. We hiked and chatted and even shared the same circle of friends at church. More importantly, we also lived near the same park.

I called out his name and said, "Hey, you! Yes, you! Why are you way out here?"

He started slowing down his bike while his companions continued into some shade just ahead. He stared for a moment, clearly absorbing the irony of the situation and trying to figure out what to say as he reached for a long drink from his water bottle as he looked up at me, still sitting high on the fence. Then he grinned and imitated me, saying, "I might ask you the same question!"

I grinned back. I felt no surprise at this response. He had reason to feel the same level of mystery in the moment. He wasn't the kind of friend who would know where I worked or, more specifically, what I would be doing that day. I had had no idea he would be biking anywhere that morning, yet we arrived in the same spot on the same day at the same time. Divine intervention? I think so. It was a very interesting form of courage—granted to me with very little effort on my part.

I could do nothing to prevent the *I-didn't-expect-to-see-you-here* conversation that followed, complete with anxiety-induced lip biting moments of *Why did I just say that, that way?*

"Well, you could say this is my workplace today. So, did you bike all the way here?"

Duh! Why'd I ask that, I already know his answer!

I knew what this man was capable of—in fact, I expected him to make a great joke out of an already amusingly complex situation—yet my mind was racing to determine the details of his ride, such as whether he had started from home, how far it was, how long it took. It was time to figure these things out, and I intended to press him for answers. I may have been a few rungs below him on the personal fitness ladder, but I believed if he had made that trip, then I could do it too.

"Wait, you work here, on this trail?"

That's his joke? Very funny.

I gave him a flat smile and said, "Yep, sure do. But today only. Normally, I work at the school near here. We have a Turkey Trot today. It's almost over. So, did you bike all the way here?"

"I did, directly from home where I met these guys."

"How long did it take you to get here?"

"About an hour."

Hmmm ... my mind was working on the math ... that equated at least an hour and a half for me—not a feasible ride in the available daylight before work hours began, not even in the spring. But no problem, I would rather take my bike to the train station in the early morning, bike the four miles from the nearest station to the school, and then ride all the way home in the afternoon when there was more time.

Curiosity invited him to make more conversation. "So, where do you actually work?"

I gave him my answer. I could have taken the conversation in a different direction, but I was too zoned in on the potential for a new exercise regimen to allow another change of subject.

"How was your ride?" I asked.

"It's a great day for it. I like the workout. I think we've made good time."

Typical man of few words, I thought. *Short phrases, missing the details I am aching to know.*

"Is it a good trail the whole way? Does it run along the train route?"

"It's on Google Maps. The trail is not direct and jogs around a bit through residential areas, but it's not hard to find. And yes, it does run close to the train route in some places."

Awesome! Wait ... sounds too easy ... but it is possible to get back on the train if there is an emergency. I was so sold on this opportunity, even though I had decided on nothing—yet.

"Good to know," I said, "How far are you going?"

"All the way to Ogden."

"Wow, doesn't that take most of the day?"

"Nope, just about four hours roundtrip. Still, I'd better get going."

Four hours? Fifty miles? Wow. Just wow. Again, maybe someday ...

"Sounds like a great way to spend the day. Or morning. Have a great ride! Also, so nice to see you today, randomly, on this trail, far from home ..." I let my voice trail off in observance of the chance meeting.

He grinned and said in a remarkably cavalier yet genteel manner, "Likewise. See you Sunday."

As I watched him roll down the path to rejoin his companions, I could not help but compare this odd (but exciting) exchange compared to some of the richer conversations we had enjoyed in the past. He was a dramatic jokester, and it had been fun to share the unexpected encounter with him. No doubt he was amused and surprised too, but more importantly, there was nothing coincidental about receiving such timely revelations from such a trusted point of view.

One day I'll have to tell him he played a key role in delivering the exact information I needed.

Now I knew I could bike that distance. And now, all I needed to know was how to navigate boarding the train in the morning with my bike. If that worked, then on good weather days and maybe even colder ones, I could hop off at the station near the school, cycle the four miles to work, and then cycle all the way home (downhill!) after work. Nineteen miles or more a day, here I come!

It was all so motivating! I felt awesome again just thinking about it.

And then it occurred to me that something had shifted smoothly within my lifescape.

Wait, God, there you go again. How did you do that?

Before I had known of the job's proximity to the trail and train line, and before I had comprehended how an exercise regimen would work, God had allowed me to figure things out and choose to stay. Now it looked like having a desire in my heart to repair my financial status and mental and physical health had been an invitation from God for me to act. He was again providing answers I needed when I needed them, if not how I expected to receive them. He was using my intentions to move me forward, likely in the direction he needed me to go. Most importantly, he seemed to be assuring me that a choice to stay at this job could work out for me, in an unexpected way. After all, why wouldn't God want me to find the health and healing I needed and the resources that would work for me at the right time, in the right place, through the right people?

The interesting part is, I think he would have shown me that for any choice I made. That's just God's way—the way he adds what he knows to what we know and thus creates awesome adventures.

It seemed like my future self would gain more from this job experience than expected, so I prayed with gratitude that this was evidence of more good things to come.

As clouds came over the mountains on the northern horizon, a breeze picked up, reducing the sun's warmth significantly. I was reminded it was November, and winter was around the corner. Maybe in the spring I could take this newly conceived adventure into real life? Meanwhile, I could still work on my strength and endurance in other ways. It would not be easy, but that's life.

I think God gives us autonomy and reason to pursue a hard thing or follow a motivation to serve, improve ourselves, or just be awesome—and then uses his power to open doors in our lives.

Or close them and open windows …

Or invite us to kick them down …

Either way, as we make choices, we may sense how these openings and God's power are working on our behalf. I used to think God would simply help us make the most of bad situations, but now I know he does that and so much more.

The way things kept working out and falling into place seemed to strengthen my ability to decide what to do when tough or stressful situations arose with the students. I was still far from perfect for my new role on paper, but one thing I knew—the full story of my experience here at the school had not been written yet, and there was more to come.

I also knew from experience that the work of finding solutions was up to me.

So, I started initiating more intentional conversations, asking other teachers and staff members about their lives, work, and experiences. Along the way, I found open doors, built new friendships, and heard key information I needed about how they survived the demands of the job.

What stood out to me most were all the crazy yet meaningful stories that seemed to happen only with our unique population of students. The teachers expressed how they looked at circumstances in their own lives differently because of those moments with the students.

Once a teacher told me about how there was a time he couldn't figure out why a student wouldn't talk in his class. It didn't make sense to him, so he started doling out consequences for non-participation. When he finally confronted the student, the response was that he had said and done a few things in class that scared the student into silence. This shocked my colleague, and he changed his ways of teaching so that he could prevent it from happening again.

Other teachers highlighted stories about the times they integrated their own personal touches into their lessons. I heard about how using certain

THE ALTITUDES OF ACCEPTANCE

visual aids or providing symbolic snacks often made the lesson ten times better. As I listened to these stories, I sensed how the running theme was the importance of creativity and being open to opportunity, and I became a big fan. It all sounded more proactive and engaging than being railroaded into a singing chorus competition.

One teacher mentioned how she started sharing stories of when students had made her laugh with her own kids on the way home. Good humor helped her family connect, and taking positive moments home helped her put everything that had been overwhelming into perspective. This conversation stood out to me because I deeply appreciated how the act of telling her stories made her eyes radiate with joy. I needed the meaningful learning experiences in the other stories too, but her stories about the effects of good humor on her mentality reflected the kind of heart-felt glow I wanted to find and experience for myself.

Their stories inspired me like seeds of potential. I was determined to plant the seeds in my heart until I blossomed and gathered such stories from my own labor of love. I started to record the teachers' stories in a Google document online and refer to them as often as I could. It was awesome to see my simple list grow while the stories revealed things I had never seen in the students before, such as clever intelligence at things that weren't common in my own experiences.

The more stories I collected, the more I enjoyed the extra boost of courage, laughter, or gratitude that came with them, and the more I enjoyed my conversations with the other teachers.

One day Allison, a teacher, shared a unique story with me, saying she shared it with her students to make a point about behavior and "the golden rule." I have permission to tell it as a "case in point" story because of how well it demonstrates the way stories deliver both entertainment and lessons.

One day Allison boarded a plane and found herself seated beside an African American man from the deep south. When he dropped his pen and it rolled under the seat ahead of him, she watched as he asked the man in front of him if he could get it for him, but the man ignored him and did nothing.

Thinking he simply had not heard the man, Allison decided to help and made the same request of the same man in a louder voice.

The man said, "I am not going to pick it up for that dark-faced negro!"

Well, Allison was not about to take something so inappropriate and full of prejudice, negativity, and impatience from a—

But the African American man reached out to stop Allison as she rose to defend him and motioned silently that he didn't want her to get involved.

So, she sat in silence fuming with indignation throughout the length of the entire plane ride while the pen remained far under the seat. Though at some point she offered him a pen of her own—and at another point, she suggested they call a stewardess. Finally … she realized that her neighbor did not appear to be too disturbed. But was it because he was used to such treatment, and did not wish to cause a scene?

At the end of the flight, the stewardesses said their usual words about how passengers needed to watch their heads because bags might have shifted or opened in the overhead compartments during the flight. No one paid it any mind, and in a moment, people all over were up and moving to get off the plane, including the prejudiced man who reached up to retrieve his bag.

Allison looked up as he struggled; it was apparent that another bag near his bag had shifted and opened while flying. Without warning, the open bag dumped a load of books down onto the prejudiced man.

Other passengers looked on, unable to help him even if they wanted to.

Allison, on the other hand, sat frozen in amazement, and when she looked at her seated companion, he was quietly hiding a chuckle.

"And what's got your eye twinkling?" she asked him.

"Karma," he said.

Allison's face filled with confusion and her eyebrows raised. What kind of answer was that?

"I am a book salesman; those are my books!"

THE ALTITUDES OF ACCEPTANCE

One might think the book salesman knew all along what would happen, but that would make him a magician, and this was a real story, and a stage act can't honestly compare to real life. Regardless of circumstances, the man did the right thing. He refrained from causing a fight over a pen. He might not have gotten his pen back in the end, but he sure did get the pleasure of seeing the perpetrator put in his place!

Now, the opportunity to see justice served on a silver platter was not likely to happen every time, but it could, if only the students chose to do the right thing—or so Allison would remind her pupils when she relayed this story to them. For me, though, this story created a sense of how little bits of whimsy and good humor could get wrapped into a lesson. How to collect my own real-life stories that presented meaningful moments was yet to be determined, but it was time to start!

The first task was to nail down criteria for collecting my own stories. Knowing I needed to keep it simple because I was a beginner brought a theme from a past job to mind—keep it simple, make it fun (KISMIF). In fact, discovering more ways the kids brought me joy sounded extremely fun—and very much like Mary Poppins: "You find the fun, and snap! The job's a game." Not only would recording simple moments of fun please me, but it would also benefit me. When I found out capturing humor was recommended by top scientists for emotional healing, I was sold.[2]

This was just the thing to pave the way to healing all that had burdened me that year.

With a plan in place, certain story-collecting triggers stood out. When students shared jokes or said things that clicked with my sense of humor, or when I observed a lesson learned or identified a meaningful experience, or even when we learned something from each other—it got written down. When I began to smile about something, or when a moment caused me to ponder, or when I saw a student's sense of humor sparkling, or when I thought of another teacher who might enjoy the story I was seeing or hearing—I knew I needed to write it down.

Some story pieces ended up first as a note jotted down on a Post-It, in an email or text to myself, or even on the palm of my hand if that was all I had. Sometimes I would even invite a student to "remind me to write something down." As a result of the reminders, the students began catching on to what my story collecting was all about. Some students started memorizing, or absorbing, my story criteria and told *me* to "write it down" to make sure I did not miss anything.

Before long, recording stories took place every day as instinctively as eating and drinking.

Later into the semester, I had the chance to stay after school and help at a basketball game. It was only students and teachers from our school who were playing, but they were playing intensely. I was sitting in the front row of the audience, watching how they hurtled up and down the court, when I noticed two of the shortest kids on the opposing team were keeping up with two tall students, both of whom seemed confused at their wild and entertaining displays of energy.

It seemed like when one tall student got the ball, all he had to do was hold it far above his head. His short opponents attempted to snag it from him with all the speed they could muster— they used every allowable hand motion and change of direction to gain a possible edge. However, the tall student had no need to fake out his guard since the small young men simply lacked the reach. Throughout the entire game, the tall players continued in patience while their expressions at the shorter players were the basis of the night's entertainment.

The echo of an unspoken, "Really?" as the tall ones worked to comprehend the way the shorter opponents never gave up seemed to invite the whole audience to erupt frequently with laughter. We knew the game was one-sided and that the writing was on the wall, but we enjoyed every minute of determination on the part of the little people. Especially me. As one of the shortest audience members in the gym, I knew which side I was rooting for but I loved the interactions!

When it was over, I noticed one of the tall players giving a high-five to a shorter player. I heard him say, "Hey, you didn't quit! That was great energy out there. Way to go!"

It struck me as a peaceful, humble way to act. However hard his life may have been, this taller athlete was a true leader. It wasn't easy for these students to give meaningful compliments, and as the winner, he didn't have to be so supportive. But apparently, he knew no game could be just about winning or losing. He seemed to be thinking what we were all thinking—that how the game is played shows the quality of the athletes.

After he walked away, I followed his example and approached the two smaller boys. "Hey, those were some tall odds out there tonight, but you showed them persistence! How did it feel?"

I didn't get many words, but their faces glowed. They knew—and I had just confirmed—that their worth wasn't in winning. It was in their will to try.

Meaningful moments like this stirred feelings of connection that were positive and hopeful. I knew where I stood with all my students and with myself.

They were no longer strangers with needs I couldn't fill.

I was okay with not being everything they needed.

I was happy to be *connected* and *enough*.

It seemed sticking to this job had beautifully transformed me. My relationship with myself improved, in part because learning to accept the students for who they were had allowed me to appreciate myself that way too—I was handling my limitations and weaknesses beneficially again!

I also started to sense the children saw things they liked in me. It motivated me to be more of those things for them—some of the best things I had ever found in me that I didn't know I had.

Although I look back and see that I only took two years to heal from emotional damage and three years to heal from my facial injuries, I also realize how important and meaningful it was to have recorded stories for all the years. The effect was the same as that of making an intentional choice to grow and pursue a solution, otherwise known as a great change of heart. I kept collecting stories because I could see who I was becoming, and I liked what I saw. Being able to move past my original blindness of doubt and discouragement was the true essence of endurance. It meant I had developed good humor, initiative, courage, connection, hard work, belonging, and follow-through.

It also meant I was focusing on what I *could* do instead of what I could not.

With this new solid perspective, I felt empowered to become more proactive in finding ways to contribute to the activities around me instead of waiting for opportunities to come to me.

One of the first projects I focused on was helping to organize the medical team. With some wilderness medicine training and first aid certifications behind me due to my past job as a hiking ranger, I joined a team to support the health and well-being of the students and manage emergencies. It was just one way to work from behind-the-scenes to help the young people stay safe and healthy and to make a difference when their emotions ran amok.

The success and continuation of this venture made me feel bold and encouraged me to keep looking for opportunities to do more. I wanted to find my own way to bring out the students' strengths and gifts, or to teach them ways to think differently about their lives, or to prepare for adulthood—all important educational lessons as far as I was concerned.

THE ALTITUDES OF ACCEPTANCE

I used to think God waited for us to want his help, and sometimes he does wait for us to ask for help, but now I know God actually requires very little from us to be able to provide a path for us. Sometimes we simply need to choose and be willing to move forward with the effects of a decision. Then, right when and where we need them, God can grant us the very best opportunities and resources within our circumstances to follow through and stick to a decision.

I also think God intends for decisions to be, in and of themselves, both frightening and empowering. The fear dissipates as we move forward and manage the outcomes, and then we start feeling good about ourselves and awesome about our decisions, which can lead to greater spiritual awareness of how meaningful life's adventure is and will become.

In my case, learning the power of stories opened the door to new wisdom after undergoing a devastating series of life experiences, which I think points to one of the most remarkable things God can do for us—teach us wisdom through a a combination of our actions, our interactions with other people, and his interactions with us.

If you ask me, adventures in life feel awesome when God is with us—and we know it.

CHAPTER 6

"TRAINING" GROUND

"Did you know some parents travel fifty miles one way to get here?"

I was in the school's breakroom and couldn't help overhearing two teachers discussing the challenges parents were experiencing with getting their children to school.

"I didn't, although it makes sense. There aren't any schools as good as this one in Provo or Weber. I bet there are students from all over the Salt Lake Valley who come here."

"When you put it like that, it makes sense why so many parents operate within carpools. If I had to make this trek daily but didn't work here, I'd be desperate for options too."

"What about the train? It would be good transportation if the students could ride it."

"That's a good question. But, if the parents could deliver kids to the train station in the morning, how would the students get to the school from the station? It's almost four miles—that would be too long a walk every morning for most kids."

"But if we could connect parents who are farther away to parents who are closer, or have the school help out with the transport vehicles, it could work."

"I bet many families would want to use the resource, but the vans couldn't fit them all."

"True—and not all the students have the skills to handle any time alone in public, even in a group setting. Might be asking for trouble. Would parents or the school be responsible?"

It was like they were brainstorming on my behalf. Train? Helping parents and students? Launching an opportunity to commute by bike and train? Sounded right up my alley.

So, if this is God's lead, I'll take it. Because what if the school can pilot a program? What could it look like? How could I help?

The first step was to find the right moment to run the seed of an idea by decision-makers.

Early the next week, I was quietly making copies for the week's assignments in the front office and enjoying the sunshine from the nearby window. I wouldn't have been there except the other copy machine in the breakroom was broken—again. I had to pause and linger when other teachers needed the machine, so I ended up being in the front office for most of the class period.

Eavesdropping was not generally my style. However, it was sometimes impossible not to overhear valuable information. That day, I found myself half-listening and gleaning a wealth of stories about memorable moments with the kids. I choked back a giggle when I heard about situations in the bathrooms and hallways and the state of the cafeteria food—apparently, the new meat patties were not a big hit. When I heard about an accident-prone student who had managed to visit the nurse for unusual, unique, and unanticipated injuries every day for the past five days—including but not limited to a nosebleed and a paper cut on his chin.

I shook my head as my eyes widened in astonishment. *How had I missed that, being on the medical team? Where else could such things happen but here with these kids?*

But when I heard one of the school's administrators, expressing concerns about driving distances and the impact this had on multiple parents and student attendance, I tuned in with both ears. Hearing these concerns for the second time this week, especially from Mrs. Chutzney, had to mean something. This had to be my chance to share the solution that had been rising in my mind, so I waited for a respectable conversational pause.

When it came, I took a deep breath, turned around, cleared my throat, and spoke calmly, concisely, and like I had all the time in the world. They say that's how you make an impression, the kind to which people will listen.

"Excuse me, Mrs. Chutzney, what about a train transportation system? The train runs almost the full distance from the Salt Lake Valley, north and south of the school. If we could navigate a program to help parents get the kids to school, it could also foster student attendance and even family retention over time."

The administrator and the secretary she'd been talking with glanced over at me, then at each other. I could see they were interested—and curiously intrigued.

"Well, you're not the only one with such a wonderful idea—great minds think alike! A paraprofessional who works upstairs is trying to form a plan for something like this, since we have no idea how it could work. Coordinating train travel for the students is not likely to be a peaceful picnic—it'll be more of an uphill climb since no one has ever tried such a program here before. Honestly, it would be great to get a proposal about this idea to the school board. Maybe you could help her?"

I nodded and smiled at her use of the words *uphill climb*—just my kind of word choice. This whole thing sounded like the kind of challenge I could thrive on.

God knew that. I knew that.

Now others in my corner knew that too.

A little small talk and a few more printouts later, I thanked them and aimed for my classroom, making plans to seek out the other paraprofessional later that day.

When I cracked open the door to her classroom, it was clear we had never met.

I smiled and introduced myself. "Hello there! I'm your sidekick in the invention of the train transportation program."

She smiled as she waved me in. "Which classroom do you work in?"

I told her and then we talked about our students, our workdays, and our families, and then we got down to business. First, she told me what she had come up with so far. "I've been thinking one group will come from north of the school, and the other will come from south of the school. I think we'll need adults to help along the way. If no one else wants to do it, we can, right? The kids and our parents won't trust the system without adult supervision."

"You're right, and yes, I'm all in for riding the train," I remarked. "I think families will really want this system to work, and they'll support it. The distance, mileage, time, and increasing gas prices are a massive constraint on families."

"No kidding! It could change everything for a family to have a fifteen-minute drive to a train station in the morning instead of two hour-long trips a day."

"Besides, longer commutes make for tricky attendance records, and for most families, train tickets will be less expensive than driving."

Soon our smiles got as big as our ideas. We laughed about some silly situations that had happened to distract our classes when students arrived late. Then we agreed that helping families manage their chaos would be a privilege, and speaking of chaos, we'd give a lot of time and effort to be able to ride the train ourselves. But that was left to be determined.

It wasn't long before our ideas melded into one big master plan. As Mrs. Chutzney had predicted, establishing a solid framework that would address as many unforeseen elements of the train transportation program as possible was not a small undertaking. The more we worked out appropriate rules for riding that took the children's ages and tendencies into account, we began to realize even with caution, we never would be able to plan for everything.

A major part of the framework was the nexus of monitor-to-student ratio, behavior, and inclusivity. We also wanted to ensure the program had the best chance of survival, but we also wanted to include as many students as we could. Since this was a pilot program and limited seats were available, we knew we would need to advise certain criteria for acceptance into the program. This criterion would need to help lessen the likelihood of behavioral issues and ensure good public relationships between our students, the train security, and other passengers. Students who didn't pay attention, fell asleep, missed their station, or freaked out due to being triggered by logistical transportation issues might prompt hard questions about school use of public transportation.

Many students would have to be considered on a case-by-case basis, but in general the program would accept students who were socially capable and in an appropriate age range. Younger children could be in the program if they had an older sibling who met the major criteria or if they didn't mind sitting near the train program monitors every day, but caution was given regarding children who were nervous in large crowds or preferred to be alone.

If there was anything we talked about too little, it was how to handle the unanticipated complex technical issues that would be out of our control when it came to the train. We expected to deal with delayed train departures and mechanical issues that could impact arrival time and increase student anxiety. But with all the unknowns, we believed the program would need to be treated as a living experiment, to allow malleability and lessons learned from mistakes and growing pains to inform all changes to the program over time.

On the school's side of operations, teacher drivers would pick up the students in cars or vehicles from the station and deliver them to the school less than four miles away. We could advise parents which train to catch at their station by reviewing the schedules in reverse. Using the latest possible arrival time at the school's nearest train station, we would work backwards and advise parents about what time to arrive at their respective north and south stations. Then the families could create their daily morning schedules, and their kids could arrive each day in time to be transported to the school all together. Since the train schedule ran on fifteen-minute intervals, a car could wait for occasional late arrivals if needed. If late behavior happened too often, it wouldn't be too hard to know exactly who to approach!

Once everything was in place, we proposed our plan to the administration as a pilot program. At the meeting, we talked about how it was essential to include at least two teacher monitors, who could not only "train" the students in the nuances of thinking and behaving as train passengers, but also perform liaison duties of communication between the parents and the students; keep up with moods and behaviors; and navigate complex issues with the students, train schedules, and the public. The monitors would also coordinate car transportation between the station and the school.

When the monitor positions were offered to myself and my partner in the creation of the program, I was excited! I felt the same gratitude as the parents, knowing I no longer had to drive the 34-mile round trip every day. Plus, I would enjoy a shorter workday, gain managerial experience, and have more daily exercise time outside due to walking to the train station each day. I couldn't bring my bike if I was monitoring the kids, at least not on most days, but the stipend for monitoring would help me afford gym membership through the winter. I could implement regular bike exercise later, but for now it was enough to know I wouldn't be burdened with commuting by car throughout the snowy winter.

In the back of my mind, a temptation arose. I didn't have to become a train monitor. If I didn't take on the responsibilities with the children, I could become a bike commuter instead. Then I might regain more physical strength sooner! However, it felt more important to gain leadership experience, and I believed I might still gain a more active lifestyle anyway. Plus, I had to admit that walking might still be better for my injuries and recovery than biking.

The more I pondered, the more I understood my inspired quest for variations in exercise and lifestyle might have been God's way of preparing my mind for an unexpected solution and to be willing to meet many needs beyond my own.

After all, making ourselves available to help other people is a divine mandate. God knows we learn to know him through other people, and other people can come to know him through us. Sometimes we recognize God's pointers and accept his invitations to serve along our way. Other times, we choose to go out of our way. In any case, I think God wants us to understand that unlikely people and unexpected opportunities are his way of opening our minds and hearts.

I used to think of God's involvement in the world as being individual and targeted, with occasional appearances on the larger world stage. Now I believe God can meet a thousand needs at once through small, simple, yet significant acts when it is his will, and especially when people are willing to do the right thing. God can magnify our interests, skills, and even our imperfections to serve other people and help resolve bigger problems. He can enhance our prospects, encouraging us to push past barriers and work within our desires and circumstances for the best good.

Looking back, answers from God have often come in a personal way that makes sense to me. God is great at speaking our individual languages. I also think God often starts us on a certain path long before we know the destination, and the adventure along the way is better for it. Because God knows us individually, he can motivate us to move in certain directions so that one inspiration might lead to another until we have won the war, not just the battle.

When we recognize and become acquainted with these occasions, we start to recognize how God makes our lives better than we can.

On the first morning of the train program, all families coming from the south arrived early at my train station, regardless of their preferred station.

THE ALTITUDES OF ACCEPTANCE

The north train group did the same so that all students and their parents could meet the monitor and discuss expectations prior to departure.

At first, the discussion I hosted felt imposing—I had no idea what I was doing! I think I came across as a little bossy. However, I don't think anyone minded. The parents and children seemed grateful to learn and to see my authority and responsibility. When I got to the part about sticking close to me and the importance of safety in numbers, the kids had so many questions.

"Miss D, do we have to sit together? Can't we sit where we want?"

"The truth is, it's better if we sit together. I plan to always sit in the upper level of the third car, and I prefer that you sit near me or at least in the second train car. There are a lot of reasons for that. If I know where you are in case of emergency, you'll be with an adult who understands. I can also help if there are problems with other passengers. Also, bathrooms are only on the second and third train cars, and the ride for many of you is between a half hour and forty-five minutes long."

I emphasized the word "bathrooms," and smiled as parents nudged their young ones.

"Another good reason to stick close to cars two and three is that I will walk through both cars to alert everyone when it's time to get off. If the train is crowded, or you need a break from our group at the end of the day on the way home—well, we can talk about making exceptions when you are all more experienced train riders."

With the basics out of the way, it was time to establish a few logistical points.

"Parents and kids, get to know your train schedule. Northbound trains move along the train line and depart each station every fifteen minutes. Please make sure you get on the northbound train from your station at the right time so that you will be able to get off at the train station near the school at the right time too.

"Now, if students get on the earlier train by mistake, they'll be riding alone and have a longer wait at the school station while the rest of us get there. If you are running late and miss your scheduled train, taking the later train from your station may or may not be a good idea. We will have school vehicles parked overnight at the station for transportation, and our train arrives ten minutes before the group from the north arrives on their southbound train. If you're running late, please, text or call me. If the situation requires it, I could hold back the last vehicle for five minutes, but no guarantees. Alternatively, you may be able to drive ahead to the next station and catch your original train there. Just let me know what to expect if you have one of those days, and I will help if I can."

Heads bobbed in understanding before I continued. "All that being said, I will assume you are all going to be riding every day. If I don't hear from you or your parents, or haven't seen you on the train, we'll assume you have not made it to school that day—"

"Miss D, what if we fall asleep and end up riding the train all the way to Ogden?"

I cocked my head and imagined that rude awakening—and how sad I'd feel if I missed waking up the kid!

"Well, mistakes happen, but that is exactly the sort of thing we are trying to prevent by providing you with rules and recommendations. Most of you have phones, so if you find that this happens to you, get in contact with your parents, and your parents can get ahold of me. If you feel tired when you get on, check in with me and sit near me. That way I'll know to give you special attention when it's time to get off the train."

"Um—what car are you going to be on again?"

"Car number three. Upper level. I'll walk around each day while we are traveling to and from school to take attendance every day, and I don't want to miss you, so try not to move around. If you need me, let me know as I walk by. Remember, I want to make sure you're safe. I can't do that if I don't know where you are. Riding the train will be a fun adventure if we take care of each other."

In the distance, the train's horn announced that it was time for goodbyes, and the first ride on the train. The train screeched to a stop, the doors opened, and most of the kids stuck close to me. Parents watched from the platform as we boarded and climbed up to empty seats in car number three. As the train took off slowly, the students waved out the windows while I made sure everyone got safely situated. All of us were experiencing that kind of nervous excitement that accompanies new adventures, and I anticipated a lot of unpredictable days were ahead of us.

In retrospect, giving directions to twenty or so parents and children about riding the train I had only been on a few times myself seemed strange, but it worked. It may not come as a surprise that every day during that first week provided a different lesson in monitoring student behavior in a public space. Some days were more difficult than others, but it didn't take long to realize my favorite teaching moments by far were conversation skills and social engagement between the kids and other passengers. I got to see into their minds, and to see how other passengers responded to them. The variety of responses included everything from changing seats, to sitting closer to the students, and even to sitting far away from the students. Occasionally, I even got to witness their pure amusement, pleasure, or amazement at so many pieces of our student journey on the train.

The early days also involved various lessons in safety measures, such as not jumping down the stairs just because they were bored. I also learned that any delay taxed the young people's patience and often led to anxiety or mischief, which encouraged me to track possible temptations—red buttons and emergency phones were potential kryptonite even for the good kids who just wanted to know what would happen. I spent some of my time during that first week interviewing the kids and preparing behavioral consequences, rewards, and mini lessons in life skills, such as personal independence and practical decision making.

Despite concerns and anticipations, there were simple interactions that contributed to the development of fun train traditions. One student, Brent, was about thirteen years old, yet I was asked to keep a special watch on him until he got used to the experience. He usually saved me a seat after I completed my rounds, and the unexpected seemed to burst out of our conversations.

One day as I sat down, I asked him, "How is your day going, Brent?"

"It's good. Did you know it is called the Frontrunner because it travels almost the whole length of the Wasatch Front?"

"Oh! I never thought about that connection, but the train going that distance literally facilitates our train program. So, are you—worried about riding the train?"

"My mom says no need to worry as long it's moving forward. Today, it's moving forward."

That was his matter-of-fact way of saying he was not worried.

"Your mom is right. I can see how much that helps you, Brent."

Here was a kid with emotional courage. It was so easy for him to be anxious, but conscientious preparation and proximity to a trusted adult seemed to help him.

I looked out the window at the scenery, and the lull in the conversation motivated Brent to pull out a very special set of NASA cards that were all about clouds. They had beautifully detailed pictures, making it easy to gaze out the windows to identify every cloud we could see. Some people might look for shapes in the clouds, but we looked for and found so much more!

For me, this was taking cloud gazing to the next level, and I was intrigued by science, so it was easy to allow this daily educational activity to become a great way to pass the time. Plus, the interactive experience kept Brent occupied and helped him relax, especially when we discovered we could look at the cirrus and altostratus clouds and make a pretty good guess whether it would rain or stay sunny during our school day. I think it gave him a sense of confidence.

During one of those quiet morning moments, I realized with absolute clarity for at least the second time in my life how fascinating I found clouds and the weather.

THE ALTITUDES OF ACCEPTANCE

Had I missed my calling to be a meteorologist? Dare I imagine that this might be why—

Nope. Not going there.

I had come too far in accepting my new circumstances to go down the *what if* rabbit hole. Besides, life wasn't over until it was over, and even meteorologists must start somewhere. So, I was far from being sure, but I added it to my list of potential futures.

That first week, the changes in my schedule and responsibilities dropped on me like a glass cup over a wayward spider. It was my job to never miss the train, and I got close to missing it two out of three mornings when I misjudged distances and literally ran too late. Other than being a major adrenaline rush, it kind of terrified me into action to discover every possible efficiency tactic.

First, I found myself calculating how long it took me to walk and run the quarter mile to the train station and planning my wake-up time based on the precise time I needed to leave the house in a way that kept me on the sidewalk. I made space for shifts in roommate schedules, determined a rigorous bedtime schedule, and planned for morning workouts. Then I biked around to discover any potential shortcuts across bridges, crosswalks, or through parking lots—anything that would speed things up if I had to take it slow through deep snowfall or avoid icy, well-tracked sidewalks.

I wanted to know my options so that I would be able to choose my route without thinking about it too much. At any time, I might be walking, nearly running, or even on the phone at times, counseling with parents as they rushed to catch a missed train at another station. Doing this for myself motivated me to also map out my driving shortcuts on the way to the train station from the school. All three possible routes crossed the industrial train line on the way, and one of the routes meandered through residential streets and dropped us right into the train station parking lot.

At the end of each school day, we met in the gym about ten minutes after the end of class, giving them time to chat or finish conversations with teachers after school. Many of them rushed into the gym with explanations of why they were breathing hard and barely making it at the last possible moment. With their energy level and desire to be with their friends, on most days it was like herding cats to get them into vehicles. However, when they dragged their feet, they became more like the slowest turtles or sloths. Some days, I wanted them to move extra fast to get ahead of road conditions, but of course they found every reason to stall. They had to get their coats, find a book, or remember where they left their backpacks—just normal kid stuff! Still, we usually made it, one way or another. On the rare occasion we didn't make it, I had twenty or more parents to call.

Now, I don't know who "they" are, but they say sometimes working *with* children is the hardest work in the world. If you asked me, I would say working *against* children is the real source of hardship. Like the rocks and rivers in life, finding a way to flow *with* rather than against the current of children is a challenge that requires an informed set of skills as well as divine influence.

As an example, the first task at the end of school each day was to take attendance before dividing and departing. One day, taking attendance seemed as impossible as putting leaves back onto trees after autumn winds have scattered them. Most of the students were in clusters or corners in the gym, waiting for the stragglers, and although I had managed to gather my southbound group into the middle of the room, some were arguing while others were over-enthusiastically helping each other with homework. To make matters worse, others were talking so loud I could hardly hear myself thinking, much less speaking.

The last student, Robert, finally hustled into the gym and dashed over to where I was standing—just outside the center of the circle painted on the gym floor. He'd never been late before, and he observed the group slowly. Then, he leaned his head toward me and without preamble inquired, "Hello, is this a sewing circle?"

Well, that's not the expected greeting, and completely out of context.

I looked at him, then my circle of students. In all my frustrated watchfulness that day, had I missed anything that validated his question?

THE ALTITUDES OF ACCEPTANCE

The latest craze for the middle schoolers was a sewing class, so as random as his words were, I knew almost all the students sewed at some point during the day. As I looked around, no one was actually using a needle and thread.

"Not that I can—"

Then, despite the fog of mental exasperation, a tune I had been singing at church earlier that week popped into my mind, carrying with it a lesson from my childhood about humming songs when feeling overwhelmed. Also, I really needed to laugh, even if I had to create the joke myself!

I ran with it and shot him a mysterious grin. Then, with cast-iron certainty, I said. "Yes, it is."

His eyebrows went up as he scanned the group, clearly doubtful of my sincerity.

Well, why had he even asked me if—oh, never mind. I'd rather sing!

"In this circle—we are sowing—daily sowing—countless seeds of good and ill ..."

As I sang the first verse of the song below, I used my hands dramatically, pointing to kids scattered throughout the gym as well as in my circle. Some were seated calmly; others were wildly running around in hot pursuit of another student or chasing after a ball that had just hit someone.

> *We are sowing, daily sowing*
> *Countless seeds of good and ill,*
> *Scattered on the level lowland,*
> *Cast upon the windy hill;*
> *Seeds that sink in rich, brown furrows,*
> *Soft with heaven's gracious rain;*
> *Seeds that rest upon the surface*
> *Of the dry, unyielding plain.*[3]

The children were collectively committing acts of diverse good and bad value—distributing their seeds, if you will. Despite my enthusiasm for my humor, the student returned a vague look.

Well then! The song had done nothing for him, but at least I regained a more relaxed mindset. I took a deep breath, went to the center of the group, and raised my clipboard with a solid, "Attention, students, please!"

Most of the students listened and were still as I took attendance, but Robert proceeded to pull out his needle and thread. He caught my eyes with a stare and an amused grin.

Of course! I said yes, so now it will become a literal sewing circle.

I met that teasing gaze with, "Joke's on you, Robert. Sure, be the guy who wants to prove me right rather than wrong!" Then I told him to put it away because it was time to load up the cars.

Fast forward to another afternoon when it was more winter than fall in terms of seasons.

I had sent all the other vehicles, save for the one I was driving, to the station while directing the late arrival of a few students. All eight students finally loaded, we left a minute or two later than desired. This delayed us just enough to get stuck at the train crossing as an extra-long, super-slow industrial northbound train made its way *clickity-clacking* and coasting through the crossing.

I sat in the driver's seat glancing at the clock every half minute, praying for our train to be just a little late. Anxious for something to redirect my mental energy and apprehension about being stuck in the car mire, I tuned in to the conversations around me.

Two young male students, Stevie and Jacob, were having an odd conversation in the backseat about a topic that was appropriate for discussion yet rather beyond their youthful understanding. Still, they were working hard to make sense of their issue.

As it turned out, I was not the only one listening. Trey was an intelligent but mischievous middle schooler with light blonde hair that curled at the ends and framed his endearing blue eyes. The effect made him appear to be far more angelic than he really was, and now, he was trying desperately to derail the two boys' conversation. Even through my mirror, I could see his eyes twinkling—that was my first sign of trouble.

Or the sign that I was about to laugh.

Or dole out a consequence. Alas, I never could quite predict what was going to happen.

I could tell Trey was in a dangerously persistent mood. Time after time, he kept dropping inappropriate comments that harassed the boys' endeavor to exchange mature statements.

To their credit, those two conversationalists were having none of Trey's nonsense. Stevie and Jacob politely sidelined Trey's choice of discussion material and ignored the implications of Trey's comments, continuing to remain focused like pros on a debate squad!

It was hard to decide if I needed to interject. To do so would mean taking the risk of ruining a chance for the boys' better nature to come to the forefront. I also didn't want to risk laughing—for them, this was serious! Finally, I judged it best to see which act would play out.

As they talked, and I listened, I found it interesting that the longer this went on, Trey was merely proving more and more to everyone in the car who was listening that nothing he said would be allowed to influence the conversation.

Eventually, Trey became strangely silent. It was not in his nature to admit defeat or stop on his own, and from my front seat, I searched my mirror for the signs that would tell me he was hatching a plan. He was prone to attention-seeking behaviors and bothering his peers, but all I heard was a sigh and an embarrassed laugh!

Was it possible? Was this the moment he would show he could be sensitive to others?

Then he said, "Uh, okay, I think I'll stop talking now. I don't know what I'm talking about."

It was pin-drop quiet for a few seconds, enough for me to process the miracle in my ears. His words were almost sensitive, although his act was possibly more out of pride than humility or awareness. But now I had the new pleasure of knowing Trey could listen to common sense—his own as well as the common sense in the behavior of others—and pursue harmony for once over the intrigues of conflict.

I had just seen him go from his usual behaviors to knowing when to let things go—and I had seen him do so quite gracefully with words and a smile. This was about as rare as a snowfall in late July—unless you were on a fourteener.

To witness a student's changing and growth firsthand—to see them display skills they didn't usually use in a beneficial and intelligent manner—it was nothing less than a privilege.

I made a mental note to later approach him to express my appreciation for his reflective moment. He had recognized a losing battle and become behaviorally introspective, and that deserved recognition. However, there was still the reason I was on the edge of my seat, waiting—

Click-clack, click-clack, click-clack.

Ahead of me, the train still inched along through the crossing.

I checked the time and noticed a few minutes had passed, and then looked around, knowing that the level of chaos that had just ended was nothing compared to what would ensue if eight kids and I missed the train.

I had a choice—take the fall and miss the train or take a risk and make the train. I was not desperate enough to do something stupid, but was there anything I could do safely?

If only we could somehow get to the other railroad crossing farther south ...

I bit my bottom lip, a quizzical frown creasing my brow as I took in my surroundings. I was in the farthest right lane next to a wide shoulder. Beyond the shoulder was an empty parking lot. Behind me was a traffic light. Cars were waiting at a standstill in a long line in every direction—

Except in the south-bound lane of the street running parallel to the tracks ...

Looking out the windshield and rear-view mirror, I reassured myself of that which I already knew—no cars were moving behind me.

Once I start moving, what else can the other cars do but let me through?

I answered myself with a victory laugh. What I was about to do wasn't exactly legal, and I hoped there wouldn't be any phone calls made about my behavior!

Feeling quite cautious yet daring, I considered every possible risk of the operation. I concluded there was no other way. My mind was hollering: *End the chaos as soon as possible!*

If I didn't get the kids to the station in time, my workday would lengthen, kids and parents would be elevated emotionally, and any number of other extraneous possible elements of chaos might ensue while waiting fifteen minutes for the next train.

If there was anything I could do, it was my responsibility to at least try.

Readjusting my fingers on the steering wheel, I breathed in a long and deep breath as though I was about to blow up a balloon. I filled my lungs and internally encouraged myself to take this risk, not because it was a risk, but because it felt right under these unnatural circumstances. Then I prayed for forgiveness for the numerous traffic laws I was about to break quite willingly.

Here. We. Go.

My first move was to pull the vehicle into the shoulder and drive forward, taking a right turn into the parking lot. Then I spun around and shot back onto the shoulder, facing the opposite direction of traffic.

Ever so slowly, I crept forward like a predatory cat, gradually rolling a little at a time down the right shoulder toward the light. I kept my eyes on anything that might inhibit my desired left turn. With a stroke of intelligent intentionality, I also flipped my left blinker on to communicate to the other cars what I was doing, hardly thinking about the children's view of my unorthodox behavior.

"Miss D, how did—wait a minute—what are you doing?"

Reasonable question, thanks for asking!

"Getting you guys to the train station on time."

Nerves of steel, Deanna, you got this!

"Miss D, you're going the wrong way!"

Actually, it's the right way, the only way …

"Don't worry, I've thought it through. In this case only, going the *wrong* way might be the *best* way to get to where we need to be. I'm sorry. Also, no more questions please. It's focus time!"

I heard them start to joke with each other about what I was doing.

As I made my left turn, one of the boys said, "Miss D, that car is following you. And that one too!" It was a curious observation; one I had missed. For better or worse, I had started a trend!

At least they aren't taking bets on whether I'm going to cause a wreck or not. Dear God, please do not take that as a suggestion. I can do without any kind of speculation right now!

I said another quiet prayer that all those following my bad example would not come to bad endings, and that the students would be able to learn good things from this strange experience.

Finally, we were on the road parallel to the train line.

I drove just a little too fast to reach the other crossing where the bars were just going up. In the distance to the north, I could see the industrial train's tail end that had passed by mere seconds before.

Whoot! Timing is everything! Oh, and God, thank you. PS, I will never do this again.

The short distance remaining from this point consisted of a residential shortcut—an easy left turn that would gain us a minute or two and help us avoid the slowdown of two traffic lights.

"Miss D! I saw our train coming when we were crossing the other tracks."

As it turned out, that minute or two would matter.

"Thanks, that's good to know." I took that left turn and powered forward.

Yikes, I thought. *This will be cutting it close. No more shortcuts options after this one. Or maybe …* "Everyone, gather your things. I need you to be ready to make a run for it."

THE ALTITUDES OF ACCEPTANCE

I zoomed through the residential area, though barely above the speed limit. I figured I had broken enough laws that day!

Next came two left turns before reaching the train station parking lot.

Hmmm—wish I had a shortcut with more right turns than left turns!

No cars were in my way as I pulled up to the platform—and the train was approaching. I stopped the car and, as if they were all pulled by marionette strings, the doors opened behind me. With eight kids piling out as fast as possible, I could feel the car's weight shift as I made use of the time to search for the nearest parking spot. If they had to run for it, I was going to have to sprint.

As they hurried to the platform, I blindly hoped they'd make it as I rushed to park in the only open spot in the first row, just down the lane several yards. It was *my* turn to make sure *I* didn't miss the train, so I grabbed my backpack and took off. I could see that the train had already slid to a stop, so I had not even a second to spare! But as I got closer and darted through the gates, I noticed Stevie—one on whom I could always rely for practical help—standing at the doorway, holding it open. The train couldn't leave until the doors were all closed, so I let my steps slow just a tad but didn't stop until I stood next to the open doorway, gasping out a thank-you in Stevie's direction.

"Well, get on the train, Miss D!"

Oh, right!

I grinned at Stevie. "Yes, sir!"

Feeling the rush of adrenaline, I hopped aboard. Stevie let the doors close behind us, and when I glanced back for just a moment, I felt like all the stress of the last thirty minutes was left behind on the platform. As the train took off, I smiled at Stevie and breathed a prayer of gratitude for the thrilling and safe ride. Then I aimed straight for the stairs, ascended to the upper level, and pondered as I took my seat.

So, I had dared to be an outlaw for the sake of the children. I had judged what was more important and somehow prevailed despite the risk and anything in me that was anxious about such a maneuver. I had acted for the right reasons, but were the means justified?

On one hand, by breaking the law, I had successfully curbed the potential for chaos among the parents like a broad side of a building could stop a whirlwind of leaves. On the other hand, I was lucky to not have to know if getting to the train station on time was worth a possible traffic violation. Maybe all is well that ends well, but I still felt grateful that this one was only between me and God.

At this point, all I could do was quell my frayed nerves. If they didn't know it yet, the kids would know if I was rattled. I knew they might go home and tell stories about me, but it would be best if we didn't discuss such matters in public. So, I would have to get control of myself, calmly ascend the remaining stairs, and then make my rounds as though it was a normal day. Once I was in my seat, I would text and tell their parents how I had to make some unique decisions to ensure we arrived at the train station.

Having never done anything like this before, in my prayers that night I reminded God I wouldn't ever do such a thing again. Then I added *unless he decided it was necessary.*

When I reflect on this story, I think of Trey's story too. Although both stories are so different, reflection on our actions made all the difference in what we learned from our experiences.

Trey learned his old tactics were not working and figured it was time to try a new, wiser, and more socially acceptable approach. In my case, reflection helped me see how the way to act was laid out in my mind like a life-force, or a pure source of intelligence, as though God cared about my problem to the degree of instantly providing me with resolution. I felt sure he had his reasons and that it wouldn't always be authorized for me to do such things.

Making it to the train had been vital to my role as train program monitor. Desperation and awareness of the consequences played a role in my decision, and no thought had been given to whether I was willing to pay the price if I got caught.

As it happens, this was not the first or the last time I had sensed the spontaneous and spiritually inexplicable. Some things we must do in life feel insane but are really inspired. Realizing the difference translates to knowing it's the right thing to do, but also knowing the inspiration or answer might be personal and make no sense outside of context.

Only God can see the whole picture of our intentions and behaviors.

We can only ever do our best to deal with every situation, and because God knows us, he can help us know how to act and respond. Sometimes it feels like we will either fall into turmoil or tenacity, but then we recognize how God matched our traits and strengths to the circumstances and tempests in our lives. That's when we come to find out we are not given anything we can't handle, and that God has everything handled, or is waiting for us to act so that he can act too.

Moments like these are when God is saying something akin to: "Hey, I can use your package, no matter the size. I can use your strengths, your weaknesses, your circumstances, your hesitations, your history—little things that make you who you are to create a moment in the storm where you save you, and others. Or maybe just to save you from yourself. I can help you step up and out or into the dark—even if it's only so that I can show you the light!"

I used to think God spoke less in moments when emotions were high and could get the better of me, but now I know there are occasions for bold acts of inspiration. Such moments are often when a deeper part of me is hearing God's guidance. I've noticed that anxiety dissipates and is replaced with the decisive, solution-oriented side of my soul. I feel led to do the right things that scare and surprise me.

Sometimes those things are not going to be as easily understood by others.

But incidentally, such things do not surprise God.

Maybe you have met someone like Danny before? Danny was one of those kids whose ability to be authentic came from a place of boldness. He amassed friends, dazed enemies, and pursued fun in life by simply being himself.

As the adult in charge, responding to his antics proved—interesting. I was either laughing, feeling exasperated, or trying to see what I could learn about troublemakers in disguise. That's right, he convinced me to believe troublemakers were entertainers in the making.

After all, it was all I could do to try not to be too entertained as I tried to guide him and other students to be their best selves. I counted it an intrepid privilege to mold this young mind and often imagined what kind of entertaining feats he might accomplish one day. At first, I had no idea how to do that, but one day—I figured out the secret.

After finding our seats on the train, Danny pulled a small sewing needle out of his backpack.

Uh oh. I had seen this movie before, and I didn't—well, I didn't mind how it ended in the past! What about this time? Life with these kids was such a "choose your own adventure" story!

My mind darted around as I imagined all the damage that small sharp things could do.

"Danny, I'd like you to put that back in your backpack, please."

Of course, he resisted my request.

So, round two. "Danny, why do you have a sewing needle out, anyway?"

Danny did not really answer my question as much as he answered my concerns, "Don't worry, it's for school, it's my mom's, and it's too small to be dangerous!"

THE ALTITUDES OF ACCEPTANCE

"Uh, Danny, you cannot persuade me that your little needle is not dangerous—it's sharp! Did your mom give it to you or did you get it—another way?"

"Miss D, she gave it to me, I promise! It's for a project in sewing class."

Right. That class *was* on my radar. I muttered, "Well, at least you got it legitimately!"

However, back to the problem, or rather round three—or is it four?

"Danny, I am so glad you are learning to sew. Honestly, my only issue is that you have something sharp out in the open right now. Knowing your mother, I bet she advised you what to do with the needle before you left home, didn't she?"

"She did. She said I needed to keep it safe—but," a glimmer of mischief stirred in his eyes, "it's kind of fun to show it off!"

He thrust it in the direction of Abe who sat next to him. The boy promptly—and somewhat dramatically—cowered into the corner of his seat.

Ah! He likes the power it gives him. Good to know, but it's still not okay.

If I had been a cat, my hackles would have shot up in warning. I didn't like being defied, even by Danny the Entertainer, but I quelled the rising heat in my mind by reminding myself this was a child I was dealing with. Still, out of my inexperience, a twinge of desperation seeped through. When it came to Danny and his antics, there were some real and reasonable fears—

"Danny! Please put that away before you put it in your mouth on a dare or something."

Danny remarked, "Uh, Miss D! I'm not going to do that—I'm not that stupid!"

The subsequent glare I gave him, with raised eyebrows and a sideways frown to indicate my substantial disbelief, was totally validated. I knew, he knew—we all knew—he had taken on crazier dares then what I had just suggested.

However, given his assertion of innocence, I fully expected him to start explaining why I was wrong, and he was right.

Instead of his voice, however, several voices from surrounding seats chorused in protest—all in favor of *my* side of this story.

I let my case rest; I had nothing more to say. There was nothing I needed to say.

The reasoning of people in his fellow age group seemed to take effect as Danny took on a thoughtful demeanor. Then he admitted, "Well actually, you all have a good point, I'll put it away right now."

When Danny put the little needle back, I watched him in silence. Abe, who had once cowered in fright, had joined the protesting voices and now seized the chance to gloat. Laughing with an excessive amount of glee, he said, "Wow, he's smart enough to know he's stupid!"

Uh, yeah, but no. Also not okay.

I threw Abe a few smoldering daggers with my eyes, letting him know he had crossed a line with his statement. When he stopped giggling, I returned my gaze back to Danny.

"So, for the record, no one is calling you stupid, Danny. Abe is relinquishing his animosity right now. But as you can see, apparently several hands on this deck agree it would be a far less-than-intelligent decision to have your needle out at this time."

He nodded and made no argument, not even a jab at Abe for the crude remark. This behavior told me at least two things for sure.

One, whether he was simply anxious to please his friends or truly conscientious with the help of his friends, I could rely on peer pressure to adjust his behavior. This being the case, I would consider guiding his friends to help me in future altercations while helping him recognize right and wrong for himself—eventually.

Two—despite his silence, there was a sparkle in his eyes. No doubt he was scheming a way to get back at Abe. Danny had a way of getting on "you owe me" kicks. He would think of ways to tease until he won a dare—then the kid would owe him a thing, like money, a soda, or whatever else he wanted at the time.

THE ALTITUDES OF ACCEPTANCE

I was not a fan of the way he lorded over others who became indebted to him, nor of the fact his cons were unpredictably contagious. People liked to follow his example as much as they liked to influence his behavior, so I had to do my best to keep up if I wanted to steer him out of trouble.

One weekend, I was inspired by an online comedy. It displayed the extreme of a Danny-con. It started with a girl randomly challenging a guy to flip a coin for money and escalated into double or nothing with a billion-plus dollars on the line—in minutes, he owed her everything.

That was the week I got my first fancy new smartphone. I felt so proud to finally graduate from stick phones and enjoyed cleaning its screen, reveling in the sheen of its black camera case, and finding ways to use its perks with the kids—like sharing the show with Danny and a few other kids on the train.

"Danny, do you see yourself in this screenplay?" I asked, hoping the answer was yes.

Danny's immediate reaction was to laugh.

"Nope, I'm never going to lose a bet like that!"

Well, of course, he'd think like that.

"Danny, has it ever occurred to you that the devastation that this guy feels is an extreme example of how others feel when they lose a bet against you?"

A moment of silence followed by an, "Oh man!" and a sideways glance told me he was getting it. The gears in his head were working to internalize the topic.

Good.

Hoping he was realizing the error of his ways, I got up and left him to his reverie. He was a good kid with an epic job of channeling his energy in a productive manner.

On another occasion, Danny was looking at his yearbook as we traveled to school. Looking over his shoulder, I found myself trying to see the yearbook through his eyes.

"This person looks like a witch!" he said with all the intensity of a teenage boy who doesn't think before he speaks.

It wasn't anywhere near Halloween, but the compassionate, protective parts of my feminine existence rallied to protect whomever it was he was pointing to.

My huff must have been accompanied by a mask of distaste because he said, "No, she *really* does!"

I peered closely at the picture. To my surprise, I found I could not disagree, but—

No, that's not nice.

Then again, I certainly could not agree with him either.

So, I thought for a moment, *I need to be wise …*

Danny had a good heart and a sense of pride. He was not out to hurt people with his comments, but it would also not hurt him to internalize a few social graces. I wanted to help him think differently about his words, to help him turn his criticism into a compliment.

… Perhaps I can tease this behavior out of him in a way he would understand … Yes, yes, I'll try that.

"Well, if you really think that, Danny, then wouldn't you agree that she could probably pull off a witch costume at Halloween much better than you can?"

The air seemed to turn into pudding under the effect of a very palpable pause. I couldn't see Danny's mind whirling, but I believed I could trust his ability to do his best to make sense of the implications of my words and let me know his thoughts on it—when he was ready.

A boy, Toby, revealed from across the aisle that he had been paying attention by sprinkling the air with a colorful and somewhat tasteful comment, "Ah, Miss D, that comeback doesn't even work!"

I held my silence but raised my eyebrows at him as if to say, *Are you sure about that?*

But what I was really thinking was, *Not supposed to be a comeback at all—In fact, I hope it's stronger than that.*

"Uh, yes it actually does, Toby."

Huh?

Danny clapped the yearbook shut as he finished speaking. He wore an honest, respectful expression but there was something jovial and appreciative in it too. He looked right at me when he said, "I know what I'm not going to be for Halloween this year."

The edges of my mouth turned up in a smile. This was a win, even if I hadn't given ideal advice or counsel. Danny had showed some level of mindfulness of his behavior and feelings toward others—albeit in a somewhat self-centered way.

Then, deep inside me somewhere—knowing Danny's tendency toward mischief—I managed to suppress an unexpected giggle as I imagined he might find a slightly meddlesome but ingenious way to recommend the costume to the girl he had pointed out—just to see if he was right.

Fortunately for me, Danny was far from being the only child who made my "training" days more fulfilling than challenging. Light-haired Danny's friend, Abe, had another buddy, Creed. Both Abe and Creed had dark hair and eyes that paired well with bright gazes and very loud voices—the kind where if their cacophony of noise was missing, the effect was alarming.

That day the train was especially crowded with costumed individuals headed north for Comic-Con. At the risk of losing my seat to the crowd, I got up to check on the two boys. As I arrived at their tabled booth, I noticed their intent interest in a little notebook.

"What have you got there, boys?"

With all the gravity of a tombstone, Abe said, "Miss D, *this* is called the *Death Note.*"

Upon further inquiry, I learned this was a toy come to life from one of their favorite TV shows. The book was used in the show as a powerful source of magic—if you wrote a person's name in the book along with a death story, he or she would experience that exact fate.

Learning this, I felt some small trepidation. Not that I believed magical powers could be in a little notebook, much less the hands of these two boys, but to say the least, this was a very interesting toy to play with in a public place. And on today of all days—the toy seemed to have more of an eerie relevance when combined with the presence of numerous characters of magical folklore and pop culture wandering throughout the train.

Cautiously, I took an empty seat nearby. "Cool. Mind if I watch to see how your game works?"

Creed gazed up at me with eyes full of purpose and spoke with a matter-of-fact tone. "If you like, Miss D. We are planning to kill off our least favorite celebrities."

Oh really? I almost protested at the word "kill" but then thought differently about it. I knew not everyone shared my sensibilities. It sounded harmless enough—for these kids, anyway!

Abe opened with an example of what they might write— "Britney Spears dies from poisoned blonde hair dye." Then came Creed's "Justin Bieber dies in a train wreck."

Hearing that last one gave me pause—so I had to interject, "Uh, boys, if you have it in for that pop artist, I won't stop you. But before you write that, consider the people in costumes sharing our ride this morning. I know it would not be the real guy, but if there is a costumed Justin Bieber aboard this train, well—"

"Well, what Miss D?"

I gave shrug, "Well, I'm just saying beware is all. I mean we're all riding the same train."

Their faces froze along with the pen in Creed's hand.

I held their eyes with intensity, watching those little windows to the brain.

They looked at each other. Then back at me. Abe gulped. Creed's ears went red.

THE ALTITUDES OF ACCEPTANCE

And the two little pennies dropped. Ding! Dong!

I smiled as the two boys sheepishly grinned.

They never wrote "train wreck" on any page in their notebook, at least not to my knowledge.

The train had come to a full and complete stop about eight miles from our normal station. Occasionally, our train would have mechanical issues or be unable to continue its route due to an obstacle of some kind on the tracks. The conductor had used the intercom to invite all passengers to disembark and wait for a backup train to take us the rest of the way. On days like this, the simple ride on the train would transform into a balancing act of managing chaos and herding children.

The first time it happened, we only had to switch trains on one platform, but I was beside myself going over and over the attendance sheet I carried with me every day. I could not lose a kid.

Losing even one kid could be the end of many things—the transportation program, the relationship with a parent, a good reputation, any amount of funding for the school—not to mention my confidence and psychological well-being. Luckily, that first time I had not lost any kids because we still all sat together. Now, a few of the kids seemed bolder about their preferences for transportation and always sat apart from everyone else. Most days, our group extended between several separate passenger cars. The more independent students would be harder to direct and keep close, especially amidst people crowding into the small staircases, waiting to exit the downstairs door onto the platform.

Consequently, I tasked myself to come up with and communicate a plan for when things like this happened. As far as I was concerned, the ability to handle chaotic train moments was a secret superpower that needed developing.

The new plan was for all students to exit their train car and walk to the center of the platform, near the seating under the canopy—no matter which car they were riding. They were expected to wait and rejoin our group, and under no circumstances were they to leave the train platform until we all left it together. I even asked two or three older girls with natural nurturing instincts to stay close to and steer one or two of my low-functioning students off the train safely.

When it happened again, my mind was focused. Get off the train. Go to the meeting place. Take attendance. Come up with a game to play while waiting for the next train. Call the administrators if it takes forever. Then—

"Miss D, I know why we have to transfer trains!"

I turned around to see who was speaking. At the top of the staircase, Abe was surveying the crowded scene, grinning from ear to ear as though he had just won a trophy for a best-kept secret.

I opened my mouth to reply as thoughts tumbled through my mind: *Can't he see how these situations make me busy? Isn't the reason obvious by now? What can he have to say about it?*

But upon closer observation, I could see it in Abe's face—the hunger for some kind of goofy but rational explanation to make it all better. This was the one thing kids did that often made more sense to them than anything an adult could do for them: using drama as a coping mechanism.

To me, it seemed so counterintuitive—how was it a good idea to deal with any unexpected or abnormal incident with a melodramatic truth?

Sigh.

Oh, all right.

I figured it wouldn't hurt to share a bit of bandwidth and lean into the drama of it all. Besides, I had to admit, these antics did make me smile, and I could use a smile right now.

"Abe, if you know something I don't know about this train transfer, you'd better own up to it, dude. I've about had enough of these things." I gave him a wink, followed by a fake serious and intimidating glare, squinty eyes and everything.

"Miss D, I hate to tell you this, but there is a vampire on this train," said Abe, and he was quite serious on the matter. He kept going with his story, talking about the vampire's disguise and the mystery surrounding him and his presence on the train. A noir novel detective, if I ever saw one.

Ha! Maybe I'll get more than a smile out of this.

His tall tale delighted me more than surprised me, and a few other kids around us began to tune in to the show. Then, a couple of the other passengers began to gasp and giggle as well.

Most people would have ignored this reasoning, but these were train passengers. They were disenchanted by the delay and of course would find such antics entertaining!

Minus the curtain, we might as well have been on stage, and Abe knew it.

He announced the impending doom with a voice of terror. "We must escape having all our blood sucked out! The only way to do that is getting onto a train that doesn't have a vampire."

Finally, the door opened.

The crowd shifted.

The sea of people flowed down the stairs, and—

Is it just me, or did the thought of vampires on the train urge people to move faster and closer to the door? I blinked and shook that thought away.

Yep, just me. That is a door, and it is about to open. Of course, people would—

"Well, Miss D, let's hope there are no vampires on the next one," said Abe.

"Uh, yes ... let's hope," I said, not sure what the proper response should be.

Then I held back a giggle. I wasn't entirely unaffected by Abe's vampire story.

Ha! I suppose I should be grateful he didn't come up with anything more ominous.

As we got swept up with the crowd, there was no more talk of vampires, and by the time we met the other students and found seats on the new train, I realized Abe had taught me something.

Can't say I saw this one coming! I have learned this via a vampire—really?

Vampires or not—faster out the doorway or not—movement needs motivation.

In this case, Abe's motivation was the same as his coping mechanism. Sharing his drama got him off the train without a hitch and made him happy. And from what I could see, navigating chaos and managing children might be somewhat interchangeable phrases, but there is always a place for good humor when motivating others to do any right, acceptable thing amidst chaos.

After a few weeks of riding the train, the children's behaviors melded into what might be expected of any train passengers. Most days, things were as quiet as a barren monkey house I had once seen at the zoo—I expected wild things to happen, but I was left with nothing to fuss over. Everything felt low-key as most of the students were napping or doing homework. Note—most, but not all. It seemed there was always something interesting or shocking just waiting for a chance to surface.

Abe, as you can see by now, was an inquisitive soul, and was prone to saying many lively and unanticipated things out of the blue.

One day as we all deboarded the train, I heard: "Why don't adults know what trolling is?"

I didn't know he was talking to me until I looked down and saw his big blue eyes staring up at mine, as innocent as could be. I had no answers—as in, I could make zero words come out of my mouth. It just opened and closed like a fish's.

THE ALTITUDES OF ACCEPTANCE

At my silence, he looked me up and down, grinning as though catching me in ignorance was his plan all along. Then came the moment I found out what trolling was!

As the kids liked to say, we learn something new every day.

Another time, I was sitting near Abe when he made a very strange noise. It was a mix of a mouthed "pop" and a holler, and it came with a very odd, somewhat eccentric behavior—kind of like when dogs get the zoomies. However, movement was contained to his chair and ended abruptly in perfect, nonchalant stillness.

It came upon him out of nowhere. To my knowledge, he had no medical history of such things, so I figured he was simply being dramatic.

"Okay—I think Abe has left the building! And *not* through the door," said Keston, who sat next to Abe. When Keston gave Abe a look that reflected the quirky strangeness of it all, I figured something was up.

Awesome. I have a crazy one on my hands. Maybe two? Ha! Tell me something I don't know.

I grinned and said, "Well, you two are good friends. Maybe you can help him re-enter the building *through* the door?"

Keston seemed happy to set to work on that task as I pulled a book out to read.

Not so many minutes later, I heard Keston ask, "Can I poke you, Abe?"

Without hesitation, Abe said, "Yes."

This is going to be good.

I shifted my eyes upward over the top of my book to watch as Keston brandished his pointer finger and shoved it speedily toward Abe's shoulder, slowing down to a king's grace right before it met skin.

Then he said with all the appropriate effects, "Ahhh. Now my life is complete!"

As they settled back into chatter about something equally random and incomprehensible, I giggled to myself and figured their lives really were complete. Watching such a delightful, quirky, and wonderful friendship was a little like seeing movie characters growing up together. There were things between them that would never be between anyone else, and it was my pleasure to witness this movie in the making.

I pulled my snack out of my bag. Across from me sat one of the most innocent, sweet, low-functioning girls who joined our train crew a few weeks after we had started. She liked sitting with Brent, so it was easy to also sit with Sally and check in with her whenever I could. She seemed to bring a sense of calm wherever she went.

She eyed my snack. It was more of a curious stare than a hungry glare, but I asked anyway..

"Sally, do you want to try a seaweed chip with me?"

My heart dropped to the floor as her adorable face changed from curious to terrified. There was a shocking amount of genuine concern in her eyes, which looked to be as big as saucers.

"Oh dear, what is wrong?" I reached out to touch her hand comfortingly.

She spoke haltingly, "You're—going to—you asked me … do I want to sink a ship?"

I gasped ever so slightly and sat back in my chair. I didn't mean to stare or go silent, but where did that come from? I was trying to comprehend how she might have concluded that such an activity might be possible for someone like me.

Then I remembered sometimes I talked too quickly. A moment later— *whoa, my own words!*

Seaweed chips were not exactly a common snack for children, but I had not realized how the sound of the words in younger ears might trigger ideas of a sea-faring life—maybe even like in the movies where pirates make and follow through with plans to sink other ships.

So, I was a pirate in her eyes for a moment, eh? Well, I wanted to be clever, but she was almost crying, so I did the only thing I could think of doing; I pulled out one of the dark, oily, thin, crunchy wafers, and turned it over in my fingers so that she saw the whole thing.

"No, dear, this is a sea—weed—chip. I think they are really good! Would you like to try one?" I enunciated every syllable to help the message sink in. "I promise you I don't want to sink ships. It's not one of my hobbies."

The curiosity in her stare disappeared as she shook her head against eating seaweed chips.

"That's okay, more for me! But someday if you change your mind, please let me know."

Sally was a calm one, but now I knew she was not meant to be teased. Some children enjoyed being teased to feel loved, but Sally needed an adult's honesty, patience, and protection. It also wouldn't hurt if I slowed my words down. Someday I would learn to make her laugh, but for now, it was enough to retain her trust after a silly mistake that almost made her tender heart break.

The best part about interacting with these students and spending time with them in a public environment outside of school was learning the importance of not taking myself too seriously. I enjoyed these kids and their antics more and more with each day, and so did many of the passengers who got to know us. I would like to think the train passengers became more conscious of others, especially children, and learned to never jump to conclusions about the children's presence on the train without allowing them to speak their minds.

While members of my group made friends with the other train passengers, I knew they weren't all constant friends with each other.

Throughout the duration of my role as train monitor, there were occasions of heated arguments, giggling fits, and severe injuries, including a broken finger and a concussion. I did my best to keep my voice patient and the kids under control, but all of us attracted the attention of fellow passengers and train professionals, sometimes for the better, and sometimes for the worse. But many passengers who rode regularly offered feedback such as, "It has been inspirational to watch how these kids are learning!" And that gave me all the hope I needed that this project was working out—at least for now, we hadn't overstayed our welcome.

As for my relationship with these young people, I found I could manage my expectations better when I based my self-assessments on what I was learning too—which meant accepting that I was learning too, often by trial-and-error about how to build meaningful friendships with them.

In total, I led the train program for about three years, but it only took one year to become aware of the effects of humor and compassion in caring for them. In the first year, I tried to implement methods for rewarding their behavior or providing consequences and discipline, which helped me identify individual traits and triggers. I was still so new to working with these young people, but I could see that they wanted to be good, but they also needed space to be themselves. In social situations beyond their control, they needed to trust that I, as their leader, would listen to their side of the story before reprimanding them. As I earned their trust, they gave me honesty.

Eventually, I found that enforcing direct consequences for certain actions on the train wasn't the right approach. General rules were important, but when behaviors didn't match expectations, all I needed to do was clarify my reasoning and then help them adjust their behavior to meet the expectations. I learned I didn't need to immediately re-establish control every time mischief happened. Together we'd find a little light and humor in the situation, then we'd revisit the rules. After we talked, I let them govern themselves and stepped in when necessary.

Most days, they also tended to keep each other in check, which helped a lot!

To understand the students, I discovered I needed to accept that they often had no idea why they did what they did. I could teach and set expectations, but they needed time to figure things out for themselves as they measured up to the expectations laid out for them. This was not a characteristic unique to this population of children, but for me, it took working on the Frontrunner with them for the concept to sink in.

I used to think the motivations of other people would always be discoverable through pinpointed conversations about their upbringing or an educated analysis of their behavior. I still believe that can be true, but now I understand that what is behind choices and behavior is much more complex, fluid, and ongoing than any single moment or action can reveal.

As I became more proactive and competent in applying interventions and learning from observations, my conversations with the students on the train and at the school became more comfortable, genuine, and fun. I started collecting stories to immortalize our train adventures and preserve the laughter. Being treated with equanimity agreed with them, and the students seemed to enjoy learning from me and with me almost as much as they loved having time to do their own thing with friends every morning and afternoon.

As the lifescape that had once been a challenge turned into a gift and an opportunity, I found my sense of purpose and confidence growing daily. I learned God can orchestrate certain moments to prepare us for whatever he knows we need and whatever is around the corner.

Evidently, I needed a literal "training ground" to become the better version of myself, from which I could rise above the despair of the last year.

I used to think we experienced despair in our lifescapes because of what is weak about us, but now I know it's because of what is strong about us. God can take despair away, but sometimes he doesn't. Life is often a more complete (and complex) experience for us because he doesn't. Instead, he simply sends his love and light through a project, inspiration, or an invitation to act. That means feeling despair can be the beginning of the process where God sets up opportunities to show us what he knows we can handle.

The Bible tells us that in the beginning, God had the power to separate the light from darkness, which tells me that even when we are in the dark about what's happening in our lives, God is not. We might get uncomfortable when life is dark, but there is nothing more likely to attract our attention in the dark than a bit of his light.

Truthfully, I don't think God *wants* us to be uncomfortable—unless it is going to do us some good. So, if you're feeling uncomfortable, guess what?

Time to get on the train and do something good!

CHAPTER 7

THE ADVENTURE OF LAUGHTER

There is one thing that every train ride, every classroom, every field trip had in common. It was necessary, but it was not exactly considered fun and was generally just a tedious process.

To offset the monotony of taking attendance, students often joked around with half-baked humor.

When it was my turn to carry out the task, I never could anticipate what might be said, but eventually I realized that the process of taking attendance is very telling about the people who are present, even though the jokes were often more about the people who were missing.

I'd dare to ask the kids in class if they'd seen Ben, or where Bill was, or why Byron was gone—in case they knew. Of course, they usually had no idea, but they told me all the ideas they had, such as—Ben was on the best date of his life, Bill had won the lottery, or Byron was finally never coming back.

Sometimes, in amazement I'd say, "Wow. Ben, Bill, *and* Byron—all of them are gone today." If the absentees were considered disruptive students by their peers, I would learn who was looking forward to not being distracted in class when they said some clever remark like, "What's wrong with that?"

Or, if I said, "Looks like the only person we are missing is Jasen," another student would say, "Speak for yourself. I don't miss him."

Wow, no love lost there, apparently.

I usually smiled at such a comment, believing they were joking, but still it caused me to wonder.

During the time I was helping an English teacher, Mrs. Carter, with her class, I noticed that when it was her turn to take attendance, the last name on the list was fun-loving Henry, who would often respond with, "Do I have to write a full and complete sentence, with periods, spaces, and capitals?" Then he would pose just like the meme where the baby gives a questioning look with hands on his hips.

Mrs. Carter would respond with pride in her occupation, "Great question! Yes—in English class, we write full and complete sentences—every single day." And she said that same thing, every single day. Sometimes, she would tie his statement expertly into the day's writing assignment. In time, it seemed this interaction was almost a necessary precursor to starting the lesson.

Later in the semester, I caught Henry laughing and grimacing as he walked into class. Confused, I asked him, "What's going on with you?"

He beamed at me gleefully, "I'm laughing because I'm in pain!"

Mystified, I inquired, "What in the name of all the worded world are you talking about?"

He quipped, "I'm in pain because I'm here—in English class!"

As he aimed for his seat, I could only shrug my shoulders and dismiss the odd exchange.

Then Mrs. Carter took attendance, and upon reaching the last name this young man spoke only one word, "Here."

That was odd. Or at least unusual.

I glanced up from my task and looked over my shoulder to see his mouth curving in a surreptitious grin, something that didn't surprise me as much as it disturbed me.

Uh oh, he's a little too happy for comfort.

I looked over at Mrs. Carter to see if her teacher's senses were tingling like mine. She merely raised her eyebrows and reminded the students to review their notes for the first fifteen minutes for the test that day.

Huh. Maybe the pain Henry mentioned earlier came from anticipating the test?

He was clever, so maybe he had derived a way out of the test that we'd discover in due time. I wouldn't put it past him to have covertly arranged for some kind of interruption of class, which would conveniently allow him to skip out on the test. Then his joke would be on us, hence that smile of his.

But I was only guessing!

Soon, Mrs. Carter asked students to put their books and notes away so that test papers could be distributed. Then, she added a request that the class finish their term essays after completing the exam.

The scene was set, and I took another look at our paradoxical student. He had just been told he'd be doing a lot of wordsmithing in one day, and yet—he still had that Cheshire Cat grin sprawled from cheek to cheek. As he dove into his test, I had to think nothing of it and moved on with my tasks.

However, when Henry finished the test in what must have been a personal best record, he handed it to me without a word and returned to his desk with unusual haste. There, he pulled out his essay.

I tried to focus on grading his test, but I was distracted, watching his unusual blissful energy transfer to a review of his essay. Then, I blinked once … twice … I was sure I was imagining things, but was he turning pages too quickly? When I barely had time to grade two questions on his test before Henry slapped his essay onto Mrs. Carter's desk, it was clear something was up.

Mrs. Carter appraised him with a stern look and then spoke with slow, deliberate clarity, "There are still ten minutes left in class, Henry. Don't you want to use it to make your paper the best it can be?"

Henry had to know what she meant by that, but he confidently countered, "Don't worry, I wrote full and complete sentences and put periods, spaces, and capitals between every sentence."

Mrs. Carter looked at him with disbelief, and I can't say I blame her; this had to be the first time he'd ever done his work so quickly without complaint. We were always willing to believe a student might turn over a new leaf, and we were prepared to be delighted, but also cautious about abrupt changes in behavior. As she proceeded to scan his work, I wondered what she was thinking. *Did he cheat?*

Then, her eyebrows lifted, and she looked him in the eyes, grinning from ear to ear.

"I see that you did. This is what I love to see. Thank you for doing such a good job!"

After Henry gave his thanks and returned to his desk, Mrs. Carter promptly handed me his paper.

"Do you see that? And that?" She pointed to two well-structured sentences and paragraphs, written in his voice and handwriting. As we looked at that paper with mirrored expressions of happy surprise, she said "I can hardly believe it. I mean, it's not perfect, but they've had a week to get this done. He must have done this over the weekend. And come up with this clever plan to make my day!"

Grinning, I replied, "Well, now you know Henry's finally got you and English class all figured out."

Not long afterward, there was a day when Mrs. Carter was absent. On days like this I oversaw the class according to her lesson plan. That day, the assignment I had been asked to give the students was, of course, an essay. After giving instructions, I stood at the back of the room, awaiting the students' questions as they began their work.

Of course, Henry was back to his usual traditions. Almost as soon as he could, he walked over to me, and with his hands on his hips and a questioning look, he asked with an air of curiosity, "Do I have to write a full and complete sentence, with periods, spaces, and capitals?"

I attempted to replicate the teacher's response. "Uh, yes. Many sentences, in this case. And whenever you wonder if you need to write a full and complete sentence in English class, the answer is yes. The answer is always ... yes." I punched that last word with a little too much power, and my heart dropped as Henry gave me a slight smile, ducked his head, and respectfully returned to his desk, leaving me to think about how I hadn't said quite the right thing.

Ah man, I must have come across as too annoyed! But Henry can clearly handle the coursework and expectations, so why bother asking? The way he repeats questions for which he already knows the answers is kind of a waste of time, honestly—but I never meant for that thought to come out and be heard.

My thoughts were interrupted as a student walked by and stopped in her tracks. She turned towards us and speedily countered with, "So—can I go home now?"

What?

I frowned, looking in her direction, and then I caught the spark in her eyes as they darted away from mine toward the door, which was still open after the first bell had sounded.

"You said, yes—yes is always the answer!" she said, making her move for the door with a bolt of energy.

I impishly jumped into her path. Then, drawing myself to my full height and folding my arms, I mirrored her grin with a light air of authority. "Wait a minute, you. It's still the morning, and I happen to know you've got a lot to do today, so—"

"So?" she asked, challenging me with a long, questioning vowel to finish my statement.

I emphasized the same word in my response to tease her and make my point.

"*So*, the answer is *not* yes—to *that* particular question. Now, please return to your seat."

As she dramatically relinquished her exit and reversed her run out the door, it looked as if she was bouncing back to her seat, and our giggles brought the feeling of a good start to the day. However, seeing her walk away with such energy in her step reminded me of how I had shut down Henry's buoyancy.

Poor Henry. What's his real deal anyway?

A thought flickered in my mind like a little light bulb, then blinked brightly.

His concern about sentence structure, word choices, or punctuation is not what it seems.

It occurred to me how repeating the same question over and over was about more than a concern for grammar. It was about his relationship of trust with the English teacher. And he had just extended it to me. I had failed. But he kindly let it go without hesitating.

Wow, Deanna, sabotage much? Not cool! You want to build rapport with these kids, you know. Sharing a joke is one thing; receiving good-humored behavior is quite another.

I knew there were some kids who enjoyed self-expression and the world of words. Those kids always loved English class. But Henry was motivated by a feeling of rapport. Displaying good humor and being clever was perhaps 30 percent for the sake of getting himself ready to learn—and at least 70 percent because his relationship with the teacher mattered to him.

As I pondered on the situation, I concluded laughter is an indicator of not only what we find funny, but also what we think is important, and I had exhibited my own sense of humor by how I naturally responded to each of these students.

For whatever reason, I had plugged into humor for her, and not for him. Yet for these kids, it seemed humor wasn't just something they plugged into or out of all day long. Because they experienced life so differently, a good sense of humor was an exceptionally powerful and essential life force for them.

Maybe I don't laugh at things that waste time, but the key is to not make anyone feel like a waste of time. Even if he is not thinking about it that way, it's important that I am. I need to be more careful.

Okay, stop this self-critique and analysis! Only I could be so serious about humor!

It was too easy to take life too seriously. I already knew good humor could disentangle me from self-criticism and relational comparisons. But it was time to learn a thing or two from these kids, such as how to form stronger links with others and embrace unexpected laughter.

Sometimes I feel that good humor is a gift, and we can learn to notice how it surrounds us. I think God is very intentional about overlapping human experiences, with the aim of helping us discover each other. Such connections don't always come with laughter and good humor, but they often do. We can choose what to do with the connections that come from it.

The effects of connection are both profound and non-trivial because they bring us joy. The art of good humor helps us reap the benefits of each other's decisions and actions rather than experience too much stress and frustration. If the gift of good humor can do all that, it's a gift worth seeking.

The truth about seeking good humor in life is that it surprises you.

During my second year at the school, on the first day of the teacher's preparation week, I was reassigned to work in the high school math and computer programming classroom. Regularly voted by students to be the "most frustrating" course in the school, I was initially quite flustered, thinking about how I had no great knowledge of either subject. I had been excellent at math in high school, but it had been years since then. I couldn't help but feel sorry for the poor kids. They didn't deserve to deal with what I *didn't* bring to the table. With a wry grin, I pictured the students teaching *me* instead.

In a flash of thought, I determined I'd have to be willing to jump out of the comfort zone and settle into the growth zone. I didn't have all the answers now, but I would figure it out.

THE ADVENTURE OF LAUGHTER

Looking over from where I sat, I noticed the tall, heavyset man who would be my new teaching partner. Mr. Dixon was a little balding, but that made him feel familiar—all my brothers were similarly losing their hair. Then I remembered he had once worked for a huge international corporation.

A gentle giant with an intriguing background, likely to be brilliant! Knowing him could be awesome.

Then I also remembered everyone who knew him better than I did talked about the man as though he was one of the most popular teachers in the school. And yet, students had said he was "mean."

How can he be both popular and mean?

I was slightly intimidated, but then, I had not become personally acquainted with him yet.

I stepped over to meet Mr. Dixon before he left the gym. I got up and walked quickly over to introduce myself and follow him to his classroom, where I asked him questions about how he worked with students and what his classroom standards were. Soon, I understood how a person of his corporate background had become a teacher, and how he earned his reputation among the students.

Mr. Dixon's work in the "real world" had given him power to illuminate learning, especially about hard subjects. As a trick of his trade, he loved carrying a stern demeanor as a front. It enabled him to command his presence and authority with the students while keeping them on their toes.

Ah, so this man had a presence that drew people's attention. At least we had something in common. I had once been told I had a presence too, but I didn't know how to effectively employ it.

Mr. Dixon clearly didn't have that problem.

In class, he would say what needed to be said in a way that was understood as well as enjoyed by the students, which allowed him to enjoy the freedom of candor to create learning moments.

In fact, one of the best parts about being paired with Mr. Dixon was seeing how he could tease the students and elicit laughter like a comedian on a stage. But he'd do it and gain respect, not applause.

One day, just before lunchtime, it came as no surprise to him when a student remarked, "Mr. Dixon, I'm hungry. What are you going to do about it?"

Mr. Dixon turned to the student with a grave face. His words had razor edges.

"I will show you."

Curious now, all eyes followed him as he made his way slowly down the aisle of seats to the back of the room. Then, pausing with a hand above the candy jar on his cluttered desk, all his gravity fell away as he grinned at the student who voiced the question.

A sea of eyes appraised Mr. Dixon as he calmly pulled a piece of candy out of the jar—and ate it.

I glanced around the room. Each face wore an appalled expression. Mine included!

Whoa! Who does that and gets away with it?

I finished my silent scan and looked back at Mr. Dixon, trying to see through his actions.

He settled the jar back onto the desk, completely unruffled and boldly apathetic.

"You're evil," moaned the student, dramatically shifting in his seat into a slouched position.

Mr. Dixon gave a fist-pump of victory, following it with a resounding, "Yes!"

I let out a breath, more like a gasp of amusement—laughter on the inside was trying to come out.

Some students were not laughing. Others were muttering under their breath. They knew zero snacks were coming their way before lunchtime. For my part, I knew this was all part of some kind of plan.

It occurred to me how Mr. Dixon generally made it super clear that he wouldn't give a centimeter, much less an inch, when students were attempting to push the boundaries. He seemed very comfortable laying down his law—and making this known without saying a word about the law. And, under all their bluster and desire to get things going their way, I suspected the students valued how he didn't let them get what they wanted all the time.

Unsurprisingly, Mr. Dixon also used good humor to teach students how to not be a doormat to other people. Once a student was unhappy and, hoping to get a rise out of Mr. Dixon, he said with abhorrence, "I shun you because you're not entertaining."

Mr. Dixon glared—before he grinned.

"Good. I intend to never be entertaining. That would please you too much."

I giggled—*but he is! I've never seen such a good show!*

Apparently, "entertaining" was not a required teacher quality, but there was quality entertainment in Mr. Dixon's classroom. It was the kind where he called all the shots, yet knew laughter belonged in learning and quality education. With a smooth style all his own, he encouraged hard work and made his expectations clear while creating opportunities to release tension.

And there were times of great tension.

Whenever Mr. Dixon introduced a new mathematical formula or programming principle, the air in the room among the students could often be sliced with a knife. The students would slump in their seats, their minds churning through the mud. Sometimes, the students tried to speak assertively that they understood—when it was apparent they didn't. On rare occasions, the students quit trying or gave in to behaviors of deep frustration, such as throwing pencils or pounding desks, but Mr. Dixon smoothly found ways to encourage them to ask questions and renew their mental and intellectual efforts.

In such moments, I felt compelled to pay attention. As predicted, I felt mortified by what I didn't know and how I couldn't help the students. I had done algebra and calculus in high school, but I was new to the specific curriculum and methods used at this school. I should have pursued math in college and become an environmental engineer or a meteorologist, but I hadn't.

THE ALTITUDES OF ACCEPTANCE

Now, I didn't want to risk leading the students astray or trigger such behaviors when it was my turn to answer their questions. I was extra motivated to learn by how Mr. Dixon was regularly called upon to be the strong arm or the compassionate father figure of authority in the hallway to respond to behavioral situations. He was undoubtedly the right person in size, stature, and nature to do a lot of good when students acted out. But when he left, I had to take over.

In the end, I found it easier to catch on to the material than I expected. I attributed the speed at which I figured things out to be an unexpected return on those early math investments in high school. I also discovered an unexpected advantage—I knew what to say when the students would fall into their doldrums and ask, "What is so important about math anyway?"

"Who are you to deny your future self this information? You never know when you're going to need or use math again in your lives—even if it doesn't seem likely now. Take me, for example … "

This answer came from a very personal space. Even though I hadn't taken a career trajectory where math would be centrally important, now I was living evidence that learning math could pay off. The students needed to understand how life is full of unexpected turns and unanticipated outcomes, that we never know where our random or intentionally gained skills might come in handy.

However, in the ongoing battle of mathematical wits, the students were not so readily convinced. This was clearly evidenced when a student showed our class an online meme that said *MATH: Mental Abuse To Humans.*

I'm sure he was hoping to make a point or at least offset his discomfort with a joke, but instead of receiving an easier assignment or guilt-ridden handholding from Mr. Dixon, there was only a quick look and a casual shrug, followed by, "Yes, I do that all the time."

His words caught the student off guard while the other kids booed and hissed. Mr. Dixon was not in any way abusive, so this comment served to teach the student there was no way to insult him.

THE ADVENTURE OF LAUGHTER

At the time, I was grading papers in the back, and I slipped him a grin. In Mr. Dixon, I had found a good teacher of humor, but I certainly had a lot to learn. I admired Mr. Dixon's ability to thwart a sneak attack over a subject he loved most, while at the same time managing to convey a key message.

In this case, *if you share your perspective as a joke, be ready for honest but droll feedback.*

Another thing Mr. Dixon did all the time, in addition to his teaching responsibilities, was coach basketball. When "life as a basketball game" percolated into Mr. Dixon's interaction with other people, I joked to myself that he couldn't help but see the world through "basketball rim glasses."

One day it happened to me! I was trying to help a student named Mike with some math, but we kept interrupting our progress by laughing about a memory from recess the day before. Our giggling caught Mr. Dixon's attention as he walked in.

"Miss D, what are you and Mike laughing about?"

Mike started with, "Uh—we were playing basketball game yesterday in gym."

His thoughts gave way to an overpowering chuckle, so I jumped in. "Yeah, Mike threw the ball at me, and I kept missing pass after pass. It was hilarious!"

A glimmer of amusement flashed in Mr. Dixon's eyes as he remarked, "Wait, so Mike made some passes at you, Miss D? And does he have a game?"

I paused, feeling just a little self-conscious until my mind caught on to Mr. Dixon's joke. I grinned, flipped my shoulder-length brown hair over my shoulder, and winked with confidence. "Well, I'm afraid he's got a better game elsewhere—but I can't blame him for trying. Can you?"

Mr. Dixon just smiled in appreciation.

THE ALTITUDES OF ACCEPTANCE

I might not be great on a basketball court, but I hoped this was the beginning of Mr. Dixon trusting me to play his humor game as good as anyone.

Students were groaning, straining against the weight of their tasks. It was Thursday, the only in-class workday for an assignment due on Friday. As far as I could see, Nelson was the only student who was completely on task. He was just sitting there, minding his own business, doing his math project as directed. Somehow, while walking by his desk, my feet met metal, and I tripped.

Nelson's pencil jostled as a dark jagged line appeared across his page.

His head shot up, and his hard stare made me gulp.

Of all the students, he didn't deserve the interruption, and he was wondering if it was intentional.

Yikes! Those suspicious eyes were almost too much.

I fought the urge to simply say, "Sorry!" A simple apology would never be enough.

Instead, I dug deep for a sweetly teasing smile and paired it with a slightly accusing voice.

"Nelson! What in the world are you doing, running into *my* leg with *your* chair?"

At first, his mouth gaped open in protest with a big "O." Then, willing to play along, he used his own tone of slightly amused annoyance. "Sure it wasn't the other way around?"

I returned his gaze with a look of astonishment and disdain. "Don't you tell me the truth, Nelson."

"The truth hurts, doesn't it?"

Nice! I grinned at his comeback and pretended to limp a little with a fake injury, "Sure does!"

That was all. Nelson returned to his task with a grin, and when I later told this story to Mr. Dixon, he pointed out, "Nah, it was the chair that hurt."

A surprised pout erupted from my lips, followed by a hearty laugh and a thank-you as I realized he was hinting at how tough I was while adding to my joke. *My* joke! It was a very welcome compliment.

Over time, it seemed to me that Mr. Dixon was something of a knight of morals, wielding a sword of power and expecting positive impacts. He could exact the best student behavior in a way that made humor fly but stopped trouble in its tracks. Students loved and respected him for how he elicited laughter and exerted authority, yet they didn't always enjoy how he left no escape from hard truths. Eventually, the students graduated from fondly calling Mr. Dixon "mean" to calling him "the meanest teacher."

As unoriginal as it was, it stuck like a magnet to iron.

As fate would have it, this nickname amplified in a marvelous way.

Several students arrived in class one day to find the desks in dreadful disarray. A group had borrowed our classroom during lunchtime. I had caught wind of the situation, but I was tired and dragging my feet a little, not excited to have to put desks in order. However, when I walked into the room, it was as though the desks had never been scattered! The students had cleared the mess and reorganized their workspaces, all on their own.

Out of gratitude, I exclaimed, "You're all angels. Thank you so much!"

And for the record, they really did look like a flock of angels: seated at their desks, facing the front of the room. Clearly, something like magic had fallen over them. As if inspired, they planned this moment perfectly, down to their clasped or folded hands.

A split second later, Mr. Dixon walked in behind me. Apparently, he had heard me speak from the hallway. The students threw glances at Mr. Dixon as if they expected him to express gratitude as well. Then came the most curious statement.

"We do not have any angels in *this* class. You see, angels can't be where Satan is, and we all know I'm the meanest teacher in the school, which means I'm Satan. So, *you* are not angels."

I tilted my head in disbelief—he was owning his nickname like a pro! And he had done so while one-upping the students in one hilarious gesture and tainting my gratitude for the students' hard work.

One assertion deserved another.

I put a sweet smile on my lips and let him know I was on to him.

"Huh. Well, if all that is true, then you should know that I *am* an angel. In fact, I seek company with other angels, and this is my cue to go."

I made my move toward the door, only to be followed by a chorus of protests from the students. I wasn't sure whether they were against their loss of angel status or just didn't want me to leave, but as I placed my hand on the knob and turned it slightly, I realized the latter idea was more useful to me.

I paused, dramatically stepped away from the door, and flashed a grin at Mr. Dixon.

"Ha! Who's the favorite teacher now?"

The protests turned into laughter as all eyes turned to Mr. Dixon. *What would happen next?*

Mr. Dixon left me and walked over to the front of the room. He picked up a dry-erase marker, acting as though I had never spoken.

In a mock protest of my own, I folded my arms, ready to glare daggers at him if he glanced back.

But Mr. Dixon's face remained neutral and mysterious. He even commenced the day's lesson on graphing parabolas, the U-shaped figures a grid. *What? No more fun pricks and digs?*

"When it comes to parabolas, the maximum [referring to the y-coordinate of the vertex of a parabola that opens down] looks like a frowny face."

Then he flipped the image and continued. "The minimum is a smiling face. You kids are always smiling, so you have the minimum amount of meanness. I am the one who is always frowning—I rarely smile—so I have the maximum meanness."

I knew better than that, so I raised my eyebrows in his direction, but I kept my silence.

With a wink, he added, "And Miss D, well, she has zero meanness. She also has papers to grade." With a flourish, he drew an arrow pointing the spot where the X and Y coordinates met in the middle.

He had long since gotten the students' attention, and now he had earned a new level of admiration from me. He totally had his fun, did his job, and won the day while playing his game in the kindest way.

What a cool guy!

I smiled, pulled the door all the way closed, and made my way to grade papers at my desk.

Looking back, I realized that Mr. Dixon might have simply been having fun, but he also taught me an analogy in the powerful way that only he could. Of all the teachers at the school, he had a front row seat to the students' bad days and good days. He could have had a less enlightened perspective, yet he chose to focus on how despite their hard knocks in life, these students smiled a lot.

This truth was something to be valued.

I was so lucky and blessed to be walking in his footsteps, to see what he saw in these kids.

Although I was able to quickly catch on to how good humor contributed to math, I can't say the same about Mr. Dixon's computer programming class. For me, being cheerful while dealing with the function (or dysfunction) of computers felt so much more complicated. The class included some of the math students, making it easy to transfer rapport with them, but I couldn't ignore one small fact.

While some of the students were better at math than computers, all the students were better than *me* at computers.

During the first few weeks, I desperately watched Mr. Dixon help resolve computer problems and answer project questions. I was willing to learn through observation—just like I had in the math class—but I was not much different than a beginner when it came to making mistakes. And when they say you learn much from mistakes, they don't talk about what you don't learn when you are getting stuck all the time.

And I got stuck—all—the—time.

I don't know how I was trusted to help the students! I so often found myself falling down a rabbit hole of simple solutions all the time, never quite knowing what to do for more complicated problems. Sure, there was the restart button, which—before anyone asks, yes, I turned it off and back on again as necessary—but nine times out of ten, both the student and I generally became more lost in the problem than we were when we started.

To my credit, most of the time, I did have enough good sense to not make the problems worse. I knew when to call on Mr. Dixon or a more experienced student to step in.

I really appreciated those moments. They usually began with a simple exchange that started with, "Mr. Dixon! I don't know what's wrong with Amy's computer. It won't—do that thing."

He never asked, *What thing?*

He never even made a show of fixing what I couldn't.

No matter the situation, he just walked over, looked at the issue, and proceeded to help. Occasionally he would point out to the student what he or she had been missing, while making sure he did so in such a way that allowed me to learn and observe.

But then came the week when Mr. Dixon was going in and out of the classroom, handling hallway emergencies a little too often. I was sure he was agitated, not only by having to be in two places at once all the time, but also by the fact that my skills weren't up to par.

THE ADVENTURE OF LAUGHTER

I hated to ask, but I had to. "Mr. Dixon, what's wrong with Andy's computer?"

Mr. Dixon raised an eyebrow at me, and I noticed his smile seemed a little raw.

There it was. The first hint I'd ever seen of exasperation. For some reason, that look triggered a fear that I had managed to keep in the deep parts of my mind up to this point.

Today was *that* day, the day he would fire me from his classroom.

I dropped my eyes—honestly, I couldn't blame him. He had been given an incapable assistant—me—and because of this he would never be able to catch a break in computer class, much less take care of all the student needs that were requested of him.

"Well, for one thing, Miss D, it's a computer."

And then he grinned. He knew he'd caught me worrying.

It wasn't fair to use my fears to get a laugh, but the revelation in the moment made it better. Apparently, I still had to work on how self-conscious I was, and he wanted me to get past it.

When the students around me giggled too, I knew they knew that I knew I had been had.

I gave Mr. Dixon a trace of a smile as I borrowed his line of thinking to practice patience and re-align with reality. He was right—not having all the answers about computers was hardly my fault.

What *wasn't* wrong with the computers? Technology was great—until it wasn't!

Mr. Dixon knew this. He also knew it took experience with computers to possess the understanding to troubleshoot problems—experience that precious few people in our classroom had. Most importantly, I wasn't blamed for what I didn't know.

When I struggle with computers now, or anything that involves layers of knowledge and understanding that I may or may not have, or be able to add to my repertoire of skills, I think about how God is more likely to reward us as much as he can for what we do know, and for the good we do, and how he will punish us as little as possible for what we don't know or don't do.

God doesn't fire me from life just because I am frustrated, unable to find a solution, or feel like groaning about the situations, people, or choices ahead of me. Like with Mr. Dixon, I can't blame God if he becomes a tiny bit exasperated with my fears and tears over my woes and weakness, yet rather than get angry, I believe God is more likely to remind me of a thousand truths in simple terms, point me in the right direction, and then make me laugh and move forward with life.

Truths like, it's a computer, it's a situation—and this too shall pass.

I used to think God was more like I imagined him to be, but now I realize he has always been as he is, with me and not against me until the end of time.

Sometimes God says, "Oh, so you're feeling uncomfortable? Good! Now, grow a little, and thank me later. Don't give up, don't give in, don't get lost. And if you do, come back."

God wants us to remember how all the bad, the good, and the ugly—all of the problems and the joys of life can't last forever, but they have purpose.

Not having all the answers about life is hardly our fault.

God made us unable to be perfect in life but he still wants us to get us as far as we can. God really does want to help get us where we are going, especially if it's eventually the same place he is. He wants us to live in the moment, the present, and if we do, he'll have more to work with in our lifescapes if we make plans, stay flexible, and welcome improvements.

So, in the same way I was learning to trust God, I decided that if Mr. Dixon trusted me to do what I could do and didn't judge me for what I couldn't do, then I would do my best to help him, bar none, just like God was doing his best helping me.

As the school year wore on, Mr. Dixon's occasional departure from class to help manage various commotions in the hallway increased. Eventually, he was absent for entire class periods. Although I had learned a lot, and the students were gaining strengths from troubleshooting problems on their own, I believed that they were missing out on a quality education in computer programming. The needs were logical, but the effects seemed unfair.

Despite accepting I didn't have to have all the answers, I still felt feelings of fairness and justice every time Mr. Dixon darted out of the classroom. I remembered a lesson I had learned while training to be a religious teacher—any time you spend on one thing takes time away from something else. It was just a fact of life, but in this case, it seemed like an expanding major juxtaposition. I wished he could be in two places at once! After all, dealing with student shenanigans was one thing, but what to do when a program went wrong was another.

Each time he had to go, I started taking a deep breath and giving myself personal pep talks.

Relax. You got this! Half of computer programming is trial and error anyway. You've been doing that all your life, you know.

Most days became student workdays. However, one day there were no assignments for them to work on. So, I looked at the lesson plan left behind by Mr. Dixon—a five-paragraph essay about the dangers and benefits of modern-day technology dependence.

Well, now—I can handle an appropriately time-consuming writing assignment!

Maybe Mr. Dixon was playing to my strengths after all.

After I issued the assignment, my anxiety dissipated as curiosity bubbled to the surface.

What were the student brains going to come up with?

As they began, I went up on tiptoe to write the day's announcements on the whiteboard. Whispering started behind me—I hoped it was just pre-assignment jitters.

THE ALTITUDES OF ACCEPTANCE

"Did you hear about what happened in the chemistry room yesterday?"

"No! What happened?"

"Jason lost an electron. He couldn't keep an ion it."

"Ha! I always knew he would have problems in chemistry."

"He doesn't have problems—he's just not bonding well. Or maybe it was the solution."

"Well, duh. If you're not part of the solution, you're part of the precipitate."

"Thought you would say *problem* right there, but speaking of precipitation, I heard it's going to rain later today."

"Awesome! I love it when it rains. I get to hang out at home playing video games."

"Whatever. You play video games when it's sunny outside too ..."

Jokes, weather, and video games? Clearly, they were just putting off starting their assignment.

I turn my back for one minute and—I get too many jokes and not enough hard work.

Not on my watch!

So, I took a minute to concoct a plan.

I needed to be taller or somehow more intimidating for my plan to work. I opted for an authoritative stance, so I tucked one toe behind the other and with a balanced, ballet-like movement, I spun around into a leap that landed me two feet away, squarely in front of the chatty duo. It felt a little weird, but it worked!

They jerked back slightly, and their voices paused in surprise when they looked up at me.

My eyes narrowed into a kind but pointed expression so that they had no doubt I was onto them.

With finality I said, "I will happily offer you each one piece of candy if you can manage to be silent for at least five minutes while writing your paper. If you can *all* make it five minutes, I'll give each of you two pieces.

If you are silent and write through the end of class, I'll give you all three pieces."

The students looked at each other, evaluating their individual and collective chances of earning mini candy bars, hard candies, and jellies. When they brought their attention back to me, one of them spoke as if representing the whole class.

"Uh, Miss D, isn't this a bribe for our silence?"

"Nope," I said confidently. "It's an investment in your behavior. It's positive reinforcement that will build your motivation to complete your assignments *and* aid my ability to keep you on the right path. Also, did I mention that it's a one-time deal? So, what do you say, are you going to take it or leave it?"

No hands went up, and I allowed them a minute to consider their options. The chattiness continued to snake through the room in whispers as they talked about the new circumstance.

Then Ivan spoke up. "Everyone, be quiet. I am hungry and I want sweet-tarts. They taste really good in my mouth."

A grin threatened to spoil my authority, but I held back as I watched peer pressure play out in the open.

Ivan's jokester friend, Jordan, retorted, "Well, you can be my sweetheart."

"Sweet-*tarts*, you goof!"

Pencil swordplay ensued followed by a few more worded jabs until Ivan said, "Ahh, shut up!"

I giggled. I couldn't help it, even though I knew despite the content of their words, and even if they didn't consciously know it, they were milking the chance to talk rather than write.

Taking my cue from Ivan's last remark, I moved with purpose to my computer. It might *look* like the students had taken me up on my offer, but I wanted to make it actually happen.

Using my computer, I quietly projected a five-minute online stopwatch onto the whiteboard at the front of the room.

Then without a word, I picked up the candy jar and strode back to the front of the room, where everyone could see me as the timer started to count down.

Let the visual do its job, I prayed in my mind. *For their good and mine.*

Heads bowed, and pencils danced across the page …

After five minutes, I walked down the aisles offering candy but maintaining my own silence to encourage theirs. In case anyone is wondering—Ivan and Jordan took sweet-tarts!

Given the five minutes had worked, I adjusted the timer to count down the minutes left in class. As each essay was placed in my hands, I relinquished additional various contents of the candy jar. When all the papers were in, I tried to place the jar exactly where it had been—

The bell rang, the students ran off to lunch, and a few minutes later, Mr. Dixon walked in.

The pile of essays sat on his desk, but he stopped short of sitting down.

He must have sensed something because his eyes moved from the significantly reduced contents of his candy jar to the essays, and then to me where I was sitting at my desk. There was no hiding anything from Mr. Dixon—I could see he knew exactly what had happened, if not in so many details.

Bottom line was, for better or worse, there were now a bunch of sugar-high kids walking the halls.

Then it occurred to me sugar could influence an increase in hallway emergencies …

Uh, had I just made my tomorrow worse? … Oh well, at least they did the assignment!

As far as I was concerned, the less I said the better, so I focused on the positive instead of the *what-ifs*. Before he had a chance to say anything, I smiled and insisted, "I want to read those papers when you're done, if you don't mind."

I'm happy to report that the essays didn't disappoint.

The computer programming class didn't always require such creative solutions, but almost every day there were interesting conversations.

From my desk at the back of the room one day, I heard Caton and Keith whispering and saw them looking at me furtively while working on their partner assignment in the corner. Alert and concerned, I pretended to put something into the cabinet near them without giving myself away.

The conversation was about something undoubtedly inappropriate.

I still didn't know the exact topic of their discussion, but perhaps they were testing me. However, by this time, I was the queen of redirection, and after this went on for five minutes, I had to do something.

"Boys, if my ears shouldn't hear what you are speaking, neither should yours."

I could see they were thrown off guard, just a little. *Had I hit the mark?*

Caton hesitated, then said, "Wait, so you really know what we are talking about?"

"Actually, yes." They appeared dubious, and rightly so. The slight untruth was pricking my conscience like a cactus spine poking straight into my shoe. I had aimed for mystery and attempted to re-direct their attention, but was I getting in too deep?

"Well, in a past life, I was somewhat of an actress, which means, I can read your lips and would know what you're saying in a crowded room full of conversations."

True or not, I *had* been on stage a few times. I also hung out with the actors in high school. And I could read lips too—though maybe not *quite* that good!

"Wait, so you believe in Hinduism?" Caton queried.

THE ALTITUDES OF ACCEPTANCE

Uh—what? That didn't get me where I wanted to go. Should have simply requested an alternate conversation topic! Now I had talked myself into a hole and needed a way out.

As if he had read my mind about needing to bring this conversation home, Mr. Dixon spoke his way playfully into the conversation. "It doesn't have to be Hinduism," he countered. "There are a lot of other religions that believe in reincarnation."

He had a good point and was going with the flow, so I went with it too, taking the opportunity to leave the white lie in the past and operate collaboratively, "Yeah, you don't have to be Hindu to believe in a past life. Also, having a 'past life' can mean lots of things."

"Exactly," said Mr. Dixon. "Now, in case you all haven't noticed, this isn't a religion or philosophy class. So, no discussions on religious beliefs are necessary. I don't need to know what you believe to know you'll do great on this assignment."

Grateful that Mr. Dixon had built a wall against the tilting conversation, I nodded my agreement. *Phew, glad this conversation is over! And it looks like the earlier dialogue is now resolved too.*

I returned to my desk, feeling rescued from myself by Mr. Dixon.

As though he wanted to get in the last word, Caton stated, "Yeah, that's right, we believe in Java. And we don't need to know what you believe, Miss D."

Mr. Dixon and the other students laughed, while I just smiled.

Apparently, in this classroom, Java was accepted as the primary language and belief system, and the principal followers were the students and Mr. Dixon. And even if I couldn't "believe in Java" myself, I was capable of advocating for student success and keeping their momentum going in the right direction.

In this classroom, a little collaboration and good humor clearly went a long way.

Before I knew it, a new school year arrived. School schedules and needs had changed, and I was asked to work with the financial literacy and marketing classes instead of math and computer programming. As an assistant, I was used to doing what I was told, so I had no complaints—I had been trained in financial literacy at home, and I believed being smart with money could make you almost if not equally as rich as being smart with computers.

While my environment changed, the kids and the age range I worked with didn't, so the same kind of shenanigans continued, along with my motivation to collect stories.

The first week or so was like any other class—attendance, learning the names of kids I didn't know, and tracking their progress with the teacher, Mrs. Decanter, taking the lead on the course section on United States government. As the unit ended, she organized student-led presentations about the three branches of government.

One set of students introduced the First Amendment. They took the time to clarify that this was *not* the amendment that gave citizens the right to bear arms.

Wait—other students are going to give presentations on the Second Amendment, so why mention that?

Molly raised her hand.

One of the student-presenters called on her.

"Oh yes, you're totally right, the second one is the right to arm bears," she said.

Huh. Surely this is not their intent—to glean audience participation based on what the presentation is not about. I'll play their game—how about a tangent and then a redirection?

I quickly added, "That's right, folks—we can arm bears. Lucky for us they are pretty vicious fighters."

"But that would be a beary stupid thing to do!" said another student.

And another, "Yeah, if we ever actually do that, we might lose our bear arms."

THE ALTITUDES OF ACCEPTANCE

Amidst laughter, I had to cut the punny business short and move on with the presentations.

"Okay my friends. Now, that we've all exercised the freedoms of religion and speech about the Second Amendment in a very silly way, I want those at the front of the room tell us all a little more about the First Amendment—and the rest of you, please listen and consider the value of your rights and your arms as you go throughout the day."

I knew we'd eventually get around to the real meaning of the Second Amendment, but at least all the students would remember this lesson!

A couple of weeks later, we moved from constitutional rights to United States history.

Knowing some things were complicated, I took extra care to explain things: "Inflation is a measure of how much more expensive the same set of goods and services might become over a certain period of time." Then I explained that there were several examples throughout the economic history of the United States and added, "So, who can give me an example of inflation?"

Casey's hand went up.

I knew him to be unusually brilliant, but he also tended to be extremely quiet, so I hesitated to call on him, but he was the only one with a hand up. "Casey."

"An example of inflation is—we bought the Louisiana Purchase, which is 1/3 of the land in the United States, for $3 million dollars, and my uncle just sold a mansion for $15 million ..."

At the word "million," he trailed off, and almost immediately you could have heard a pin drop on the carpet in the classroom.

Casey's example was so accurate that I had no doubt that everyone understood *exactly* what inflation meant. This young person had taught an entire lesson in one simple sentence!

THE ADVENTURE OF LAUGHTER

Wow, teachers strive for such simplicity, but kids inspire it.

Speechless, I smiled and reached for the pile of worksheets on the desk in what felt like slow motion. I thanked Casey and passed out the worksheets, inviting the students to hone their new knowledge and drive it a little deeper. If that was even possible.

Halfway through the school year we hosted a holiday celebration for the children.

It was to be a day full of long-anticipated crafts, movies, video games, and sometimes decorating cupcakes as a reward for good behavior and completing classwork. At least one of those activities was fun for every student, although some struggled with the change in daily structure.

When I wasn't trying to be outside or in the gym while on duty to observe and monitor the students, I usually ended up in the video game room. Before this job, I had never supported video games, but I soon learned the environment of a video game tournament was an excellent way to observe how they acted with their peers when they felt less constrained.

As I entered the video game room again that year, I noticed a student I knew, Andy, had just lost a tournament. Amid the excitement and disappointment, I heard these words: "Hey, you just got beat by a woman!" They came from a student who had been passively watching the tournament. "Don't you know you'll get a reputation for that?"

Andy responded with an indifferent, "Yeah, well—didn't you know, that's actually why dinosaurs went extinct."

What in the world?

My eyes shifted to the screen that had the scores. I could see Andy's skills at the game were represented by a dinosaur fighter while his opponent in the game was a female fantasy figure, selected by one of the other boys in the class.

THE ALTITUDES OF ACCEPTANCE

I giggled. *How did we go from losing a tournament to a debate on the fate of dinosaurs?*

At the center of my amusement was the fact that in a way I could relate. Maybe I should have been a paleontologist—dinosaur track sites intrigued me—and as a woman, I happily accepted that vote of confidence—giant dinosaurs exterminated by little women!

However, the only other female in the room, a student I hadn't seen sitting in the corner playing on an iPad, began muttering about the colossal difference between the dinosaur on the screen and the much more realistic photo in a paleontology book, before concluding in a matter-of-fact tone, "Just so you know, he should not be wearing clothes."

Oh my, did she really just say that?

The silence across the room indicated everyone had heard her.

"The dinosaur that is. Not Andy." The budding paleontologist—or realist prodigy—in the corner quickly amended her statement. I glanced around. I needed to make sure none of males in the room were taking her literally and taking off any clothes to enjoy some attention.

No such folly occurred. Sometimes, winning is based on what doesn't happen.

As far as what actually did happen, her simple statement reversed the awkward silence into a giggle fest. Meanwhile Andy went from not knowing what to do about losing to being able to agree with her completely. He relinquished his controller and walked over to where she sat. Apparently, Andy recognized a friend who liked dinosaurs as a win for him that day.

I enjoyed watching those two talk and laugh about that book for the rest of the time before lunch. I hope they became friends for life. It was a smart move on Andy's part, to recognize, embrace, or actively celebrate the big and small wins in his life, even if it wasn't the one he expected or hoped for.

THE ADVENTURE OF LAUGHTER

We never know what good or great things might eventually transpire in our lives. Sometimes we just need to accept each win and enjoy all the rewarding moments of life as they come.

During the last semester of school, I was walking between the staff breakroom and the financial literacy classroom at the end of the day when Jaron, a student, stopped me in the hall.

"Where can ... I ... find a ... rolling chair?" he asked, a bit winded.

There was a strange look in his eyes. Something clever was brewing, and we both knew such chairs were only used by teachers, who occupied them in every classroom.

"Sorry, Jaron, I actually have no idea, but all the ones I know about are ... well ... good luck finding one not being used right now."

He respectfully said thank you and moved along, continuing his search.

What does he have in mind?

My work pressed me to return to my classroom, and I proceeded to grade a stack of papers, aiming to get done with them before the day was over. I forgot about the chat with Jaron until a commotion started in the hall about five papers into the stack.

Sneaking a peek out the door, I took in a breath along with the strangest sight I had ever seen—at least in the halls of the school. It was strange, but also somewhat delightful!

Two boys wearing red and blue hats and roughly cut paper mustaches were pushing a wheeled chair down the hall as if they were finishing a race.

Whoosh!

I felt the wind go by as a second strange apparition whipped past my doorway in a blur.

The only thing I recognized about the third boy, Jaron, was his shoes. The rest of him was entirely wrapped up like a mummy in toilet paper! Apparently, Jaron had been successful at extricating a chair from a classroom—as well as recruiting a pack of hellions.

My first thought after getting over the shock was, *What kind of teacher would allow such a thing?*

My second was—*oh, that's me, I'm that teacher—this is an accident waiting to happen. Do something already! ... But what can I do? ... What kind of teacher am I if I do nothing? ... But I kind of want to see how this unfolds.*

My third thought was one of sheer amazement. *Where did they get that much toilet paper?*

So, there I stood, unmoving, and fixed to the ground by incredulous astonishment.

One of the students from my classroom, Sam, came out and approached me. I could see a question in his eyes about his assignment, but it disappeared when he observed the hallway happenings. He gawked at the curious apparition for a moment, inhaled deeply, turned his gaze on me, and finally asked, "So, Miss D, what's going on here?"

Still watching the mummy roll up and down the hall, I could only say, "You know, Sam, I actually don't know. You see what I see."

As a ping of subdued concern about whether my delayed and frozen reaction to the incident was potentially sending my class off course, Sam's remarkably confident voice said, "I'll tell you what's going on here."

"What?" My eyes turned away from the incident to look at Sam.

"Nature is out of balance, that's what." He was all matter of fact—no judgment.

The boys with the rolling chair were close enough to hear his statement and began laughing hysterically. Their giggling distracted their focus from their antics so that the careening vessel lost control. I almost jumped into the hall to try to help, but—

BANG! SMASH!

Jaron's figure rolled off course and into a wall of lockers. His mummified body bursting from its bonds left a brief cloud of white toilet paper dust in the air as he collapsed to the ground next to the wheeled chair.

His two companions laughed their way over, almost tripping in the weakness of their muscles from too much hilarity. Their joyride over, they all started to help Jaron finish unwrapping, first removing the paper from his legs, then his shoulders, and finally his head. One of them jogged over to the cafeteria to get a trashcan, and the three boys stuffed the toilet paper into the trashcan, nearly filling it.

Note to self—lecture these boys on how expensive toilet paper is from tree to store!

Also, why was this so fascinating? I couldn't believe I was still watching. Sam was too, and it seemed like he was pleased to see balance returning to the hallways.

Aside from not being able to do much more than stand there and laugh, I knew someone could have gotten hurt, and they could have been in trouble, but they weren't. I had no precedent from which to judge—although it wasn't the first time I had witnessed befuddling situations in the hallway. Plus, it would be too harsh to shroud the glorious hilarity of such a moment with reality.

Besides, being a teacher was about more than just playing by the rules all the time.

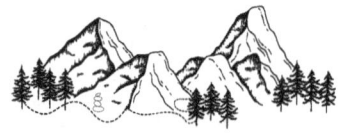

The burden of grading papers can breed procrastination. I was on the verge of shoving a stack of papers off to the side and choosing the more pleasant and equally important task of checking in with the students who were taking the biggest financial literacy test of the year when I heard several art class students across the hall exit their classroom. It wouldn't have been a big deal for them to be taking a walk—if they hadn't been shaking paint cans while our classroom door was open.

Then again, I figured it was my fault the door was open during a test.

I apologized to my classroom for the annoyance I could see on some of their faces. I moved in the direction of the doorway to close the door, only to see Maggie, one of my students, jump up.

I reached out to stop her, but I was too late.

She blurted into the hallway, "Shhhhh, we're trying to sleep in here!" Then she closed the door with pizzazz. On the other side, all went silent—the students had more or less tiptoed their cans outside!

Uh oh, had she really been trying to sleep? Shame on me for not noticing during a test!

Then it dawned on me, and I cracked up. *Note to self, Maggie knew how to get it done!*

I would have aimed for some kind of compromise about that noise, but Maggie had mentioned sleep. All the students in and out of the room knew there was no real sleeping going on, but that was exactly what made her word choice such a marvel. If, by chance, sleeping was happening ... no student would risk having a reputation of interrupting and undervaluing sleep!

Near the end of the financial literacy course, it was my job to invite the students to write their closing essay, an answer to the question, "What does the 'good life' mean to you?"

Their response was to be in terms of hoping or wishing for the future. I expected comments about family or career or education, but when Darcy's assignment came back to me for grading, his essay was titled, *I hope to grow a beard.*

He had completed the paper in exactly the way I'd asked, despite the unexpected theme. Feeling amused, I said to myself (and an imaginary Darcy), "My friend, as a male individual, I'm sure you'll have better luck at reaching that 'good life' dream than half the US population."

THE ADVENTURE OF LAUGHTER

I moved on to the other papers and thought of Darcy's paper no more until the next year when I was walking by the gym doorway. One of the male paraprofessionals was chatting with Darcy about a few torn corners of a piece of paper that were taped to the left side of the clear glass double doors of the gym.

My coworker was saying, "I think that used to be a flyer for the dance."

"Really? Why didn't they take the pieces off? That party was so yesterday."

"I don't know, but we're going to get slammed in the face by the gym door if we don't move out of the way soon. Second period gym class is almost over."

My coworker moved away from the door, but Darcy didn't follow him.

He turned back to face the door where Darcy was peeling off the corners and stacking them so that the paper corner points angled downward, longer and longer—on his chin.

"Well, it's a beard now!"

The other paraprofessional couldn't contain his amusement but turned to try to hide it and there I was, grinning at the scene before me.

He said, "Wow, it's like I waited to hear that statement my whole life!"

"Well—I've been waiting to hear it since last year."

That comment earned me a quizzical look, but I offered no explanation—just a sly smile.

After a few moments of perplexed silence, I leaned away from him and simply walked off, finding it fun to leave him wondering.

What I knew about the mystery behind Darcy's beard was on a need-to-know basis after all.

Those gym doors became the main event in another story, the story of the first day back to work from family vacation. I had been gone maybe a week, and that morning I entered the gym through a single door opposite the double doors near the main office. I saw a student, Jamie, running toward those doors. I wasn't sure what his hurry was, but I couldn't help but watch him go. He had an interesting gait, loping and bounding along.

I cocked my head as I tried to figure out how to help him with his posture someday.

Then, like a premonition of danger, I noticed something missing in those doors.

"Jamie! Watch out, there's no—"

Too late.

He went to push the door open, aiming for the glass above the long handle that spanned the width of the right door, only there was no glass! The momentum of his tall frame tipped him over the handle and forced him through an opening where the glass pane had once been.

When had this glass on the door broken? Apparently, very recently and while I was out of town. The school had not yet put the usual temporary plywood cover in its place.

Having clotheslined himself, poor Jamie hung from the door handle. Slowly, he rotated himself tightly around the narrow handle, twisting to avoid breaking his ribs, then catching himself before the lower half of him arced all the way through the upper half of the empty door, flipping him completely over.

Jamie's feet landed on the floor while he was still hanging on the door handle backwards.

It wasn't that Jamie was normally a klutz, but he sure looked graceful as he sailed back down to the ground. I rushed up to him as he pushed from his legs and gathered himself up, switching over into a pushup position. I tried not to smile when he very firmly grasped the handle on the other side of the door for a moment, as though he was trying to resolve to remember to use it next time, instead of pushing on the glass. In his face, I could see a permanent change happening—his fingerprints would probably never be found on the glass of any door again!

THE ADVENTURE OF LAUGHTER

"Jamie, are you okay? Do you feel pain anywhere? Do you need the nurse?" I hovered near him, not sure what to do for him as he finished standing and shook out the shock from his head-over-heels moment. Then he giggled, likely picturing how odd he had just looked.

"Nope, I'm good, I just forgot!" His imperviousness was really something.

"If you say so! That was quite a ride you just took. How did you like the trapeze?"

He was backing away from me toward the outside doors as I finished speaking and just said, "I know, right!" Then he turned around, clearly ready to burst, eager to share his crazy story with his friends.

Or he was just in a rush to play some basketball.

Near the end of that day, I was standing near the double doors again. I was wondering who else had seen what had happened because there was wood on them now.

Then one of the lower functioning students, Corry, walked by and stood next to me.

"Greetings, Miss D! What—did—you do—for your—trip?"

Sensing the measured cadence of his words, and knowing he was not prone to initiating conversations, I had a feeling this student was practicing his conversation skills.

So, I answered in a way I hoped would help him keep the conversation going. "Thanks for asking! I had a wonderful time. I went to visit my parents, helped host a bonfire, climbed a mountain, attended church, got an allergy attack and a sinus infection, cleaned my room, and ..."

My voice trailed off as Corry's face took on a scowl full of disbelief and disgust.

"No way—NO way! You ... you're an adult; you don't have to clean your room!"

I blinked. He was almost furious. Not at all what I anticipated, so I cautiously responded with, "Actually, yes, I do. And it was kind of a mess this time."

At first, Corry didn't respond, but almost immediately his hands went to his face in despair, outright misery, and devastation. "No—no—no! That's the last thing I wanted to think about today! Cleaning my room is the worst! I thought I would get out of it when I'm an adult!"

He finished with, "I don't think adults should have to do things they don't like."

"Well, Corry, speaking as an adult, that's a nice thought, but in fact, adults make messes, and having to clean your room lasts your whole life. Sometimes they even have to clean whole houses." Then, I tried to ease the conversation by saying some adults got maid services, but he was too ruffled to hear me and skittered away.

In the end, to go from diligently practicing conversation skills to terrified despair in mere moments would no doubt be a shock that could trigger only a desire to escape.

As for me, I had shoved a new reality into his worldview, so I needed to find a way to revisit this incident. I wasn't sure what to do, but as I mulled over all the possibilities, a tune I had heard in my own high school days seeped into my mind. The first few words suggested, "Clean up your room, you slob, what a mess, get a job ..."

The tune got stuck in my mind all day. It wasn't that Corry was a slob, but my concern for his poor mother reminded me how my first day back was a mere snippet of all the stories going on around me.

Things don't just happen in life. They happen because other lives touch ours.

Through building connections and being present with other people, I have learned there is such a thing as Godly humor, and it is all around us, the way God is all around us. It doesn't always feel holy but it's never without meaning. It understands but doesn't support self-deprecation, and it always reflects wisdom or truth. It is usually most exquisitely and authentically located beyond any wooden stage—it might be found in a comedy show, in someone else's facial expression, in a movie, or even in witty wordplay. If we are willing and able, we may find it everywhere throughout the lifescapes we live.

To me, Godly humor is like a lens through which we see how minor our troubles really are compared to how important our mountain, or our lifescape, really is. I think God intends for the role of laughter to be part of the adventure, no matter the mountain.

I like to think of Godly humor as a candle, casting a soft glow throughout a dark room. It's a soft, generous, and intelligent kind of glow that moves through our minds like music moves through a room. Seeking Godly humor is good for us because it raises our spirits, and often shifts our circumstances toward the kinder perspectives, peace, and joy that surpasses our understanding.

If Godly humor can do to life what music does to movement, it must also be magical.

I don't know about you, but when I think of all the laughter within my lifescapes, life's adventure sometimes feels more like a magical dance than a mountain—carefully choreographed with movements and music selected just for me.

CHAPTER 8

THE MAGIC OF DANCE AND GOOD HEALTH

I don't remember the exact song, but it's in my head—somewhere—along with the memory of my two bare feet balanced on my father's boots ... my left arm wrapped around his right arm ... his hand collecting me in half a hug ... the tune, singing from our record player ...

Our new home had a large square kitchen, and its hard floor of yellow vinyl tiles seemed to glow under the overhead light as I leaned into the whirl of the waltz. As I worked to memorize the pattern my father guided us in, I realized it was much easier to remember when there was enough space to really move. We had danced before, but never quite like this, and with each second, I fell more and more in love with the feeling of twirling around and around and around.

Dad had trained in dance at Brigham Young University, and all of us kids loved watching and learning from Mom and Dad as they danced all kinds of ballroom dances. It became tradition for us to enjoy a night of family music and dancing together. That night, my mother watched us from the stove where she was stirring dinner in a pot. Giggles from my siblings came from the living room and where they stood watching in the doorway. My father's smiling eyes were blue, like mine, and calm, happy to see me there. I couldn't help but tip my head back, laugh, and smile at him.

THE MAGIC OF DANCE AND GOOD HEALTH

This moment was magical! How could I make the joy of dancing last forever?

I figured the first task would be to learn as much as possible at home since there were no dance classes in my Colorado public schools. So, I learned the basics of waltz, swing, and foxtrot.

I had to wait until I was in college at Brigham Young University to take dance courses almost non-stop. I even competed in annual competitions a couple of times. Not only was it great for physical fitness, but I loved how it gave me the balance of a bird, the strength of a ballerina, and the flexibility and posture of a princess. I am pretty sure it positively influenced my social confidence, endurance, and creative expression. It brought out the best in me, and when I went home to family dances, it was my turn to keep my dad on his toes for a change!

Eventually, by the time one of us was married and three of us were in college, our dance parties outgrew our beautiful big kitchen. Fitting more than two couples in there was impossible, yet we still enjoyed creating our own playlists and favorite songs. So, we decided to move our dance party to the gym at our church building and invite our friends.

Once we nailed down a date, my brothers prepared their equipment and my sister—who aimed to make a career out of drama, theater, and singing—suggested we use a fog lamp as a table centerpiece so that we could produce real fog from water vapor and enhance the gym setting.

The gym was one of those usually found in church buildings, with multi-purpose accessories like basketball hoops and stages, but all we needed was the floor. When I turned off half the lights, and my sister turned on her glowing fog lamp, the room looked just right for dancing. My brothers started their music playlists, and our night of fun began.

I was making one last sweep for decorations when I investigated a box my sister brought.

Hmmm ... what was she going to do with a brimmed dress hat and a broom?

A familiar song started to play, something that reminded me of my dance lessons, and as I was about to stand, the items in the box were snatched away.

"I'll take those!" my sister musically whispered.

My blue eyes met her hazel-green eyes. The flick of fun residing in them reminded me of an emerald in a storm—or maybe Oz.

The drama queen was at it again!

At first, we all just watched. My feet tapped to the music, and I glowed with warmth and energy from the inside, but it wasn't ready to come outside yet. It was too much fun to watch my sister in her element. A vaudeville tune was a wonderful opportunity to display her acting talent and creativity because it was like acting out a story through dancing. She knew how to roll a hat up her arm and place it on her head with a flair while spinning across the floor, a blur of sparkling black.

I didn't have much stage experience, but a lightbulb flashed on inside my soul when I realized the next tune was a jazz tune! That was my favorite music to play with, and though I knew it would be a challenge to keep up with her, I jumped up and caught the hat when she tossed it up near me. She hadn't been expecting that!

And so began a playful partnership as we traded the hat between us while dancing as though we had taken lessons from Gene Kelly or Fred Astaire. With the help of our creativity and synergy, the hat soon transformed into something far more shiny, tall, and black, and even the broom handle in the corner appeared to have a pair of pearl white knobs on both ends, just like in the old movies. The broom-handle baton joined the hat to twirl with us while all the cheering and laughter told us our family seemed to be well entertained.

When the next song came on, its lyrics flowed like a story, and we kept up with our movements, mirroring and echoing one another in style.

Dancing without a care in the world and sharing the experience together like this was delightful. It was more than a lifestyle activity, and more than just a piece of my lifescape. It seemed to cleanse, restore, and give us a little more courage to get out there and face the world.

It was easy to approach dance wholeheartedly, and I decided to work to keep it in my life. Knowing that it was healing and invigorating for me was quite the motivation! However, I never became a professional dancer, which

I regret often enough, yet it has become clear to me that God wanted me to dance because he has supported my interest in it.

In the years since college, I have danced mostly socially, taught lessons here and there, and made many friends. When my friends and I talk, it's clear how dancing lifts our more fragile feelings to higher ground, provides relief from life's problems, adds meaning to relationships, and helps us connect with others at a level where movement transcends words.

In my life, the ability to dance is right up there on the priority list with hiking. Both have become essential to how I enjoy quality of life. Hiking in the mountains satisfies my hunger for adventure while dancing frees the smallest, hardest-to-reach pieces of my heart and mind. The physical strength gained from both activities unites and forms a muscular sense of grace and excellent balance. It can be a life-saving combination of effects! In fact, when I trip, I rarely fall, and I attribute this to my "dancer skills," as I call them.

Balance in life matters, in more ways than one!

Speaking of balance in life, there have been times when all the time, money, and social connections related to dancing were encompassed by more challenges than I wanted. Over and over, I learned how even precious things we enjoy doing can be a burden at times. But the personal and physical benefits of dancing always brought me back to the dance floor.

I have found several ways to share my dance skills over time, but I never expected such skills to come in handy at the school. Yet that was where it became possible for me to combine my dance skills and bachelor's degree in restorative, fulfilling ways.

Many of the students were reluctant to perform well in gym class, but they had to have physical education credits to graduate. Some students preferred forms of physical activity that were less sports-focused while other students needed ways to develop and practice their gross motor skills. The school needed options for the students, so the dance class was created. A parent who had been trained in Europe as a dance instructor was chosen to lead the class.

By the time I began working at the school, the class had been fully functional for several years. Knowing how to dance had not been in my original job description, nor had it been on my resume, but the administrators were dedicated to putting their staff where they could be the most helpful. One glance at how I moved while chaperoning the school dances put me on the short list to be assigned to assist the dance teacher as often as time would permit during my second year of employment. Then, for the entire third year, I was scheduled to be the daily class assistant.

As with Mr. Dixon's class, I was given opportunities to lead the lesson far more often than I expected, but in this case, I already possessed a natural, well-practiced ability to teach dance. As I shared my perspectives and experiences with social and ballroom dancing, I felt much more confident than I had ever felt when left in charge of math and computer programming classes.

I guess it's no surprise that familiarity with anything breeds comfort, but in God's realm, being comfortable at any time is a short road with a steep drop right into—the growth zone!

Little did I know there was a reason the dance teacher had to be gone so much that year.

Over the summer, I heard very little from the school until teacher prep days arrived. I think it was my second day back when I overheard the concerned voices of two teachers talking in the teacher's lounge.

"Hey, did you hear about Miss Crista?"

"I heard they finally figured out she has a life-threatening cancer, and the treatment this year is going to be severe. There's no way she will be able to teach the way she used to. But they will have her do other things."

So unexpected! Miss Crista couldn't teach dance anymore. All the students loved her.

A question burst out of me. "But—there aren't very many other teachers who could teach dance, and class starts next week!" I paused and took a breath. "They must already have a new hire for the job—don't they?"

All I could think about were requirements for course longevity and the quality dance instruction I hoped would come to these kids. Even after two years in the class, there I was, acting like *I* wasn't qualified for the job—at least not compared to the highly credentialed Miss Crista!

They didn't respond right away, and they were looking at me expectantly. In their silence, my mind dipped into some troubling new thoughts. I was usually way too hard on myself when it came to my own talents, and the dance teacher's role had never been full-time. If they kept the class, the best financial decision would be to fill the teaching role with someone already on staff.

So, under these circumstances, why shouldn't they pick me? And if they do pick me— It's almost the first week of school and—gulp!—I know nothing about this.

A wave of nerves washed over me as the potential pressures of unexpected responsibility hit home. I glanced furtively at my friend, one of the paras I had worked with in middle school the year before. She smiled at me and took on a playful, mysterious demeanor. Her eyes were sparkling.

"Uh, Deanna, so you know you're not assigned in the middle school classes this year?"

"Honestly, I have heard very little about my schedule, but I do know I have been placed only in high school classes this year. And I was just getting used to the chaos of middle school too!"

I bit my bottom lip, pushed my hair back around my ear, and looked down.

At the core, her words didn't surprise me. Being reassigned without preference was common, no matter how much the administration tried to meet requests. It was just going to happen that way sometimes, and three years had taught me to accept that.

She gave me a smile that held a hint of hesitation. "So, you really haven't heard?"

I raised my eyebrows. "Heard what?"

"You're the new dance teacher!"

I blinked, feeling uneasy. *There it is. I'm the new dance teacher…*

I swallowed hard and just stared at my friend. I didn't like the timing or method of this discovery, but I believed her.

THE ALTITUDES OF ACCEPTANCE

Teaching isn't about money, but isn't there a small stipend that comes with part-time teaching? Stipends are like a treat, and as much as I hate to admit it, I am a bit of an eager puppy.

When I finally spoke, I thanked her for letting me know. We talked for a bit longer, but she had things to do and soon left me to my own thoughts.

A mental fog of maybes and what-ifs took over. It was time to find one of the administrators.

After a conversation with lots of questions and need-to-know revelations, I realized the administrators wouldn't have assigned me if they thought I couldn't do it, and that they were indeed planning to pay me. I appreciated the higher level of responsibility and the additional resources. While I never found out why others knew about my new role before I did, I learned the timing and missed communications related to the decision were mostly due to complications with Miss Crista's situation—which was, of course, forgivable.

Soon, I felt I had at least one solid vote of confidence. Maybe two, if you counted my friend whose enthusiasm for my new role showed she believed in me. Beyond that, it was up to me to navigate the details and develop skills in classroom management and instruction.

Luckily, I am a creative girl, and the more I thought about it, I realized I had developed a dance teaching style over the last two years while assisting Miss Crista. I could use some of her methods, make some changes to the structure, and adjust the content to match my dance expertise and training. And if the students experienced temporary disinterest or disappointment, I could live with that. They would get used to me eventually.

Besides, it was about time I put my dance skills into the service of others.

I might not have chosen this route of teaching for myself, but it was given to me. This had to be God's plan, or at least it was a bit of his light showing me what I could do given the chance.

And I could take a hint!

Sometimes, that's how God steps in—when we feel unaccustomed, incapable, inadequate, or simply out of sync with the opportunities laid upon us, he triggers an external—or internal—shift so small that it changes our perspective of what's feasible in a big way, if only to move us in the direction of doing what's needed instead of what's comfortable.

As I began figuring out what my lessons might look like, the more I realized my skills were more than sufficient. For one thing, I would always have more experience than the kids. I also knew enough to be effective. I began to see myself succeeding—or, at least, I discovered an abundance of potential for success, plenty of room to grow, and lots of positive rapport with the young people.

All I really needed was to do my best, learn as I go, ask for help when I needed it—and, of course, let God take care of his marvelous side of things—which, by this point, I knew were mysterious on purpose, and usually for my own good.

In the days of teacher preparation prior to the school year's start, the administration and the clever, resourceful English teacher met with me to share how new connections had been made with the local dance company, Ballet West. A relationship was now in place to allow the company's outreach educators to visit our school's dance class for two days each week. They would train our dancers in choreography for a region-wide youth performance.

Aside from the awesomeness of being unprecedented, the idea sounded more than thrilling for the kids—and kind of perfect for me. If, by chance, I failed to be as interesting a teacher as I hoped to become, the class would still have a marvelous experience! Plus, the sheer operational size of the change would make anything else I adjusted in the class so much smaller and would not be nearly as daunting to the students returning to the course.

THE ALTITUDES OF ACCEPTANCE

As things usually go in the first year of anything, I decided to frontload the students with an introduction to three new structural elements. One was an exercise to help those who had taken the class in the years prior, allowing them to share what they liked best about the course—so I could learn what kept them interested. The next was ten to fifteen minutes of high intensity cardio after attendance each day. I borrowed several series of movements sprinted over short distances from my high school track team and called them our ABCs, with each letter representing a set of exercises and stretches that were perfect for a dance warm-up.

Finally, I wanted to implement a third combination of nutrition and take-home assignments for both extra credit and homework. Miss Crista had taught a lot about nutrition, and I figured I needed to do that as well. I believed it would help students understand how dance and health were interchangeable and connected on multiple levels. After all, balanced nutrition served me well over the years, and my dancers would be supporting a higher level of physical activity. So, I needed them to gain positive relationships with food, a benefit I hoped would be lifelong.

However, I didn't know how to teach health information effectively.

Although I had taken a few college courses in health-related topics, had my own ideas about what the students might value, and had learned a lot as a child about nutrition from my mother, I still felt limited. Teaching a class full of different physical bodies with potentially different nutritional needs and resources didn't feel like a task where one could simply use intuition. I needed more than a refresher course in nutrition, or so it seemed.

I wanted to find some kind of tangible, logical nutritional tasks that could be easily integrated into the lesson plans and help the concepts of dance and good health hit home. As homework, such an assignment could help students receive full benefits from new knowledge as they independently applied what they learned over time. I also didn't want to implement things from sources online without knowing what mattered most.

Keeping the matter of teaching nutrition on the back of my mind, I spent the first three weeks teaching my dancers the basics of the waltz. It was the dance I knew best, and it wasn't hard to learn, which I hoped would help us all feel comfortable as we got used to each other. The waltz was also an exercise in learning to develop social and spatial awareness, which I knew would always be important in our small classroom on the stage!

To be honest, I wasn't sure how things would work out, but again, that's the nature of faith—starting out before you know how things will turn out. And when God approves of a path we have chosen or accepted, he doesn't leave us alone to meet the path's demands.

Instead, he uses the path and its demands to provide a chance to grow.

Due to unexpected changes among the teachers, there was a shift in my schedule during the fourth week of school. I was asked to help in the middle school health class. It was a happy surprise since no other class could have more perfectly aligned with what I needed at the time.

In just a few weeks, I had all the elements of a good nutrition lesson ready to go. I had learned which food log tracking documents and updated food pyramids might be best, and I had developed plans for visuals and assignment ideas that would help the students learn.

However, I also had a problem.

How am I supposed to get these students to take the nutritional information to heart?

I needed to gain their buy-in—somehow.

And that's when humor in the health class began to teach me the way.

"I will turn this rock into a potato."

The health teacher had just completed a lesson about tracking personal nutrition and had given an assignment to encourage the students to identify their favorite healthy foods. A young man near me had, without any warning, raised both of his hands.

In one there was a tiny rock. In the other, all he had was his pencil.

Oh-kay! Hmm, what was this guy talking about? The comment was clearly a bit off the mark!

Potatoes were nutritious enough to have prevented entire continents from succumbing to starvation, but no one had said anything about rocks turning into potatoes.

If that were possible, the Irish Potato Famine wouldn't have happened!

Still, it was not totally out of the realm of creative thinking. Unsure whether I was taking him a bit too seriously, I decided to do a little redirection while getting a little more information.

"So, Jack, you like potatoes? Potatoes *are* healthier to eat than rocks, but turning rocks into food is not really a thing, at least not in the world I live in. What do you mean, turn a rock into a potato?"

"Because … that's what the magic does!"

Uh-huh. Yep, I'm taking this too seriously! Or am I? Things we can't explain do happen …

I wondered if he knew the children's story about stone soup by Ann McGovern. However, no one in the story ate the stone. Nor did the stone transform into food. The story suggested that a little mental magic could create a feast.

"Hmm. Well, Jack, what kind of magic are you talking about?"

Instead of answering, Jack tapped the rock with his pencil. Only then did I realize he was *showing* me his answer.

"A wand? You mean to tell me you have a magic wand?"

Wow, this conversation is getting stranger and stranger! Also, if Jack is going to use magic, he needs to know about the rules.

"Jack, isn't that kind of food transformation against the rules in magic, like in Harry Potter? Making food out of a non-food substance is kind of against the rules in our world too."

THE MAGIC OF DANCE AND GOOD HEALTH

Then the magic of gardening occurred to me. Rocks and organic matter degraded into soil, and soil supports plant life, and plants are the only thing that can create energy from sunlight.

That's magical indeed! God's power takes patience on our part to reap the rewards.

I was about to apply more patience and try to get Jack to think his way into the class assignment and think about gardens and healthy food, but then I saw his face.

It wore a look that said I could go now.

Clearly, Jack preferred the magic that had no rules and no strategy when it came to food.

I backed away, but I couldn't help dropping one last piece of good sense.

"For the record, Jack, a living potato plant in a garden usually provides more than just one potato, and if your magic wand can only make one potato out of that rock, you're getting the short end of the deal."

"Miss D, if I make a potato out of this rock, I can let it sprout and then have six potato plants. I'd say you're getting the short end of the deal if you don't let the magic work!"

Oh!

I stared at the rock for a second. I hadn't noticed six holes in the tiny rock that looked like the eyes of a potato. I looked up at Jack and saw his exasperation had turned into amusement.

All I could do was smile and say, "You keep the rock until tomorrow, Jack. What do I know—your magic might come true!"

Note to self: Bring Jack a real potato tomorrow.

I used to think when kids answered questions with unrealistic, unfocused remarks, they were simply not applying their education well. But with a few years of experience, I understood how sometimes I could not understand their depth of thought until after a peculiar conversation.

It wasn't that their viewpoint was flawed; it was just unexpected. And I needed to employ a little good humor to see what they were seeing.

It also occurred to me that some students were in situations where nutrition wasn't feasible without some kind of magic wand, whether because of parent schedules, lack of knowledge, or financial limitations. My high schoolers would have greater understanding, which would make it easier to keep my expectations and their assignments realistic, but I needed to be mindful and allow them space for simplicity, creativity, resourcefulness, and flexibility.

From that moment on, I decided creative answers deserved a place in health and dance, especially for this group of young people. Whatever it took, I was willing to try.

Like the health class, my dance class needed to understand the importance of informed personal decision-making when it came to nutrition, and I could teach through simple conversations and stories. Maybe we'd even laugh together. Simple conversations and stories seemed to be excellent tools for showing students how to apply concepts in realistic ways. Good humor seemed to help them remember things.

As a perfect example, after talking about calories and sodas one day, one of the older middle schoolers, Chase, told a story about gathering a few things from a store for his parents.

"So, I got the peanut butter and the apples and the bread and went straight to the checkout counter. You know how it goes, the only register open has a person ahead of you with a lot of stuff to buy, and you only have three things! Well, I saw that the cart was full of Rockstars—and absolutely nothing else! They weren't in cases or anything, which I thought was weird, and it took forever to ring up all those cans.

"Anyway, while we waited for the cashier to ring him up, I asked him if the Rockstars were for a party. The man said no, and that he was a nurse and worked crazy hours, so he needed the caffeine.

"I tried to ask him nice questions about his job, but all I could think was that a nurse should know what Rockstars do to the body, right?"

The teacher said, "Likely that nurse did know, but didn't have time to cook. Good health practices and time are always at odds with each other."

Another student cut in. "But there are healthy fast options, and snacks too. How much money did he spend on those Rockstars, Chase?"

"Eighty-six dollars!"

A collective gasp rose from the mouths of almost every listener in the room. Including me.

I started thinking out loud in case it would be helpful. "Wow, at $2.50 a pop, and one Rockstar a day, he had to have about thirty drinks, enough for one month—if he only had one a day. By my reckoning, he could have bought enough peppers and tomatoes and oranges and apples for about three months with that kind of expenditure!"

In the moments of silent processing that followed, I added, "Such a waste of a good opportunity for better nutrition!"

But Chase was grinning at me now, for some reason. "Miss D, of all the things—of course you'd list those. You eat peppers like they are a candy bar. As for me, I was thinking brownies or a bike!"

I grinned—somehow, I felt admired by his personality behind those words!

The health teacher pointed out, "Wow, Miss D, now we know what your shopping list looks like! Also, my insurance costs about $86 each month."

I nodded at how he pointed a cost relationship I hadn't considered. Then I giggled as students started listing out other nutritional ideas. Milk! Eggs! Nuts! Beans!

Without them saying so, I realized their comments were straight from their parents' shopping lists or based on observations of what was in their refrigerators and pantries at home.

Then I burst out laughing and immediately drew a grand number of perplexed glances.

So, I explained, "Well, it occurred to me I am a shopping health paradox! Despite eating peppers like candy, the first two things on the grocery list that I started making over lunch period are—wait for it—toothpaste and sugar."

Their perplexities translated into raised eyebrows, especially from Chase and the health teacher, who said, "Well, if you have to buy toothpaste, you might as well get sugar. And if you're buying sugar, you better be getting toothpaste too!"

Giggles from the class signaled it was a good time to move on to another part of the lesson.

Later, a little pondering pointed out how the mere mention of sugar on my grocery list made me a valuable kind of imperfect in the eyes of those who respected me for eating peppers instead of candy bars. I didn't mind. Realizing I was human was a good thing all around.

When it came to teaching nutrition to the dance class, I wanted that real element of nutritional decision power to hit home—eating healthy didn't always mean no sweets. It meant learning to appreciate the value of healthy foods, even when students didn't like them or weren't used to them—to eat to live rather than live to eat, but also to enjoy life with balance and boundaries.

Finally, I was ready to teach my first lesson about the food pyramid and what made a balanced diet. At the end of the lesson, I provided a ready-to-go tracking sheet and challenged them to track daily food and water consumption—not just for calories but also for awareness.

This proved to be very hard for some because it is hard to track anything for two weeks.

In the end, the effort revealed eating situations that alerted me to some health red flags, which I had to report to parents and other teachers. But for the most part, those who did the assignment figured out what and when they weren't eating. They did their best to communicate about it and make changes to better maintain their energy throughout each day. Definitely a win!

Beyond nutrition, I did more than just teach movement—I taught the class how to exercise to music, kind of like Zumba. I allowed requests for songs and created a few Zumba routines, incorporated some line dancing, and taught about how to identify their own stylistic flairs. It was like providing physical training that could enhance their lives well beyond their high school years.

During the autumn season, I had the most fun when I taught a modified version of the line dance from the famous Thriller music video by Michael Jackson. They loved it, and it was awesome how they channeled it into a flash mob at their school's winter dance party!

As we got used to each other, emotional days and squabbles among the students increased. Occasionally, they weren't happy with how I was operating, and we dealt with those moments with a little compromise and negotiation. But for other issues, it made sense to give them mutually agreed upon natural consequences. Following discussion, we agreed that if their behavior stole my teaching time or a student's chances to learn, they owed ten or twenty pushups per infraction. I liked it—the penalty was daunting enough yet fitting—a discipline system that hopefully helped them improve their physical conditioning while enhancing how they supported their dance team and valued class time.

As the school year ended, the students felt pressure as they anticipated their first large-scale regional performance. It was the culmination of a lot of hard work—in my mind, the equivalent of climbing a mountain to the peak.

As our school's liaison with Ballet West, I coordinated logistics with each of the students and parents, and on the appointed day and time, we gathered in the largest gym at one of the biggest high schools in the area. All the schools that partnered with Ballet West were present, gathered on one side of the gym curtains. The performance would take place on the other side, and through the transparent strip in the curtain, all the nervous faces from my dance class eyed the dance floor and the filling bleachers with concern.

"Hey everyone, remember it's only a different place, not a different dance! You know what to do, you've done it all before, and you'll be great! Give it all your heart. I have confidence in you!"

"Yep. I know I can do the moves. I just don't know if I can do the people! Sometimes I'm afraid they'll look at me, and sometimes I'm afraid they won't!"

Briana had said what they were all thinking.

I smiled. "Whether you want to call that pre-performance butterflies or anxiety, it's perfectly normal. You want to be noticed for all your hard work, but you don't want to be judged if you make a mistake." Then to all of them, who were fidgeting or starting to pace, I added, "You could do this in your sleep, and it doesn't have to be perfect! All you need to do is dance what you know with a smile. And you know a lot. If it helps, dance like I'm the only one in the audience!"

Next, I invited them to focus on taking care of themselves before the performance—to drink water and use the bathroom. Finally, they were waved over to take their position on the dance floor, and then it was my turn to fidget!

An age went by as we waited for the music to start. When it finally did, I watched them all closely, specifically during the hard parts. They knew and performed their dance moves and as well or better than the other kids!

Afterward, I asked them about their experience. Briana said, "Miss D, I didn't know how it would work, to dance the same moves with people who weren't with us in class, but it worked and felt awesome! And now I know I can dance in front of so many people."

Most of the students agreed, with one adding how sad she was that our group would never do that dance again! That was a really good point, so I made a note to schedule a performance of their hard work at least once before the end of the year, maybe at the next school dance.

In class over the next couple of weeks, I taught a few new ballroom dance steps. The energy was different now, and I sensed the magic of energy and personal accomplishment in the students. The way they believed in themselves had changed.

They had gained a kind of courage that mattered.

The world might want to box them up, or their hardships might threaten to pin them down, but they now sensed the nature of doing hard things, and that doing a great job didn't imply perfection or a lack of fear. The fear had been real, and they hadn't been perfect, but they had grown. It was my privilege and pleasure to help them grow.

I was growing too.

I saw many things differently than I had before. After seeing the students perform alongside each other, I could see I believed that *normal* was a social construct, *inclusion* was a divine mandate, and both were part of the gargantuan mountain that made up human life.

When it came to my students, I hoped they would forever challenge the way the rest of the world looked at them, even beyond the dance floor.

The second year came, and everything was still fun, new—and improving. I made it my mission to renew the old lessons in delightful new packages—and find new things to teach. I even learned from the Ballet West teaching methods and tried to adopt a few.

As I channeled my energy to fulfill this mission, I prioritized the students' best learning potential. As a dancer, I had always preferred partner dancing over other dance genres like modern dancing, and along the way, I had missed a few lessons in choreography. And yet, all my experience with swing dancing showed me how both planned and impromptu movements are integral parts of developing confidence and personal strategies for expression in dance.

That confidence and self-expression was the platform I wanted to work on that year.

Outside of class, most of my students were working on conveying emotions properly. Inside class, all of them had favorite songs. The task of thinking through a song to extract rhythms and match the most applicable movements from a repertoire of dance moves they had learned from me or Ballet West or even YouTube was an experiential lesson in choreography, and it seemed like a promising method of challenging them to reach inward for emotional expression.

THE ALTITUDES OF ACCEPTANCE

From what I'd seen so far, the students could do it if they persevered.

So, I started formally assigning final examinations each semester of that second year. The assignment combined physical fitness and knowledge of movement with the challenge of choreographing a song of their choice. I hoped the autonomy in the experience would help them keep their choreography training and experiences with them in years to come.

The students showed dedication to practice, and when they executed their dances, I was pleased by an excellent show of skill level, spatial awareness, and physical ability. Perhaps it was because I knew them all very well, but I found it easy to grade each student based on individual merits, their ability to follow instructions, and their own personal improvement—and all without comparison to other students.

I think that's why God can judge us based on our own merits—because he knows us so well, far beyond any human relationship. God sees us as children of individual worth with personalized gifts, abilities, and purposes that are unique to us and our will to pursue them.

I know my students initially chose to be in the dance class for the same reasons anyone in the world might choose to learn to dance. They had always wanted to learn, or they liked me, or they wanted the company of their peers. However, regardless of why my students entered class, the most important reason was whatever reason they chose to stay. I may never know what those reasons were, but I do know that despite many trials or failures, they chose to keep going even though the work of dancing was not easy.

I can only hope they felt what I had found in dancing—the empowerment to pursue life as they knew it with a little more energy, determination, and courage.

On that note, there was one thing that we did in class almost as much as dance, and it's the thing that life needs more of too, all the time.

Laughter.

Life needs all of us to be more diligent about enjoying a good sense of humor, and I can't imagine any time in my life where dancing couldn't deliver a smile to my face.

THE MAGIC OF DANCE AND GOOD HEALTH

Not to say there weren't times when I've cried as well. My students also experienced days when tears flowed, they felt intimidated, or they weren't up to the day's exercises right from the start. Things that are empowering are like that—causing times of sorrow and times of joy. On those days where opposing forces seemed overwhelming, I told them how dancing is like life—what you get from it matters but what you put into it multiplies. That's why when it's hard, you try harder.

Looking back, that meaningful advice applies not only to how I approached teaching the dance class, but how God approached teaching me.

For most women over the age of twenty-five, it is normal and natural to be concerned about marital status. During the years I was teaching the dance class, I hesitated to talk much to anyone at work about dating experiences. But as it turns out, young people pick up on things. So, when a favorite single teacher consistently maintains singlehood for over two years, they become curious.

At the time, the dance class was being taught on a stage, which shared a curtained wall with the gym. After the last class of the day, I was cleaning up while Danny—the same smart and mischievous youngster whose well-loved personality reduced the effects of annoyance—was conversing with Mr. Reyes, the P.E. teacher. They overheard me sharing some good news with one of the other paraprofessionals who was sitting on the edge of the stage.

"Hey, Gabby, that great swing dancer from my social dance group agreed to come visit the school and help me teach a few dance steps—I'm so grateful, the young men really need the help. I might be good at swing dancing, but I never quite nailed down the leading role. The bad part is, he's working on his dissertation these days, so I'm not certain how soon I can convince him to come."

THE ALTITUDES OF ACCEPTANCE

"Sounds like he's the perfect guy—with an imperfect life schedule!"

I laughed. "I don't know about perfect, but I sure don't like his schedule!"

Smiling in return, Gabby went on her way. Then Danny stopped talking with Mr. Reyes and leaned over to me in surprise. "Uh, Miss D, you have a boyfriend now?"

I blinked at him—twice—and folded my arms. I didn't love his interest in that subject.

Was it just me, or was Danny trying to pull up the weeds of my untold life story? The only person allowed to pull up those weeds was me.

But knowing Danny, and knowing he meant well—most of the time—I decided this was an unintentional social faux pas.

So, I said, "No, I just have a good friend coming in to help the dancers."

"Ah, come on, Miss D! You have to get a boyfriend. It's important! You don't want to be alone the rest of your life!"

As if I don't know that already! Now he's pushing his luck. Should I put my hands on my hips and stretch up to my full height? No, that wouldn't do—Danny was far too tall.

Flustered and feeling resistant, I reminded myself that the truth and reality were more important in this case than my feelings and pushed past those feelings.

Ignoring my mental image of Danny's incessant weed pulling and replacing it with an innocent child playing in the mud, I responded as though I had just patted him on the shoulder in class when he got a correct answer, "Ah, Danny, you know what? You are absolutely right."

The gym teacher, Mr. Reyes, had been looking over some paperwork nearby after Danny had left him, but I guess he had easily overheard the conversation and wasn't satisfied with how my response addressed Danny's curiosity. His head came up and he spoke in a gruff tone.

"Danny, I think you need to get a new filter."

That odd statement made me giggle.

Of course, Danny pretended with a grin not to comprehend his meaning.

"What?" He spoke with the roguish attitude of a rascal laced by the innocence of youth.

Although I appreciated Mr. Reyes for his recognition of the problem, I strove to keep both poise and authority in the situation and figured the best way this would all be forgotten was if I interjected with the language of forgiveness.

With a wink, I said, "Thank you but it's okay, Danny's right. He's just looking out for me in the best way a teenage boy knows how."

"Huh, if you say so."

I noticed Mr. Reyes keeping his eyebrows raised toward Danny. I had zero doubts that when I was out of earshot, he would still give Danny a severe talking-to.

Nodding toward Danny, I indicated my agreement and considered expressing gratitude on behalf of all the future women in his life, but I stopped myself from jumping the gun. The boy really did need a more tactful mentality behind his observations, yet I couldn't inspire that change without coming across as angry. It was better to let Mr. Reyes's words do the work.

The truth was, despite the discomfort I was trying to hide, I was far from angry. I had been honest, and Danny was right. I was healed now, and it wasn't on my agenda to be alone forever. Yet while I had found and dated some excellent men, so far, the right man for me was not to be found.

When we were riding the train home later, Danny was quite mature about apologizing for his earlier behavior. "Miss D, I'm sorry. You know I just want you to be happy, right?"

I accepted his apology and told him I was grateful for his honest concern and willingness to let me know how he really felt. Then, he just glowed!

As I look back on this incident, I feel confident that Danny learned an important lesson that day. He deserved to feel good about having the courage to apologize, and both he and I were now certain of something all good men and good people know—that making the effort to communicate and apologize can go a long way. It's important to acknowledge errors and do right by other people.

THE ALTITUDES OF ACCEPTANCE

On that note, this incident also taught me an important lesson too.

Having a dance class at this school was inspiring lessons of social awareness and emotional intelligence among those who weren't even taking the dance class!

As I exited the stage one afternoon, I saw one of my students, Carson, in the hallway with one of his friends, who was not a member of my class.

The train program wanted me right away, yet I stood there in the doorway, curious. Carson seemed to be teaching his friend what I had taught that day, but something seemed off, and I felt like they both needed some encouragement or guidance. Yet, as I started listening in on their conversation, I didn't quite know what to say. I couldn't tell if they were just having fun or really trying to figure it out.

"One more time. Remember, ballroom dance frame has a triangle, but it looks like a circle."

"What does that even mean? A triangle *and* a circle?"

"Three points of contact, like this …" Carson clasped his friend's right hand in his left, grabbed his friend's left hand and dropped it onto his shoulder, and placed his own right hand on his friend's upper back. I noticed how his friend kept laughing as though he thought it looked and felt silly despite going along with it.

And yet, Carson was trying to show him why it wasn't silly at all.

As I stood there watching, my student's candid demonstration turned into less of a ballroom dance frame, having deteriorated into play fighting or an odd-looking upright manly embrace. Three points of contact became holding onto one another, which morphed into pushing each other down the hall. At least they were moving in waltz-like circles!

THE MAGIC OF DANCE AND GOOD HEALTH

I already knew this was evidence that I had more work to do with this student of mine, but it was time I revealed my presence.

"Hey guys, what are you doing?"

Carson tried to look at me as he and his friend spun around and around, before he looked back at his friend. Lifting his head up within the centrifugal forces, he glanced back at me as soon as he could.

"Uh ... dancing, of course!"

His sly grin seemed to indicate that he knew I had been there for a while.

I smiled back and said with a tease, "Hmm, somehow, I missed that in your movements. This might just be the dance teacher talking, but what you're doing looks more like a wrestling bromance!"

At that comment, the two boys split like twin tornadoes and ran down the length of the hall in opposite directions.

I wanted to yell, *Wait, guys, bromance doesn't always mean—what you're thinking! Seriously, I was just teasing!* But the thoughts never made it past my lips.

The nearby teachers who had observed this interaction laughed aloud—less at how quickly the hallway cleared of young men and more at how flushed my face had become.

To them, all I could say was, "Uh, I think this moment just landed in the hall of regrettable dance fame. Maybe I should have said bro-dance? Not sure. I'll fix it tomorrow!"

I had wanted to explain to the boys that they were doing something cool, at least in the dance world I knew. It was more common in swing dancing, but two men dancing together was not unheard of. Some great male dancers were so confident in their skills that they adopted the art of switching back and forth between the lead role and the role of the follower, which was strangely easier between men than in a mixed couple. It usually turned into just two guys in a friendly battle—an imaginative way to show off talent and ability. Dancing like that was fun and fashionable yet severely undervalued—just the thing two boys might enjoy if they didn't balk or get scared away.

I never wanted to say or do things that might affect young friendships negatively, but instead of helping them see what they were already naturally doing, and congratulating them on their intuition, it seemed I had teased too far and landed even further from where I wanted to be.

I couldn't let the unsaid and slightly misunderstood situation create a negative experience for those students, so the next day at lunch, I found Carson and his friend—who I had learned was named Henry—sitting at the end of a table, a little apart from the others. Taking a page out of Danny's book of self-awareness, I made my apology.

"Hey, I think it was cool to see you dancing together yesterday. I didn't mean to make it weird—assuming that's why you darted away? When I go dancing in town, the best male dancers often dance together to teach each other tricks of the trade that come with leading and following. Many of them are very good at it, especially the swing dancers! It looks cool—like a battle of dance skills—and I was thinking you guys could do it too!"

"Oh, okay—I never heard of two guys dancing together like that. I was just trying to teach Henry."

"I think it's awesome that you are teaching Henry what we learn in class. Sometimes we learn better when we take time to teach other people what we know."

"Yeah, and dance frame is so important, Miss D. I think I made a mess of it!"

"That's okay. You've only been doing ballroom dancing for a few weeks now, but today we're going to start fine-tuning it, and I'll let you in on a little secret."

They both leaned closer.

"I've been dancing for years, and I still must practice my dance frame all the time to maintain it. So, don't get discouraged—just keep working on it."

As the bell rang, an idea inspired by this conversation popped into my head.

I had plans, and I was working hard, but as a dancer, I knew the value of practice and good feedback, and I wasn't the only one my students could learn from. If I established a peer review system with all class participants working in pairs on their projects, I could create a system of checks and balances that would help my students think through what they had learned with another person. In fact, I had seen many dance styles improve by the powers of observation.

The idea felt awesome—this particular mountain wasn't as hard a climb as I'd thought!

As I continued this mountain climb and taught dance for two years, an unexpected event occurred that represented a major crossroads in my life.

Not long into my dance teaching career, a string of days began when my stomach churned, causing me to feel sick and miserable every afternoon within two hours of lunch. It started almost overnight, and I realized feeling this way right before I had to go teach was making me more anxious than I really was. I figured my stomach issues were just a temporary effect of the added anxiety and stress, but the longer it continued, the more it seemed anxiety was an effect rather than a cause, at least in this case.

Up until I turned twenty-eight, I had been able to eat everything and anything. My favorite meals included cheese, meat, crackers, and veggies, which I ate for lunch nearly every day, especially in the summer and autumn seasons when I needed a sack lunch, and it was too hot to cook. When I started suspecting food was the issue, I targeted my lunch meals and bought a new block of cheese and a new type of crackers, thinking it was a mold problem, or something like that.

But the stomach problems continued.

It's not fair! I can't live like this!

But I knew a lot of people who did live like this. I just never thought it would be me.

I had a mystery I needed to solve, and luckily, I had some very educated suspicions.

THE ALTITUDES OF ACCEPTANCE

After a few phone calls with my mother and grandmother who both lived with dairy intolerances, I believed I was likely experiencing a genetic situation triggered by some kind of change in my body. I began experimenting without dairy and gained some relief, but I was still not at the top of my game. My mother, a dietitian, suggested eliminating gluten next.

Although I was motivated by the fatigue, headaches, and increasing struggles with anxiety that were connected to my stomach upset, changing my diet has been one of the most difficult changes I've ever had to make.

When I think of how my case was too severe, too soon, I sometimes feel robbed. There are people in the world who are much more careless with their diets, but I was the one who now had to be even more limited by necessity than I had been by choice. I missed cheese and craved bread all the time. Completely rethinking my health and nutrition required new mental energy to focus on what I could eat instead of what I couldn't.

Luckily, now that my income from the dance class was accumulating, I could afford calcium supplements and dairy-free and gluten-free substitute items as often as I dared.

As hard as it was, in time I realized I had been given a gift of understanding. A few of my dance class members also had gastrointestinal challenges triggered by other health issues. Using online resources they did not possess, I conducted research for myself and on numerous occasions discovered ideas that would help all of us.

As I paid attention to the stories of my students in the dance class, I found additional strength and motivation in their stories and examples. One student shared how her parents frequently insisted on buying treats like Twinkies instead of carrots. Their reasons? The healthier options were too expensive and went bad too quickly.

She said she had once been able to take a stand at the grocery store and ate only healthy food for an entire week. Many of her mystery IBD symptoms had subsided, which made me proud, but then she reported that her parents still didn't buy her healthy food. I understood financial struggles and hoped that they might rise above them one day, yet the situation was disturbing! All

I could do was encourage my student to be patient with them and find ways to empower herself.

Here was a girl who wanted more for herself and to improve her life down the road, and here I was, trying to provide a young girl with the education she wasn't getting at home. With a dietitian for a mother, I never had to do without such education and resources.

This was another way I knew how much my life had been blessed.

Other students had allergies to food dyes, dairy, gluten, nuts—or everything!—and as I listened to my students' complicated relationships with food, I realized how life sometimes invites us to learn to live without and become more disciplined within. That insight eventually turned into another angle on an old lesson—that with the onset of any of life's changes, it would always be important to focus on what is gained through a necessary change than on what is lost.

That lesson came to mind with a few others that were evidently uncommon, that nutrition mattered even when it didn't taste good and eating to live well was more important than living to eat. Understanding and accepting these concepts long before my intolerances of dairy and gluten began was a true saving grace.

In fact, as the years have gone by, I have come to understand that I was given a gift in disguise. I will always miss the comfort and deliciousness of cheese and bread, and the flexibility of a diet where I could eat anything. Yet having an oversensitive physical response to certain tasty—but less healthful—foods is a gift because it invites discipline, self-preservation, and other reasons to make intentional choices in favor of a strong body that functions optimally.

THE ALTITUDES OF ACCEPTANCE

However, knowing what your optimal personal health looks like doesn't mean you can achieve it all the time. In fact, it is daunting yet common to face periods of life when optimal health just can't be reached for one reason or another. But there are still things you can do to maintain good health and work toward better days.

Once there was a season when usual numbers of students were going in and out of hospitals for various reasons. Hospitals seem so common and yet so foreign to most people and their families, but they were never taken for granted by our students. In fact, being in a hospital for multiple days is one point on which most children with autism can relate to one another.

We, the staff, did our best to keep the situation from depressing our students. It often meant guiding chatter with a lighter touch when it came to overhearing those hard conversations.

While monitoring the lunch line one day, I heard, "Hey, did you hear how he had to go to the hospital again this week? That must be miserable."

"Yeah. But I think hospitals are great if they have food!"

Somebody was hungry!

A young girl behind them piped in. "I like their chili cheese fries. It's better than eating cheese!"

"Do you eat cheese plain sometimes then?"

"Yeah, I do! Sometimes I eat it with apples!"

Hearing their comments made my mouth water, so I joined the conversation.

"Same here! Cheese and apples were one of my favorite treats in Canada. It's also great for summer lunches. Do you guys like apples? What are your favorites?"

All of them liked Gala apples for their sweetness and juiciness, or golden apples for their flavor.

Children after my own heart! I loved apples, and I still loved cheese even though I couldn't eat it anymore.

Then the first young man observed, "You know, I've never seen hospitals serving applesauce."

The other students lapsed into silence, as though trying to remember any occasion they had applesauce in their years of hospital ventures.

Another teacher nearby saw fit to add to the conversation. "Well, it's not really in a hospital's best interest to serve apples."

The students looked at him in confusion, then curiosity.

Then came the clincher. "You know, an apple a day ..."

The room lit up with giggles.

Everyone knows *an apple a day keeps the doctor away*. But it had just occurred to everyone that hospitals might be in the business of illness, not wellness.

Or were they? I laughed too, but now the concept intrigued me.

Was my coworker right? Were there really no apples in hospitals?

I brought up the idea with my dance students later that day, who immediately laughed too, but assured me that occasionally their hospital meals did in fact include servings of delicious applesauce.

It might have been my state of mind at the time, but I wondered if, given how many of the students endured (or enjoyed) diets filled with sugar, the reported deliciousness of the applesauce was due to the amount of sugar in those little single use, foil-topped containers they described. Speaking of which, it had been kids who taught me how to make spoons out of the foil tops of those applesauce treats, and while that was more resourceful and inspirational than silly, it spoke to the fact that kids were very familiar with the treat.

In that moment, I seriously considered anonymously petitioning or emailing all the hospitals in the area to increase their provisions of applesauce—the pure, unsweetened kind.

I didn't do that, but I sure liked the idea.

I liked how social awareness could be enhanced by a sense of humor.

Recently I heard a friend say, "Humor and social confidence are children of the same parent. Someone who is naturally good at making others laugh has an innately solid foundation of emotional intelligence, or a good understanding of human communication."

THE ALTITUDES OF ACCEPTANCE

If you think about it, having good humor is tied to having good health and emotional intelligence. Altogether they create the ability to think and behave in a reasonable way and to make good decisions. Appropriately prioritizing all three leads to having sound judgment in practical matters. I like knowing how emotional intelligence is deeply connected to the things that make us feel good. Emotional intelligence helps people develop good interpersonal relationships. It also influences solid health foundations because of its influence on mental health and discipline.

That isn't to say emotional health is more important than or matters more or less than physical health. What I mean is, they grow together. You can't improve one without influencing the other; and you can't lose one without losing some portion of the other too.

I observed this in my students as they diligently worked to improve their spatial and social awareness. Their emotions were connected to how successful they were with helping each other overcome obstacles, including the occasions when they ran into each other on the dance floor. I enjoyed facilitating the growth of my students' emotional skills as they communicated about movements and choreography, and it was my privilege to witness how even the shy and uncomfortable ones learned and mastered the steps.

I admit there were times in my life when I would have been disenchanted to see someone with autism on the dance floor, and yet I've always believed that anyone who feels shy or hesitant about dancing can overcome those feelings by taking dance lessons. Dancing is about more than skill. It's about learning to put your mind and energy into the flow and rhythm of the music.

Some humans might start dancing as soon as they walk, but all humans can benefit from dancing. Even when people don't yet know what to do on the dance floor, no one wants to be left out. I saw this in the eyes of a few of my students who started out as wallflowers at all the school dances. After taking my class, dancing on a stage, and combining enough emotional, physical, and mental intelligence, they changed their wallflower status. Dancing became less about standing out or fitting in and more about doing something awesome that shared what was in their hearts.

Often, the problem is not the difficulty of the dance.

It's how we feel, or how we see ourselves fitting in, that presents the greater obstacle.

In life, we all create molds for ourselves; who we think we need to be, who we surround ourselves with, and what we think we should become for our future. But when we spend years *folding* and *refolding* ourselves or others into self-perceived molds, instead of using our intelligence to be more proactive than reactive, we miss so much of what life is *unfolding* before us.

In retrospect, when I was struggling and healing from that barrage of temporal setbacks, it seemed I was blind to life unfolding right in front of me. I couldn't see where I fit in, but I kept fitting dance into the life I was living. Like my students, I felt I didn't have my frame correct and things seemed to be falling apart, yet I still felt a magical connection to that smooth waltz I had learned at an early age at my father's feet. I craved that connection to the deepest parts of me more than anything. For a long time, the dance floor was the easiest place to find that connection.

There is magic in dance. It is this kinetic energy that keeps you linked to the present moment—literally moving with the flow and the notes of life. It's easily shared with others, and it is closely connected to what enhances a relationship or saves a life.

This is the same magic that turns a stone into a potato, producing creative responses and pathfinding skills through life to help us rise above the limited views that may initially surround us. Experimenting with your own abilities or with the people who invited you to dance might add a bit of magic beyond your wildest imagination to your lifescape. Or it could cause a situation you'll have to learn from—but at least you danced!

THE ALTITUDES OF ACCEPTANCE

This is the same magic that motivates us to deliver the best within us even when times are hard or scary. We can trust that when life may seem to be working against us, it's very possible that things are working for us. It tells us life is less about looking a fool because of what you do, and shows us how to seek out the best rhythms, the most fun and promising partners, and the best guides as we learn the steps of each dance.

The same magic exists in good health, the kind of magic that warns and protects us. There are innumerable deceits and distractions that can deter and diminish our health. Our daily choices are evidence of whether we are strengthening our physical, emotional, and social health. In life's adventure, it can be easy to trade aspects of our health for other experiences, even important ones. Then we find that achieving balance and establishing boundaries can make or break our well-being.

As we work to become our best self, both emotionally and physically, we discover not only the *best*, but also the *worst* of ourselves. Such a process doesn't happen overnight. It's not always happy or fun, especially because everything we do or say affects the lives of others. Sometimes we even trip over our own feet or step on other people's toes—not just the toes that belong to the father who is teaching us how to dance.

When two people are dancing, the lead and follow relationship is all about collaboratively working together with their different skills and abilities. Within their roles, one initiates movement and the other responds in fluid motion, creating beautiful patterns to display how they are feeling the music together. *One, two, three,* and *four*: they must incorporate spatial awareness, discernment, flexibility, and adaptability. *Five, six, seven,* and *eight*: finding the musical rhythm in their dance and building upon what they have together is critical to the overall experience.

THE MAGIC OF DANCE AND GOOD HEALTH

In a way, life's adventure is a dance we choose to take with God. When we choose God, we find ourselves in places we never thought we needed to be so that he can bring out the best in us. Whether it feels like he is our partner or the teacher, it's our job to learn how to recognize his voice and apply his instruction. In dance, that's called being a good follower, and it is a very real skill for all dance students. If we turn toward God, not away from him or against him, we will follow better. We may even get better at knowing his ways—how he guides us through the adventures of life.

Are we eager to face him and get our dance frame right? Can we master good health practices, correct posture, and achieve harmony in our relationships so that our dance has the best chance of flowing down the hall?

Or are we not dancing at all? Are our hearts in the journey? Are we trudging along taking steps without real focus or intent? Are we dancing into the people we should be dancing with?

Even if we started out waltzing on God's toes, trust me—he does eventually want us to be able to move on our own two feet. He hopes we learn to dance in perfect frame and step in perfect rhythm. Whether on an actual dance floor, or at the top of a mountain in our lifescapes, I think God wants us to pause and enjoy the views that were once intimidating and out of reach—to know each of those views is filled with individualized, intentional moments that show us he's been there.

That's how we feel the magic.

CHAPTER 9

GOD'S ADVENTURE IS US

The sun's morning light was stretching into the horizon, accenting the feathery clouds in pink, making the child in me wonder if God's artwork reflected an affinity for cotton candy. However, despite the warm sunlight and happy pink clouds, I sensed a cold foreboding on this late winter day. As I began my early morning walk to the train station, my adult brain had taken note that the bundles of fluff decorating the clear blue sky were high cirrus clouds, with altostratus clouds approaching in the distance. Therefore, today, I was fairly certain, would end in a snowstorm.

All of which was fine by me.

I had grown up loving storms in all their bittersweet and beautiful splendor. In learning about them, watching them, anticipating them, fearing them, and witnessing how they can change and impact both the natural and human world, I had determined that weather was either a complimenting or complicating factor to every outdoor activity, yet I had gained trust that God is in every storm and knows what to do with his storms. By their very nature, storms can't be prevented. Consequently, they demand our readiness, so I have also learned to practice survival skills whenever the opportunity arises.

Those clouds signaled opportunity, so I slipped an extra winter beanie and umbrella in my backpack. I was also wearing a thicker coat, wool socks, and my new leather boots. In fact, as I walked down the clear sidewalk, I imagined the ground covered with a foot of snow on my way home—the perfect chance for my new boots to prove themselves.

As usual, I arrived at the train station about two minutes before the train pulled up, bought my ticket, and climbed aboard—only to walk right into another kind of storm.

Looking at my phone, I noticed a text from my fellow train monitor.

I can't make it to the train today, but Simon's parents texted me. They told me he is very distraught and is having a rough day due to an emotional situation brewing at school. Can you help?

Of course I could! I knew Simon as a gentle giant, yet learning to deal with emotions or situations was a difficult task for him. So, as my train sped out of one station and toward the school, I thought about ways to talk with him. When my train arrived right ahead of Simon's train from the north, I stepped onto the platform to wait for him and watch all the passengers disembark.

There he is!

"Simon!"

He was barely ten feet away, but without so much as a hello or even a bye, he passed me, muttering about something I couldn't make out, and aimed for the first car in the pickup lane.

I tilted my head. *Right, rough day indeed!*

Then I considered my options.

One, I could run him down and demand his attention.

Two, I could run after him and adopt his pace and let him know I knew something was up.

Drawing myself up to my full height, I thought it was best to pursue that second option, but it was like Simon was galloping off the train platform. Taking extra-long strides, I caught up to him at the ramp, reached for his arm, and tapped him lightly to get his attention. He looked at me, but said nothing, then looked away and increased his stride to twice the length of mine.

"Hey, Simon, I heard that something is really bothering you, and I'd like to help."

The cars were just ahead. I knew if we didn't talk about it now, the opportunity to help Simon withstand the storm brewing in his heart might be gone.

THE ALTITUDES OF ACCEPTANCE

He slowed down but kept walking.

I persisted, "Simon, you're not in trouble! I just want to help. You seem upset. Is anything going on at school?"

"It's hard, Miss D."

"What is?"

"That guy, he's a jerk. He was talking to my girlfriend yesterday, and I think he likes her. Keeps trying to get her attention. Even gave her a hug. In front of me. It makes me so mad."

I asked one question to make sure I had the right adversary in this situation, and "that guy" was one of my train riders who had not been present that morning.

"So, you feel like he is being a jerk to you on purpose? Like he's trying to hurt you and get her?"

"Yes."

His single word answer made me feel nervous. It was sweet of Simon to want to protect his relationship, but this was clearly a high-pressure situation for him.

Will he attempt to get rid of his rival? What is he willing to do to get rid of the opposition?

"Wow, that's a hard situation, Simon. I feel the best answer is going to be one you and your girlfriend decide together. Could you talk with her about how you feel about his attention, and even his intentions? If you are clear about how you feel, it might help her evaluate any actions she needs to take to help protect your relationship."

He nodded, and I wasn't sure what else to say. We had reached the nearest car, and I took a step back as he climbed in. I decided to walk around to talk to the driver. In case that other guy was at school that day via another form of transportation, I wanted to forward the message of the situation and alert other teachers that I had resolved pretty much nothing between the two.

As I watched the car drive off, I felt a pang and wished I had kept Simon with me.

I brushed off the feeling and gathered the remaining kids, moving them toward my school vehicle while thinking about the conversation. The two were such different boys, and both were loved by their families. One came from wealth and the other from a family of five children and fewer means. To have both young men attracted to or at least competing over the same girl seemed like an age-old tale in the making!

Once upon a time, two men had fought over me. I remembered how flattered I felt as the prized dance partner. I loved seeing how they styled their dance maneuvers to impress me, however, I was troubled as their interaction verged on the intensity of a real fight. I must have said or did something that showed them what I thought about their behavior, and in the end, one man surrendered me to the other.

On the other hand, this girlfriend seemed to be a bit oblivious, but surely there was something in her actions that might inspire the boys to resolve such a thing.

I had seen Simon's angst and irritation, and it disturbed me. I worried even more after I saw the other boy at school. It felt like the dam was about to burst.

Eventually, feeling out of my depth, I texted the school's counselor to see if he could help navigate the issue, since I knew it wasn't my place or within my skill set to facilitate any kind of score-settling conversation. As the day progressed, I did my part to minimize the contact the boys had with each other, however, that stressed me out—I felt like I was encouraging them to ignore problems rather than face them.

By the time everyone gathered to be transported to the train station at the end of the school day, I had neither heard nor seen whether the situation had been resolved, and both boys were present—at opposite ends of the gym. Other teachers offered to help me drive the students to the train station, so I made a point to ensure the boys would ride in separate vans.

However, I remembered too late my earlier wish to keep one of the boys in my school vehicle.

THE ALTITUDES OF ACCEPTANCE

As I drove to the station, the snow was threatening to fall out the bottom of the clouds, and by the time I reached the station, both storms—figuratively and literally—had set in.

I would have preferred the storm to hold off for an hour or two, but the wind blew, the snow stuck like feathers to the ground, and the boys argued near the bottom of the platform ramp.

Seeing them together, my senses went on alert. I parked as quickly as I could, ensured my students closed all doors, then rushed to the storm I hoped I could handle.

But I was too late.

From too far away, I saw Simon punch his adversary in the face, knocking him out cold.

When I finally reached them, Simon was still standing there, staring at the other boy who was lying unmoving on the icy concrete. Simon's face was a maze of shock and fear.

I caught his sadness, his fearful stare. Our eyes locked in a moment, then his tears tore at my heart as words escaped me. In a situation like this, for someone like me, talking to someone like Simon—words couldn't come from anywhere but a calm place, and that calm place—at least for the moment—had no words, only an odd peace knowing Simon's anger could no longer survive under the weight of his actions. He knew he'd crossed the line. I was in no danger.

After that passed, irritation took over. *I knew I should have kept one of these boys with me!*

I shook that off fast—I couldn't blame myself. Spreading blame was like spreading water, it would get everywhere too quickly. Plus, maybe Simon's storm cloud would have burst right here, on the train platform, no matter what I did.

My second thought triggered my first aid training. *What if he's unresponsive?*

I knelt beside the young man, called him loudly by name, then shook his shoulders gently. I was about to assess for further injury when his hand came up to cover his bloodied nose. Pulling out a tissue from my backpack's hidden stash, I looked him in the eyes and asked, "Can you tell me your name, what day it is, and where we are?"

He was able to answer satisfactorily, so I asked him for his side of the story.

I wasn't surprised to hear all about his own innocence, declaring he'd been run at and popped in the face without warning, and quite frankly, I believed him, but not for the reasons you might think. That's exactly how I imagined it would have happened—a blow gusting in without warning. I suspected the battered boy's innocence was marred by sparks and jabs in Simon's direction, yet only one punch had been thrown.

As disappointed as I was, I felt grateful there had been no chance to return a punch.

Other train passengers had gathered, so I asked for some space, only to notice one walking away with a phone to his ear. That looked like bad news to me, but I couldn't worry about that.

I had a job to do.

As the crowd backed up, I directed the rest of the students to board their respective trains without me. Only after they marched away did I notice the school counselor, who was walking quickly in our direction from the parking lot. Apparently not eager to drive home in the mounting storm, he had made the decision to ride the train and had driven his own car to the station.

Thank you, God.

The snowflakes were falling faster, blowing right into my face and splashing into my eyelashes. It was winter, it would be dark soon, and between blinks, I handed my extra beanie and the umbrella to the student who had been punched. Then I invited him to wait for me by the rails at the bottom of the ramp. I pointed Simon up to the train platform. I tucked my cold hands into my coat pockets and quickly explained to the counselor what had happened.

Then we both noticed a police car pulling up.

He didn't miss a beat. "Miss D, I'll ride northbound with Simon. I'll call his parents and figure things out with the police."

That was exactly what Simon needed, and for that matter exactly the help I needed too.

"Wow, if you could do all that for us ... all I can say is thank you!"

"No problem, if this had happened at school, it would have been my job anyway. I am just glad I was here. You get our friend by the rails onto the next southbound train and get him home."

I nodded. *Whew!*

As we both moved to take our respective actions, an overwhelming sense hit me— my friend had been motivated by the storm to be exactly where and when I needed help. *So awesome!* Even though I hadn't listened enough to my feelings earlier, God was still taking care of things.

To the boy who hovered near the railing, I asked, "Hey, how do you feel? How's your head?"

"Not too great in my head, but I can walk."

Hearing that, I found myself not as worried about him as I was about the call to his parents.

The conversation was anything but smooth.

"Hi there, thank you so much for picking up. I am calling from the train station because something happened, and your son was involved."

I continued explaining, and as soon as I finished, their alarm exploded to the surface.

"How—could—*you* let this happen?"

The charged atmosphere was like the sky before a lightning strike. I could feel the pressure of their frustration making it hard for me to think. I bit my lip, feeling their blame chiseling away at the calm I had mustered. All I could say was the truth.

"I understand you're frustrated. I blame myself too. This morning, I knew the young men were at odds. I wish I had done more to help them resolve it, such as keep them apart or even told the school to make other arrangements for both boys today instead of riding the train."

"Yes, you certainly could have done more."

Ouch! Being transparent wasn't helping. Emotions were running high, but they had to know that blame for the shocking situation didn't belong to just one person, didn't they? And I needed them to know that managing the care and safety of their son was my priority.

"I checked your son for injuries. He was knocked out but is not bleeding and is fully responsive. He may have a concussion." Luckily, I spoke with more composure than I felt.

"Can we speak to our son, please?"

"Yes, of course, he's right here." I stopped worrying about how they felt about me when their son responded to all their questions with coherence. I could tell they were more focused on determining the level of urgency—did he require an emergency room or an after-hours clinic?

After talking with him, they decided he could ride the next train home. As he gave the phone back to me, I took in my surroundings. It was getting colder, darker, more snow was falling, and the next train's horn had sounded. We could see its lights hovering in the distance.

"If it's all right with you, I'd like to stay with your son all the way to where you pick him up at the station and deliver him in person. The train is nearly here."

They agreed it would be better if he didn't travel alone and thanked me for taking an extra hour of travel beyond my train stop. I sensed genuine gratitude, though it seemed obscured by the belief that I had been part of the problem. Honestly, I couldn't help but think the same way.

That train ride proved to be as silent as the snowfall outside, despite my questions to keep mild conversation going. My young travel companion didn't have much to say, so in between monitoring his symptoms, I watched the darkening sky outside my window. Fighting back the tears of despondency, my mind started questioning everything that had happened that day in full force.

How could I let this happen? I echoed to myself. *Really, a fight on the train platform? A policeman on the case of a neurodivergent child? What could I have done to change this outcome?*

In all the planning for this transportation program, I had never suspected having to deal with such an altercation. Curious about the other side of this situation, I texted the counselor on the other train. He had emailed the administrators and recommended to request both youths to stay at home the next day. He expected a temporary expulsion, at least for the aggressor, but had reason to believe the police would recognize the situation as a juvenile crisis rather than an assault. He also said he'd put in a good word based on how I handled the situation. Beyond that, much was still up for discussion between the families and the school.

I pondered all this and somehow held it together until I delivered the boy to his mother, whose few questions I answered with professional decorum. Then I was free. I hustled back to the train platform to wait in the driving snow, willing the next train to show up soon and take me home.

As the adrenaline of the emergency faded, the weight of it all was shed through my tears. I hardly cared as they chilled my cheeks and threatened to freeze my eyelashes together.

I dug out my umbrella again and felt the storm start to chill me to the bone. Shivering, I thought how I had been completely out of my comfort zone, yet that wasn't why I was crying.

What will tomorrow bring? My tears were more related to how I ached for the pain of these students and the unexpected unknowns now written into their futures. Both boys were in pain for different reasons. Pain had purpose, but I hated seeing the kids in pain.

It felt like the beginning of the end, and it was.

Although I was involved very little over the next few days, I was eventually asked for my take on the situation. I spoke the truth as I had seen and experienced it, and in the end, both boys were given consequences. As expected, the boy who landed the punch was given time off from school.

On a happier note, I think his relationship lasted through the end of the school year somehow. That seemed beautiful in a youthful romantic type of way.

It wasn't long after this event that I sensed a pending shift. I wasn't surprised to hear the administration intended to evaluate the effectiveness of the train monitoring program, and I knew the fight incident had been the breaking point. The constant stream of unknowns and complexities related to train monitoring had created more liability than the school could afford, and it was time to rethink its structure and sort through all the successes and chaos of the program.

After all, pilot programs are intended to help determine how best to organize the real thing.

The school administration acknowledged all efforts in the program's implementation. My associates and I were recognized and appreciated for our willingness to handle so much chaos. They recognized the motivation I had to keep the program going, but they concluded that what I was doing was more than should be expected of train monitors in longevity.

Frankly, I agreed. If we reformed the program, it had to be less labor-intensive.

The final kicker was when we talked about how this wasn't a partnership with public transportation. Despite the monitors' presence, the school could assume no real authority on the train. Since the parents and families were, after all, the *public* part of public transportation, the bulk of behavioral responsibilities needed to be on the parents and the students, not the school.

All that said, many children were now able to ride safely and responsibly. That was the crowning success of the pilot program that would directly benefit families. In all cases where parents had confidence in their child's social independence and travel experience, families were encouraged to

THE ALTITUDES OF ACCEPTANCE

allow their children to continue riding the train. The school had purchased a bus and the services of a bus driver to continue providing transportation. This added an expense but reduced the load of responsibility on teachers to drive before and after school.

Under these shifting circumstances, some students continued to ride the train while others did not. As for me, at first it was hard to appreciate and accept the changes. The cost of gas and distance were still a deterrent to my driving every day, so I still rode the train but only according to my schedule rather than the school's needs. While on the train, I could sit on my own without children, which felt very strange compared to being on alert for student needs. In the end, I concluded I had reached the moment I had been dreaming of for over two years.

I could now bike to the train station and the school. My mouth had healed, and I had been gradually increasing my physical activity into a very active lifestyle. I could endure ten miles of biking per day easily, so I started riding my bike to the train station every morning.

Everything about it was delightful—except for the wind factor.

It was the early spring, but I felt like I was living a version of the oft-quoted idiom, "walking to school in knee-deep snow, uphill both ways." The wind always seemed to be blowing against me! However, I knew how to keep challenges simple and make them fun, so to entertain the students, and get a better workout, I often tried to beat the bus against the wind. On freezing days, I of course joined the students on the train and bus. Less than one year later, I started biking all the way home from the school—all nineteen miles of trail—several times a week.

At about the same time, I started earning higher hourly wages due to my extended employment with the school. This, added to the fact that I could now make myself available to new experiences and longer workdays at the school, somehow superseded the monthly stipend for train monitoring. My cost of living hadn't changed much, so I was able to earn equal and eventually more money than I was earning while monitoring train program.

Looking back, I can see how my needs were being met, one after another. I don't have to tell you who was taking care of me. God has a way of making all things work out for our good, according to what we need, when we need it, and how we need it—no matter what.

Up to my fourth year at the school, I remained intimidated by stories I had heard from teachers who worked in the younger classrooms. I knew that despite my four years of experience, I still lacked a full understanding of early childhood brain development, and I believed I would be more into playing with the kids than teaching them. I also feared how I would respond to kids screaming without apparent reason or escaping the building on my watch.

I had to admit, my fears were valid. Things like that really happened. But when I was asked to assist with the elementary afterschool program in the winter, it turned out I was more prepared than I anticipated. It was a new level of chaos since every day involved some kind of unexpected challenge, yet with each opportunity, I realized all I could do was my best and learn along the way.

One day, as I walked over to the elementary school, I looked up at the sky and felt very close to God. It was a perfect day, one of those rare cold days with sun and no wind, and I recognized the same feeling of peace, fulfillment, and acceptance that came when I was high on a mountaintop.

Out of the blue, I got a distinct impression God wanted me to be outside that day.

I thought that was odd since it seemed sort of—well, obvious. On a warm, sunshiny day, where else would I want to be? Then it occurred to me that being outside would be hard if everyone voted to stay in the gym and do indoor activities. There was a chill in the air after all.

THE ALTITUDES OF ACCEPTANCE

When I saw the children practically bouncing off the walls, I suggested to the other elementary teachers that we go outside. They were not difficult to persuade—they had been stuck indoors with the kids for most of the day. As soon as the announcement was made for an outdoor day, I dashed outside to stand sentry near the door as children took off in every direction, amusing themselves with large bouncing balls, jump ropes, chalk, the jungle gyms, or the soccer field. A few children simply wandered around, talking to friends or to themselves. For half an hour, all the teachers walked around too, helping kids find occupations and activities. Then we stood together, and I curiously inquired whether anyone had a great story from the classrooms that day.

"The last time I was here one of you was telling me about that hilarious stunt a kid had performed at a pizza party. Remember, the one where the kid—"

A child's scream—a blood-curdling cry of terror no adult wishes to hear—erupted and startled us, ending the peace of the afternoon like the flight of a bird into a glass pane.

Spinning around in every which way like a herd of buffalo circling up and looking for the threat, we searched the faces of the children for any sign of danger, terror, or shock. A moment later, I noticed the kids closest to me were standing agape, and I followed their stares. That's when my eyes found the terror-stricken face of one of the adorable little boys in the group—Theo, a well-mannered kid who deserved nothing bad in life.

Only twenty-five feet away, Theo hovered several feet above the ground.

Looking closer, I could see the little guy's arm above his elbow had vanished between two metal bars in the jungle gym. He was not only swinging at an impossible angle, but he was also too small to reach any of the other poles. I gulped down a gasp as his legs thrashed, then winced as I imagined how each movement pinched and squeezed Theo's arm. If he somehow loosened himself while in that position, he would fall and face a fate worse than a broken arm—a broken skull.

Clearly, mere movement and the hard ground below were his enemies, and their threat would increase with time. My mind was full of colliding thoughts—first, a silent plea for him to stop moving. Second, the motion of turning and rushing toward him. Third, the moment at age three when I had discovered for myself what it was like to hit hard ground from that height.

I still remember the pain, the hospital's black surgery table. Feeling like a fish in a bowl with all the doctors looking at my head. How they put my cranium back together with fourteen staples.

No wonder I had always felt extra compassion for Humpty-Dumpty.

There was no way I was letting that happen to Theo, not on my watch.

"There!" I pointed. "It's Theo. He's hanging, might be hurt! I'll get him."

Even though it felt like I'd been looking at him for an hour, it had been mere seconds.

I started running, remembering who was watching me that day, who had wanted me to be outside. But if I hadn't pushed to be outside, then maybe this wouldn't have happened.

But it was happening, and someone had to do something. And I was here to do it.

Dear God, Theo is so little. He's a good kid. He needs your help. My help. What can I do? If there's anything—with your wisdom, please, please help me know what I can do!

A familiar resolve slipped into my soul, replacing all hesitation.

Like a fox, I darted through the grass, and around the two girls standing in front of me. Then I leapt like a deer over the concrete edge surrounding the woodchips of the playground area.

Along the way, incredibly vivid mental pictures flooded into my mind. One was of my rock-climbing experiences; another was of a few first-aid training scenarios I'd been in. The last one was of a wild west movie moment, where a cowboy dangled from the edge of a cliff by his arms. He had only been able to escape when he found a foothold and took the—

Wait, that was it! ... Hanging people are in danger because of their own body weight ... But am I tall enough?

THE ALTITUDES OF ACCEPTANCE

Somewhere in that mix of memories, the truth about hanging people had slipped through. I just hoped Theo's weary arm would last until I got there. Even though I was a very short person, I understood that if I could lift him up above his elbow's point of suspension, then the danger would be over. If I could just do that much, maybe it would be enough.

The short distance I sprinted felt like a mile, but gravity didn't have a chance against my strides, which at this point had to be about the same length as my height.

When I reached Theo, I felt absorbed in the storm that was his life in that moment. I thought about climbing up above him and trying to lift him up that way, but I hesitated, not knowing if that was the right way. Then I caught a glimpse of his tearful, silent plea for relief—a visible echo to his scream—and it was unnerving to see such terror.

It made me want to reach up and hug him.

Which gave me an idea. In one motion, I reached up, wrapped my arm around his waist, and anchored my feet. Then, I lifted his entire body as high as I could above my shoulders.

When Theo was high enough to sit on my shoulder, he pulled his arm out from between the bars, all on his own, as quick as lightning. Then he clung to my head as I slowly crouched down to place his feet on the wood chips.

Once there, I grasped his shoulders lightly and turned him to face me, searching for something in his eyes. In them I found the thankful hug his arms and autism probably couldn't give me. Then I stood, finally releasing a deep breath, and looked him up and down.

"Hey, little buddy, are you okay? Do you hurt anywhere?"

"Miss D, I—I was so scared. My arm hurts, right here."

He pointed to a spot right behind his elbow, where his tricep and bicep had been trapped.

Another teacher walked up with a clipboard and some paperwork on it, and I knew what that was about.

Ready to write things down for our report of the incident, she nodded at me, as if to say *go ahead, ask the questions.*

I crouched next to Theo. "I'm sure it hurts, but it'll feel better now that you're not stuck. Do you mind if I feel it? It looks normal, but I need to find out if your injury is serious."

Theo nodded, and I rolled his short sleeves up just a little. Then, I pressed my thumb and forefinger lightly around his arm at the spot where the bars had been. He didn't wince at all.

Considering the position in which he had dangled, I pressed again on a slightly lower spot and watched his eyes for signs of shock or pain. So far, they seemed clear and normal.

Then a little yelp came, and his eyes squinted at me.

It's not broken, but there must be a little tenderness, or a tissue tear in there somewhere.

"Good news! Your arm is okay. It's not broken, but you might have a little purple bruise today. Tomorrow it might feel sore. The skin might turn yellow, or maybe even green! That's cool, right?"

Theo grinned and cocked his head while the teacher writing the report sighed in relief and chuckled at my odd use of bruise colors to get a laugh. Then, it occurred to me Theo had been hanging on the *outside* of the bars, not a place where the little ones usually spend much time.

"Theo, you were on the outside of the jungle gym. How did you get there? Can you tell me what happened?"

"Well, I wanted to see if I could do what he was trying to do—fly!"

He pointed to one of the older youths who was much taller. Earlier I had seen the taller child climbing up the bars to the top, then leaning over the edge, hands free and arms out like an airplane. He had been leaning way too far past the railing for comfort, so I had stood under him and waved him off his perch.

How interesting it is to discover that while his obedience to my instructions had been quick in coming, the older boy's wayward behavior had still influenced another's desire and almost caused life-changing harm.

THE ALTITUDES OF ACCEPTANCE

Wanting to fly was common among children, and adults have to inspire the common sense that will keep them safe from such notions.

"Theo, sometimes big kids do what little kids shouldn't. Sometimes people do things no one should do. Some things seem like fun but are actually very dangerous."

My words were falling on distracted ears as he eyed all the other kids playing. When he leaned over to pick up a few wood chips, I asked, "Do you want to come sit and talk more with me for a little while?"

"No, it's okay, I want to play a game now!"

"Okay. We'll get ice when we go inside soon." Theo was making a little family out of wood chips and building a little house for them. Playtime was going to be over in a few minutes when the sun went down, and he was anxious to play rather than be still. I couldn't blame him.

"Okay. That sounds good. By the way, I'm so glad you called for help."

"I know," he said without hesitation. I smiled—only these kids were able to speak with such a matter-of-fact tone! It made one think he planned it that way—but it had to be resilience talking.

Since he appeared content to be on his own, I moved away, thinking about where Ziploc bags and ice were in the kitchen. Later it occurred to me that if I had stayed longer to watch him, maybe something would have come up to reveal his true feelings about the incident. Behaviors tend to have stories attached to them, both stories we tell others and stories we keep to ourselves. But I had no desire to hover or make a mountain of what appeared to have been little more than a molehill to him, so I followed the example of the rest of the teachers and began walking around the playground, avoiding distracting adult conversations!

It was time to reflect and express gratitude for how this moment had turned out.

For one thing, how did kids try to fly, fail, get terrified, then show such great resiliency right away? I kind of envied their belief in their power to do anything, though it saddened me too. That might be a version of resilience, but it can also be a precursor to losing our courage as we begin to trade troubles—our childish beliefs for adult insecurities. Life chisels away at our confidence if we let it, but it also creates adults whose version of flying comes only with hard work full of mountains and valleys and the pursuit of impossible dreams.

Speaking of insecurities, the world teases people about being "chicken," but I don't think most people realize there is so much more in the statement than just how timid and lacking in courage the creatures appear to be. Chickens are birds, and prior to being domesticated and bred as a source of food, they actually flew farther distances. Now they've evolved to have almost no reason to spread their wings—unless it helps them to run away.

As an example, consider the little lost chicken in one of my family's stories.

Somewhere near the city I grew up in, my parents had been searching along a mountain road for good camping spots for my father's Boy Scout troop. Without warning, my dad screeched the brakes.

GASP! Mom about had a heart attack.

"Dear, you're in the middle of the road! We're going to be hit by the next car!"

He chuckled as he turned on his hazards and opened his door. "We haven't seen a car in hours. Besides, there is a little lost chicken back there."

My mom stared, blinking in surprise as my dad climbed out of the truck.

Had she heard him wrong? Did he say dog? Because that would make more sense. A dog could easily get this far. She could even imagine a dog being accidentally forgotten. But a chicken?

A chicken all alone, so far from any farms, campsites, or other probable chicken residences within miles, was in obvious trouble.

She had to see this, so she opened her door and walked around to the back of the truck. Sure enough, the most common little chicken dressed in white feathers with black spots stood facing her about fifty feet behind the truck, head cocked, looking lonely and confused, but interested in her husband who was creeping slowly toward it. It looked so out of place!

Mom knew that with so many predators in the surrounding wilderness, the defenseless creature would never survive. There was no way of knowing how long it had been there, but left alone and unable to fly, it was probably wondering how it had gotten here and what to do with itself.

Dad crept closer while the chicken seemed to give his advances consideration, and he almost lost his balance when the chicken erupted in a flurry of feathers and darted away to the other side of the bush!

Dad dashed after it.

Round and round the bush they went, with Dad's head popping up from behind, followed by the occasional burst of feathers.

"Hey, chicken … *cluck, cluck* … come here, chicken. Time to go, little chicken!"

With all the up-and-down motions of their chicken dance, the event was a regular carousel, and soon Mom was crumpling in laughter.

I'm sure Dad added words to his chicken-whispering about a nice warm coop with other chickens, or the chance of getting some grasshoppers to munch on. As I'm writing this, I'm aware of how my dad's own chickens tend to follow his voice literally anywhere he wants them to go, which seems to say his person and voice are somehow interesting to his little feathered creatures.

But this chicken didn't know my dad's voice, so it ran away. It was determined not to be caught, and to avoid the hands of my father who knew what was best for it. I still laugh to think it resisted rescue for about half an hour, then I laugh harder when I realize how determined my father was to pursue that silly chicken!

Finally, it rushed into the bush where its wings and legs became entangled and unable to move. Dad reached in and pushed the branches aside. The chicken then jumped up at the chance of freedom and landed right in Dad's waiting arms. He carefully cuddled it to his chest, before promptly walking back to the truck.

Mom clapped in celebration: for the chicken, for the full workout of sprints and lunges my dad got, and for obtaining a moment in life she still can't stop laughing about.

Then, curiously, she asked, "So—what are you going to do with it now?"

"Have you hold it until we get to the next farm."

Me? she thought. *But chickens and I don't really get along...*

When she saw his grin, she realized that apparently this was her comeuppance for laughing and not helping.

So, hold it she did, right on her lap all the way to the little chicken's new home (which turned out to be a friend's farm). It clucked a few times at her, then settled as it realized it was safe.

The little lost chicken, finally allowing itself to be rescued, saved itself from an unknown fate, and as a result its life moved in a very different direction than it had been going. Truth be told, if the chicken had not resisted, it would have taken that much less time to save it, and it would have kept a few feathers in the process. But I'd say the way things crystallized made the memorable chicken caper quite comparable to the real live experiences of people.

Some moments in our lives might reveal us to be like the lost chicken, resisting God's invitations to aim for his safety until we are stuck in fear and paralysis from insecurity. In such moments, we might look and feel like this chicken caper, and we can only be saved by letting God lift us out of our own traps. I hate to think of people succumbing to the circumstances of life instead of seeking out the joy that is available to us through God. He intends for us to reach the measure of our creation, and we discover it by allowing ourselves to be caught and changed by him.

THE ALTITUDES OF ACCEPTANCE

I used to think God had some kind of magic wand that influenced everything for the better only when it suited him, but now I know it's more likely that God is constantly, actively inserting moments into our lives to draw us closer to him, to prepare us and help us master and manage our paths and decisions. God might not show up in the ways we think he will, but he is always expertly creating his masterpieces in us, between us, and because of us.

When Theo had called out, a flood of memories had provided the clarity through which I had known what to do to help him. I think these were evidence that God can use past experiences to help solve problems in any moment. He had handpicked those memories and made sense of them at the speed the incident required—who else could have known me and my memories *that* well?

Speaking of speed, I had been able to act so quickly that it felt unprecedented. Normally I preferred to be analytical, slower, and operate with a plan. But God knew I also had a calm head on my shoulders during emergencies, and that I moved much faster with trusted information. So, he showed me the wisdom I prayed for, and I acted. I lifted Theo up because I loved these kids, because pain is awful, because I knew the way to resolve the core problem.

It felt very similar to how God handled me and my challenges as a loving Heavenly Father.

Feeling so close to God earlier that day and feeling distinctly like I needed to be outside was evidence God knew what was coming, or just a matter of *right time, right place, right person.*

It might have been that God was creating a lesson for me, or for Theo. Either way, I knew I was supposed to go outside, and the incident would not be easily forgotten.

Later that day, as the intensity of the moment faded like a wisp of smoke into the afternoon sky, I knew as many times as we get lost or stuck in this life, God is able to use every single incident to help us learn to hear his voice and get closer to him. God knows the best way to lift us up, and the best part is that he can and will because of who he is and because he loves us.

I used to think finding God was the preeminent adventure of anyone's lifetime, but now I know that God has an adventure too that lasts our whole lives and into forever. *God's adventure is us.*

His adventure is to return us to him and make us free.

Free from sin, from sorrow, and any pain inflicted upon us by others—or by ourselves.

Free from the harsher effects of the storms of life, even if he doesn't hold them back.

But how—and why—does he do it?

In retrospect, after I have pondered the stories of Theo and my dad's chicken, I am amazed to recognize the answer to that question is not only in these stories. It's found all over the scriptures too. The boy and the chicken had done one very normal, natural, and instinctive thing—a thing that illustrates a divinely fundamental lesson God intends for us to experience over and over, in each lifescape, and throughout our entire lives.

When they allowed themselves to be lifted up, *they were able to free themselves!*

CHAPTER 10

THE ADVENTURE OF PERSPECTIVE AND REALITY

*I*n the middle of the room, I stood alone on my tiptoes, my right arm fully stretched above my head. The end of the pull-chain for the light in the ceiling fan was dangling just beyond the reach of my fingertips, and all my stretching and tiptoeing did nothing to aid me in my predicament.

In all my days as an apartment renter, I had never seen such high light fixtures or such a short pull-chain, but this ceiling fan was the only way to have light in the apartment's main living space. Luckily, I'm a resourceful individual. A simple fix would do the trick, but for now, I simply made a mental note to ask the landlord about adding a length of chain to what was already there.

Not a dealbreaker. Right?!

Stepping into the bedroom, I opened the closet and felt my mouth drop open.

Seriously!

The single closet shelf and the clothing rod were built so high that even a six-foot person might have to stand on a short stool to use them. Turning around, I discovered that the light fixture in this room also had a very short chain.

Wow, was this whole apartment built for a giant?

I sped up my apartment tour and targeted the bathroom next.

THE ADVENTURE OF PERSPECTIVE AND REALITY

There I found the toilet paper holder was so far across the room from the toilet that I would have had to stand up and take a step to access it. Nothing doing! It was such a first world problem, yet it was an inconvenience I couldn't overlook. Then again, I could—

Uh, no! Why am I still somehow thinking I could make this work?

I wasn't desperate for a place to live—this was me being normal, also known as being resourceful! To that end, maybe I could buy a standalone toilet paper dispenser ... or not. The bathroom's accessibility for giants only didn't stop there.

The *bottom* of the bathroom mirror was at my eye level, and so was the light switch on the wall next to the door. Behind the door I could see shelving built into the wall, and the lowest shelf was, of course, at my shoulder level. With nothing but a four-foot by two-foot blank wall below it.

I gave up on the bathroom and entered the kitchen.

I stopped in my tracks and stared. Then I laughed.

The countertop was at chest level—for me!—and the bottom of the cabinet system, which included a microwave, *started* at my head level and towered to the ceiling. There would be no reaching the lowest buttons or handles without a stool.

There was no way a five-foot person would live here easily or conveniently. Not that I was opposed to the daily workout of jumping up and climbing stools, but I did feel opposed to how this apartment made me feel short. This was literally a built-in perspective that would no doubt be appreciated by someone much taller, but it completely collided with my own reality.

I had never been tall and would never be tall. I knew *being short* was one thing, and I could live with it quite well, but *being made to feel short* by an apartment was a new experience.

The person who had renovated this apartment had clearly catered to tall people. Or, he simply might have been a tall person himself or aimed to create a home for the giant in his life. Apparently, no one had expected a short person to come along. I had climbed the beanstalk and been amazed by the size of the palace, yet in a world of twisted fairy tales, I didn't feel much like Jack. It seemed the effects of this peculiar experience kept me from extracting the golden reward.

There was only one thing left to think about this unconventional anomaly.

Perspective is reality.

My mother's words of wisdom surfaced, bringing their usual powers of reasoning to this circumstance. My feelings and my perspective were on a collision course with another's reality that didn't match my own. In fact, I was using a short-person perspective to assess an apartment made specifically for tall people, and that didn't work.

No wonder I felt so self-centered and dismissive.

When there is tension, or when people think, act, and believe differently from others to the point of confusion, the root of it all might be individual perspectives and realities. These are real, and they are influenced by what is true from certain points of view. They impact what we think and believe, and I had been taught to understand how my own limiting perspectives needed to be expanded when a different angle or viewpoint presented itself.

Sometimes, things really are that simple. All you need is a new perspective. In this case, I left the apartment laughing for the joy of the tall person who would find the place someday.

In life, perspectives and realities really are at the root of complexity. No single person or perspective is an exact replica of another. In fact, even people who were raised in the same household, or who work in the same science lab, or are a part of the same religion, or have similar beliefs about raising dogs will have to sort through their differences as they communicate.

We all want to be able to share our lives with other people, but perspective affects how we navigate our relationships with ourselves as well as relationships with others. Being able to communicate about how we are seeing something is important. With our perspectives, we can be critical catalysts for change or face limiting handicaps against growth or connection. Owning our perspective and striving to see life through the eyes of others tends to drive passion, empathy, and choices over time. I believe pouring one's own perspective into another's lived experience might be tempting at times, but sharing, treasuring, and collecting perspectives can inform choices, friendships, and all avenues of life experience.

When two people try to comprehend the insights they gain from communication, they might start to sense how those insights differ because of the influence of each lived experience. They might also start to understand how each reality is imperfect. Maybe they'll also realize that beyond both of their realities, there is a separate and greater reality, and each person's perspective is stretching and expanding toward it.

That reality is the home of God's truth. Truth beyond our own understanding.

God's truth is vast and boundless in how it can enhance and inform each of our realities. How do I know this? Because even when I think I know myself—or others—or a situation—through my own perspective, God shows me there is *always* more to know. More to see. Another angle. Another way of seeing someone that is so much better than the view I started out with.

I think that is why close relationships, family relationships, and marriages affect us so deeply. The more mountains we climb together, the more opportunities we encounter through which we learn about the world and each other. There is something precious to be found in seeing the world through the eyes of our loved ones and learning to benefit from other worldviews. But that's a topic for a different book ... for now, just be honest, sensitive, and wise about the stories you tell yourself and share with others.

Those stories are the ones we end up living.

Not that self-fulfilling prophecy is thing. It can be, and I have experienced a few lifescapes where I felt deep spiritual confidence about what was coming next. But even with God's guidance and help, we are responsible for building our own stories. We can't underestimate the importance of making choices and learning to reconcile with our realities and the realities of others, and of adapting and adjusting our perspectives in pursuit of a more complete version of God's truth.

Truth is higher and bigger than us, yet too often it is viewed as relative. People are inclined to think truth should be informed only by their own perspective, and this feels natural, but it is not enough. As an example, when I was in the giant apartment, my views of what makes an apartment livable were based on my own perspective, but someone else's perspective was behind all the high ceiling fixtures and cabinets. Neither perspective made sense to the other. It wasn't until I stopped trying to force my perspective onto the reality of that apartment that I started to understand the lesson from the other perspective.

Even though perspectives are solitary by nature, they require other perspectives to grow and improve. Life was created that way for a reason.

Some perspectives and realities between people don't align in this life, and that can create dealbreakers in friendships and new learning opportunities. But sometimes when you cut past the surface of any perspective and carve it with care, you might end up with a multifaceted diamond of truth that creates understanding between people.

In fact, assessing different or contrasting perspectives with reasoning based on God's truth can lead to a complementary situation where one plus one doesn't equal two—it equals four!

You don't have to get to the end of your life to finally understand that you are so much more than just one lifescape, one path, or one way of thinking.

One of the first truths I ever had to accept started at a very early age. When I was born, I was the same size and weight as my elder brother had been two years prior. As tiny premature babies, we could have slept in shoe boxes for the first two weeks of our lives.

Judging from our births, we should have turned out more similar in height, yet over time, individual genetic packages won over, and he grew to be almost six feet tall. I, on the other hand, reached almost five feet tall—four feet, eleven inches, and three-quarters, to be precise.

Life as a small person means there are people who look at me and think I'm adorable, or who think I'm disadvantaged, or who simply see the opportunity to stream short jokes. From each of these responses, I have learned it is often on me to show taller people that there is more to me than meets the eye, and to never let anyone take advantage of me because of my height.

Unless it's for a good reason!

Once in the fresh produce section of the local grocery store, I was contemplating the prices of peppers and greens on the shelves to my right.

"Would you mind grabbing two leeks for me, please?" asked an adult voice to my left.

My eyes located the leeks on the top shelf above the greens. I grabbed two of them and turned to my left—

A splash of shock ran down my spine as my brain said "Wow!" but words never came. I had never seen such a tiny, fully grown woman! People were always asking *me* if I qualified as a midget or for handicapped parking, and I always said no—because it was true—but this tiny lady could have said yes without hesitation. She must have been thirty-five years old and stood at a height of no more than four and a half feet. On her face was such a polite expression, and I noted it held no shame or embarrassment related to her request.

As for me, I felt a rush of guilt over the shocked expression I couldn't hide, yet I managed to offer her a smile as I handed her the leeks. I couldn't tell if she recognized our mutual plight, but she said thank you without any hint of amusement or irony and moved along with her shopping.

Now you know what it's like for tall people, the voice in my head whispered.

No kidding! I was always asking tall people to reach things for me. And people *were* startled by my height and acted instinctively, just as I had been startled when I saw the shorter woman, who clearly saw me as an ideal candidate for assistance.

Well, *startled* wasn't quite the right word. But at the edge of my own perspective, there was something important to learn.

Being needed to help the woman reach things on the top shelf had felt far from normal. And when I was in that giant apartment, contemplating the world of a taller person had been tough, to say the least. Now, I was wondering what life would be like for an even smaller person. For one thing, it would take a lot more personal conviction to live without expecting to get squashed!

To put this story into perspective, a scripture comes to mind—the one where God says that by small and simple things, great things are made possible. Where God is concerned, it's not the size of a person or situation in life that counts.

It's what he can do with the *who*—the heart of a person—that really matters.

In the world today, it's easy to think greatness can come from pursuing lofty accolades, huge paychecks, or a larger-than-life existence. God knows we need a lot of things to live, and beating the bottom line in life's financial circumstances is important for self-reliance—yet hearts that love money are hearts that struggle to love him or want him near.

There are others who think that by engaging in surface-level modesty, self-importance, or self-degradation, they are setting themselves up for greatness. In my experience, they simply haven't discovered what their kind of small-mindedness is preventing them from becoming.

Most people experience a portion of their lives feeling small inside. In those moments, greatness is farthest from their minds, but at the forefront of God's grandest plans. He acts in our lives until we discover our hearts are still lost or looking for the right perspectives—a frame for reality that helps us become the greater package of who we truly are.

THE ADVENTURE OF PERSPECTIVE AND REALITY

When we believe true greatness comes from the heart, we become good stewards of self and property as well as accept our personal limitations. When we focus on the small things we do every day that put our heart in the right place, we set ourselves up for happiness. All in all, once we find ourselves in the right place, there's no stopping God from making us great.

After that day in the store, I knew I needed to find more opportunities to do the small things that mattered to others, including things I could do simply because I was small—because I was *me*. I could show a little more faith and use the height God gave me to be useful.

The next day I took my car to the mechanic's shop. Having a new perspective on the matter, I realized that moving my seat down and back would be a thoughtful way to help the usually taller-than-me men who worked on my car. Another time later in the week, when my tall friend needed help cleaning her kitchen, I automatically focused on her lower cabinets. It was so much easier for me to reach what might have been much harder for her.

And the list goes on and on. I just kept noticing and doing things that were well suited to my stature that also saved trouble for taller associates and friends. Many of the things I did were things I had done in the past but often with that feeling of being stuck with tasks only short people could do—jobs the world assigned to me based on something I couldn't control. Eventually it got easier and easier for me to feel more tranquil about the effects and social perceptions of being short.

It turns out that when we struggle with things we cannot change or control in our lives, we can alter how we feel and act instead. Except for when our perspectives and realities align with God's truth, it may sometimes be necessary to modify even those perspectives that exist in us because of our backgrounds and histories.

THE ALTITUDES OF ACCEPTANCE

Even a small shift can move us into the realm of greatness.

Once I began working consistently in the high school, I was surrounded by students who were much taller than me. Despite what I had so far concluded about what really mattered when it came to my size and these kids, it was still daunting to think that according to their perspectives, I might be viewed as just one of the kids!

As a result, I often worried about the best ways to prove my authority although I was small.

One day, while reading the students' English textbooks, I ran across a story that cast a new perspective on the issue for me. It was about a famous man named Oliver Wendell Holmes.

Mr. Holmes was known for his political prowess and leadership through service on the US Supreme Court, that he was a defender of the First Amendment, a medical reformer, an author, professor, lecturer, inventor, and a believer in experience over logic. Also, he wrote some amazing poems and advocated playing as a recourse against growing old. Finally, I discovered he was a little over five feet five inches tall, and I found it interesting that so prominent a fellow would not be much taller than myself!

I admired how Mr. Holmes handled his perspectives and his reality. As he attended a large meeting one evening, he was clearly the shortest person in attendance.

A man, likely a tall man with some nerve, said to him, "Don't you feel strange being so short among all these taller men?"

"Yes," Mr. Holmes replied, "I feel like a dime among pennies."

Now that was a way to make a statement of self-worth against perceived value! I agree, Mr. Holmes—when others use obvious factors to establish value, they miss our true worth.

THE ADVENTURE OF PERSPECTIVE AND REALITY

The joke in the story was that size isn't everything since a small dime is worth more than the larger pennies. But the message I took from it wasn't about comparing the worth of people. I hadn't gone through life thinking I was worth more than other people, and I was sure Mr. Holmes didn't do that either. I also knew "perspective is reality," yet I had still struggled to see my own self-worth in the eyes of God—even after knowing great things come in small packages and appreciating how many larger packages were of great value too.

The message I understood was that Mr. Holmes established his self-worth based on how he chose to see himself among others, rather than how they chose to see him, because of his height. According to Mr. Holmes, self-worth was about keeping perspective, not keeping up.

So, the key to dealing with being the shortest teacher at the school was making space for the right perspective, yet there were many layers to the problem that created my perspective.

For starters, short people can be invisible to others, both intentionally and unintentionally. Students had already been confusing me with other students, and occasionally I got pushed aside in the packed hallways. It reminded me of my own high school days.

Back then, I often been the last one selected for dodgeball teams in gym class. It wasn't fair, and all excuses were shallow—yet this had motivated me to learn how to throw balls *and* hit targets. Once my peers knew I could do that, I earned my place. Then, it didn't take them long to find out I was a smaller, faster target, which made me harder to hit.

In the end, I became a valuable player *because* I was short!

That was how I kept perspective then, but now?

I am still short, but life is short too! I need to make more of the whole package of me.

Besides, the problem was familiar.

To solve it, I needed laughter and a healthy dose of self-worth.

I'm not sure exactly when it occurred to me, but somehow, I came to know for myself that good examples of self-acceptance helped the students develop the inner leverage of new perspectives—the tools they needed to push against flawed assumptions about autism and to recognize what was in their control.

To just exist and be unseen, to avoid responding to the incorrect and inaccurate assumptions of others, and to give in to pressure—these will always be the *easier wrong*.

The *harder right* is always a small step that shows great faith.

My authority could no longer be undermined by my height. I had the power to resolve any outstanding anxieties about being small in a big world—and to confidently command attention and earn respect regardless of my height—and to have a little fun while I was at it.

One day in English class, a student named Riley had been in and out of his seat for every reason under the sun. He reminded me of an aspen leaf that quaked at the slightest breeze, unable to be still, so long as there was reason to move. By the end of the class period, Riley was all but bouncing out of his seat!

I, on the other hand, was avoiding having to get on his case about being still and working hard. It didn't seem necessary since class was almost over, and I *had* to get some things done at my desk before the next class. As the clock ticked, I was so focused I hardly noticed when my teaching counterpart left the classroom without warning. When I finally glanced up to check on things, I concluded she had likely dipped out for the bathroom and was about to go back to my work when Riley got up to do a little song and dance by the door.

"Oh-oh yeah! There are no teachers in the classroom! We-ee are free-ee!"

He was so distracted that I was able to sneak up behind him to say, "Uh, hey there, Riley. You celebrate too soon! I'm still here and not going anywhere."

He whipped around and said nothing, but his glare spoke volumes of disappointment. I tried not to laugh at his embarrassed expression as he sat back down. At least I wouldn't laugh until he did. At least, I hoped he would see it as funny—eventually.

For the remaining three minutes of class, he was as still as a leopard on the hunt, ready to explode but nonetheless under perfect self-control.

It felt more important to be impressed by this than to worry about why he had forgotten me or had thought I was a student instead of a teacher. Instead, I focused on the gift he had given me. Under the right circumstances, my height and the fact that I didn't stand out in a crowd would allow me to wield the power of quietly stepping into the right place at the right time. With or without words, I could impress upon someone that I was not to be missed or undervalued. Perhaps I could use it to help resolve problems with little more than my unexpected presence.

Since then, I have learned much from the use of this kind of authority. When responses have been hilarious or had exactly the desired effect, I've been grateful. However, in certain situations, showing up without warning seems harder on people than intended. It has become clear to me that our traits and our quirks might create unique approaches that work for us, but aren't always the right approaches for every occasion or every person.

Over time, I've been learning how to wrap authority into my element of surprise, and to recognize when it might be a gift to be invisible. It's clear that becoming intentional with my talents and techniques will no doubt require years of sensitivity, practice, patience, wisdom, and a lot of divine assistance.

Another way to navigate what we can't control in life is to let go, own the truth, and let the pieces fall where they may.

I remember the day a high school student in a plaid shirt halted his trip down the hall just to grin at me on his way to class. He was just standing there, no more than two feet away, trying to make sense of what he was seeing, so I said hello and waited until he spoke.

"Uh—hi, Miss D. It's, uh, really weird that I'm taller than you!"

I grinned. *You don't know the half of it, my good man.*

I was tempted to speak my thought, but instead I said, "Really? Well, I agree—or, another way to look at it is … maybe it's weird that I'm so short!"

The hallway around us was crowded, but it still came as a surprise when another student decided to use our two feet of space and literally walked through the middle of the conversation.

Hearing our exchange, he stopped to turn around and add, "It's weird that … I have a face!"

He delivered the word *face* like a punchline before he moved along down the hall.

All I could think was, *Is it?*

I raised my eyebrows toward the student in the plaid shirt, but he just shrugged his shoulders and went to class.

If it mattered, we'd all have been created to be beautiful, tall, and rich. But we weren't. Instead, we were all made with faces, and we look like God. Each face represents a unique life from which a story is growing. The world might perceive some individual differences as *weird*, but to God, such differences are intentional and normal, and some are simply mortal. So, enjoying weirdness and looking at differences through God's eyes is a sure way to know what the *worth* of every soul is to God.

Speaking of being rich and knowing what people are worth, there came a day when I was helping the social studies class learn about retirement, investments, and bequests—or rather, how to plan where all their worldly goods go when they die.

THE ADVENTURE OF PERSPECTIVE AND REALITY

After describing how finances work and that retirement should be respected and prepared for by saving money, the teacher said, "You will want to tell many people where all your money is."

She meant loved ones and money managers, of course, but one of our more unsuspecting young ladies in the class cut in with, "Mini people? We should tell mini people, like Miss D?"

Before the teacher expressed that that had not been her implication at all, I took advantage of assuring the kids that this was a great idea!

"Yes, that's quite okay with me. I intend to live forever and would definitely like to know where all your money is when you die. After all, living forever is going to be very expensive."

I then bestowed a wide but innocent grin upon the class that was staring at me.

"What? Mini people are cool. They deserve your money. Especially me, for dealing with you guys every day!"

I could see they weren't convinced, so I gave in.

"Fine, I know what you're thinking—of course, you should give your money to your future children! That's fine with me, they are mini people too, or at least will start out to be. And if you do, no worries—I'll make sure they know who I am when they grow up. Remember, I'm living forever!"

A whole classroom of eyes rolled, and to this day, I am fairly certain not one of those children in the class will tell any mini people such as myself where their money is.

And all jokes aside, I wouldn't want it any other way.

Not long after the first year at the school, I found myself on more than one occasion almost tripping over children who were standing behind me. They would stand so close sometimes that if they had been a saguaro cactus, my shoulder would not be the only thing wearing prickles after each encounter!

If I discovered them, they'd give me strange looks and say things like, "Not today."

Then they would disappear without saying a word—until the next time they had a chance to drop by. Some students came weekly, others monthly. None of it made sense to me.

So, I asked one of those kids what the purpose was, and he said to see if he was "taller than Miss D yet!"

Eventually, I realized many of them were middle school students who I had never met, who didn't even know my name. Instead, I had been pointed out by their peers who called me the "measuring stick."

I felt a bit disadvantaged. *Why did so many kids look to me as just a "measuring stick"?*

At first, I saw this as a distraction from learning, so I attempted to dissuade the behavior, trying things like wearing two-to-three-inch heels and keeping my back to the wall. Well—walls only went to so many places and in so few directions, and it sounds strange, but for the first time in my life, I started getting frowns when I wore heels. In fact, it appears they brought me a bit of a bad name because they made the students feel shorter without notice. See, I was an adult—I wasn't supposed to be growing. They were!

So, my next question to find an answer to was, *Why me?*

I had the reputation of being kind and calm—and was super unlikely to snap at them for being treated like measuring tape. So, that was one possible reason.

I also knew children, especially middle school children, needed to know and discover things about themselves. That had to be why they looked at passing me up like a rite of passage.

And then I got it—a taller, possibly still-growing, high school student would make a poor choice for a measuring stick. So, if a short, non-growing adult teacher was available, she would provide a far better and more accurate long-term target—that is, over the course of a school year.

Once I understood that this seemingly bizarre situation was not about growth competitions or winning the genetic lottery, but rather the individual's growth upward, I became a big fan. There was even a deeper part of me that almost cherished their progress.

Eventually, like a drop of intelligence in my bucket of social awareness, it occurred to me that the kids, largely without knowing it, were operating along a simple truth: they ALL stood a good chance of passing *me* in height. In that way, I was a unifying anchor, not a dividing line. These young people felt the burden of being excluded from so many other things in life, and I came to see it meant a lot to them to be included in the "taller than Miss D" club.

I learned *not* to say things like, "Well, young one, I hate to tell you that getting taller than me might not be so much of an accomplishment."

Instead, I would be more jovial, saying, "Anyone who can be taller than me, should be taller than me, if at all physically possible."

Or, "After you're done with me as your measuring stick, *you* are your best measuring stick!"

If they gave me a curious look in response to that line, I would follow it with, "Not just for measuring your height, but your light. I bet you'll get brighter every day if you try hard to be the best person you can be!"

Then they would smile at my vote of confidence regarding the light of their intelligence, and I'd have the pleasure of witnessing their faces glow.

In time, it seemed like I was known by the nickname The Measuring Stick by every middle school class—or at least all of the school's population that was still shorter than me.

Most of the time, nicknames come from a good place.

Sometimes we are lucky and have a favorite person who gives us a favorite pet name. The one I'd had in high school—Little One—had come from my favorite high school librarian. Others, I believed, were based on my height as well as foods I liked—or so I thought! But of all the nicknames I have ever received in my life, living up to the role and title of The Measuring Stick seemed to be the most important one of all. I think this was because it mattered and created fun for so many of my favorite people. It also led to several very comical occasions.

For example, one day Cordon, a very tall male student, was crawling along the floor at the back of the room beside the teachers' desks. I couldn't tell if he had lost something because he wasn't looking at the floor with any kind of haste. He just kept looking around, all over the place. I was sitting at my desk, entertained by the weirdness unfolding in front of me, but when Cordon moved into Mr. Dixon's line of vision, the strange movements caught the teacher's eye.

"Cordon, what are you doing?"

Cordon responded with, "Seeing things from Miss D's perspective."

My mouth dropped open. *Uh, I'm right here! Literally a low blow, dude!*

Mr. Dixon looked at Cordon, then he looked at me with raised eyebrows, as if asking if I had inspired this behavior. I just shrugged and shook my head. I was just as lost as he was. Best case scenario, Cordon thought I could see things no one else saw. If so, I couldn't complain, but I also wasn't going to get involved if I didn't really understand what was really going on either.

I looked down at Cordon and up at Mr. Dixon again, hoping something to say would come to mind. Finally, I settled on my amusement and spoke slowly for emphasis, as though I had all the time in the world. "Well, Mr. Dixon, all I can say is, I respect Cordon for trying to see things from others' perspectives—even if it gets him down."

Hearing this exchange, Cordon's position on the floor shifted.

"It's not a bad view, although it does cause one to look up quite a lot."

Mr. Dixon raised his eyebrows and teased, "I can tell you one thing you need to look up right now!"

He meant Cordon's research assignment, of course, but I locked eyes with Cordon and said, "It turns out looking up is quite important in this life, wouldn't you say?"

I knew we all shared the same faith, so the look confirmed two things—first, that I was genuinely aware of the good-natured joke on behalf of

Cordon, and second, our mutual awareness of how important looking up to God in prayer was to navigating life's adventure.

Afterwards, as I pondered a bit on Cordon's moment, I realized he had taught me a new angle on my perspective—encouragement to *look up* is great counsel for anyone dealing with a reality not of their choosing.

All my life, looking up to people and things was part of my everyday experiences, in more ways than one. I had looked up to others to reach things I couldn't. I had looked up to those I admired. I looked up to loved ones for help and guidance, and I had looked up to mountains and seen potential, a future, hope, and personal power. I had also looked up to God for wisdom and healing.

Being small had built layers of resiliency that were strengthened because of how I was looking up. I could teach children to change perspective and believe they were important because of how I was looking up. The truth is, at any altitude within every lifescape, we might be enjoying the view but still need to look up to know where we are, and no matter how down we might feel, it is hard to feel lost when one is looking up to God.

I rarely had to work outside of normal business hours.

But when I did, it was for special events, like the student dances on the weekends.

Sometimes I planned the dance; other times I helped monitor hallways or classrooms. At one of the dances, my job was to stand beside the front door and keep the kids from any tomfoolery and make the darkness outside less inviting than the light and music within.

It sounds like a very simple job, however, according to Mr. Dixon and some of the students, I still wasn't very good at being intimidating.

I was determined that I could figure it out—eventually.

THE ALTITUDES OF ACCEPTANCE

I took advantage of the opportunity and experimented with various faces and postures, crossing my arms, raising my head, and standing straight and tall. One of the high school students was resting on a seat in the lobby. I didn't know he'd been watching me when he said, "Miss D, it's like you are Gandalf and doing the 'You shall not pass!' stance, except you don't have a stick!"

I looked over at him and stood as tall as I could, all five feet of me—without heels as I was now prone to be. With my chin stuck out in the air, I said, "I don't need a stick. Don't you know? I *am* the stick!"

Giggles erupted from the other students and teachers standing by, along with a sharp *harrumph* from Mr. Dixon who stood just inside the gym doors, as if he was trying to hide a laugh. How he heard the conversation above the sound of the cha-cha slide, I will never know!

More importantly, there seemed to be a real power in what had just happened!

The way I had just owned my nickname seemed to have built a respectable yet invisible fence in an instant. As students continued going in and out of the gym throughout the evening, they'd talk about what I'd said and laugh. As long as I was standing there, no one showed any desire to make an escape.

I didn't even have to try to look intimidating.

A sense of wonder sparked. The moment had created some kind of mutual understanding!

I had heard their stories of attending public schools prior to their days at our charter school. Those schools were not well-equipped to take on the needs of children with autism, and they had often been eschewed for various neurodivergent qualities, such as their social incapacities, emotional disparities, sensory peculiarities, mental health challenges, and so on.

I could relate.

I was aware of my limits, and the things I might never get to be because of the reality of being short. I couldn't become a professional ballroom dancer in college because of my height, and I knew the students knew they were not likely to not have the same choices or opportunities in life as children who were "taller" than they were in the neurotypical sense.

It would be very hard to face. But at least they all had a face!

And they were facing it together. At least for now.

My height has never been in my control, but how I lived with being small was always completely within my control. Similarly, the students had not chosen to have autism, yet they had a choice in how they lived their lives. This seems like such a tiny truth, but it can go a long way.

Apparently, these young people didn't need measuring sticks for the reasons they thought they did. In my opinion, the only measuring stick they needed was the one that said they were better than they were yesterday. They had a choice—they could develop perspectives based on the world that did not understand them, or they could learn to see their own worth and have faith that their differences were also their gifts.

Not long after that evening at the dance, I was helping in the math classroom when Mr. Dixon was demonstrating how to find the mathematical area of shapes. His diligence in getting the students to talk and participate in the lesson was impressive, but it wasn't working.

So far, he had succeeded in getting the students to understand the different parts of the equations, and the students understood the length of the rectangle was critical. However, they weren't getting the rest.

Finally, Mr. Dixon decided a physical demonstration was needed beyond what the board could provide, so he called upon a student, Roger, to stand.

Moving his arms in the direction of Roger, he asked, "Now, class, what do you call the measurement from Roger's head to his feet?"

Only silence followed, but it seemed deafening to me.

THE ALTITUDES OF ACCEPTANCE

I was always looking for opportunities to encourage learning and participation, and this tough crowd needed to be primed and ready for math language.

So, I said, "I know, it's his shortness!" I kind of called this method of teaching "target practice." I aimed at the wrong target on purpose, hoping the students would feel inclined to help me find the right one.

Mr. Dixon gave me one of his scrutinizing stares, telling me he had no idea what I meant. Then, as my brain raced to find another way to say something helpful, he turned to acknowledge Cole, the only student who had raised his hand.

"Whatever, Miss D, you're crazy! It's his height!" Right, Mr. Dixon?

The class speaks!

I didn't care so much about what he said or how he said it. Someone in the class was finally participating! But then I saw Mr. Dixon's eyes twinkle—a signal of mischief. I began to cringe a little as he placed a hand on Roger's shoulder to invite him to take his seat.

Then, he responded to Cole—but his eyes were on me!

"Yes, that's right, I am talking about Roger's height. Shortness is only how we measure … "

He paused for just a second and gave me a sly grin. "… Miss. D."

I had unknowingly set a trap for myself, and clever Mr. Dixon had walked me right into it.

I giggled. At this point, what could I do but agree and play along? "Uh … go ahead, why not? Being short means I'm simply more than eyes can see."

Despite the unforeseen twist in outcomes, I sensed I had done my job right. Whether due to my words or my mere physical existence, these students would never forget what *height* was as long as I was around to remind them what *shortness* was.

THE ADVENTURE OF PERSPECTIVE AND REALITY

In the years since working at the school, the adventures of perspective and reality have continued, and I have learned, as Shakespeare so aptly put it, that there are more things in heaven and earth than can be dreamt of in one's own philosophies.

I think that means few things are impossible, and many things are limited only by our ability to conceive of them. It's difficult to believe more than what we see, or to see our own limits. We allow real evidence to change our perspectives only when necessary. The world around us, and even our loved ones, offers a lot of options, opposition, and opinions when it comes to challenging our perspectives or creating new realities for ourselves.

All too often, getting lost in advice is easy and making decisions is hard.

Then, the perfectionist in all of us is found, drowning in a bucket of hope.

However, God has his way of reaching in, lifting us up, wringing us out, and hanging us to dry on the line of trust. When we feel like we are hanging on the line, we feel precarious. It's possible to fall off or back in, but the only real solution is to recognize that God is in control. Then, if we choose to align our perspectives with him, he'll help us improve our realities and find a more solid foundation. Being willing to go through this process with God is the best way to get cleaned up inside—where it counts. That's the way God works.

This is the nature of God's truth.

With our limited perspectives and realities, we live as though we are all measuring sticks. However, we are never just the measuring stick or the measured. As we assess our circumstances, we find it necessary to constantly sort through our collection of perspectives to decide what about other people and our experiences matters most. Along the way, we fear learning that our reality is incomplete, that this time we might have to accept we are living in an imperfect world.

Knowing that we are all the same, and yet we are all different. Feeling how deeply we want to fit in but also stand out. These concepts tell us we don't really know what normal is, or if normal really matters. Sometimes, we

THE ALTITUDES OF ACCEPTANCE

aren't sure if we want to be normal—if such a thing is truly attainable. We cherish our discoveries of like-minded people, but we also need those who think differently than we do.

Looking at the world and other people only through our individual perspectives is like walking into an apartment built for tall people with the expectations of a short person. The disappointment might feel real at first, yet if you pay attention, you sense discomfort. Your reality is limited by what you do not know or have never experienced, but that doesn't mean you have to live there, in that new reality. It's okay to uncover a reality that is not meant for you. In fact, it's wise to make peace with your realities, help others make peace with theirs, and watch out for the moments when realities are on a collision course with each other.

This happens all the time within the human dimensions of government, religion, and science. These affect all of us in one way or another, and for me, they are an important application of how God intended for us to exchange our perspectives and share our realities. We are meant to exchange perspectives with others and learn to improve how we manage reality—the things in our control as well as beyond our control. I also believe everyone holds a perspective that can help bring any reality a little closer to God's truth.

In fact, the rush to find answers and solutions means we are still working to understand God's truth. The better we become at comprehending our own perspectives and realities, the more we can contribute to the collective complex issues and join in the adventure on the world stage. Looking at the world with God's truth, because of who we are and who we want to be, helps us appreciate other people and measure ourselves only against ourselves—not others. We realize that people and their perspectives are the hardest and best parts of life's adventure.

If you look closer throughout your lifescapes, you'll see that God created many pathways through which you discovered, as I have, the hardships and perks of being *mini*, whether that is because you are also short, or because you have ever felt small in a big world. You'll also be able to identify the hardships and benefits that come from being you among the *many*.

THE ADVENTURE OF PERSPECTIVE AND REALITY

However, while all people have gifts and strengths, no one has all the gifts or all the strengths. We all have limiting perspectives and tainted realities. In fact, the same people we love and admire for their experiences, wisdom, and intelligence have, at times, been constrained by imperfection, misinterpretations, or mistakes—even if we can't believe it. We need other people, and other people need us, but we learn things *from* some people and other things *because* of other people. The best part is, we may not always align with other people, but once we align with God, he'll guide the adventure of growing through our perspectives and realities.

There is a personal power in each of us, an illuminating gift that exists because of who we are to him. As we learn to recognize that power, we can come to know what is true and will bring us closer to God. It also lets us know what is not true and cannot bring us happiness. Listening and learning from that power, whether we follow it or not, is the real adventure of navigating our perspectives and realities.

There's nothing wrong with stretching a little higher to turn on the light, yet if we are short, God doesn't expect us to choose a higher light fixture or to live with one. God wants us to learn, but he doesn't solve our short problems with a giant's apartment or a home full of stepladders. He knows it doesn't make sense to solve our problems by making it harder to turn on the light.

Instead, he applies his truth to our individual circumstances in a way that we will understand. It's his way of helping us create the reality he most wants for us, a reality that says the unchosen experiences that kept us down before, and even the ones that made us stretch up on our tiptoes, can be experienced and shared with others as a gift instead of an obstacle.

CHAPTER 11

TRUST THE PATH

Considering how God shines light into our darkness and helps us gain new perspectives takes me back to a college adventure some years before starting work at the school.

During one summer of my undergraduate degree, I worked as a camp counselor in southern Utah at a ranch resort near Zion National Park. It was late June, and my birthday was coming up that weekend, as well as the completion of a full lunar cycle. Since the full moon aligned with my birthday, it seemed like nature's gift! I was aching to celebrate with an adventure, but I was a new employee and wasn't sure what to do! I had been canyoneering, hiking, and riding horses with other staff every chance I got, but I was still hesitant to plan my own adventures in a new place.

When I wasn't working, I was observing and enjoying the people around me. That Tuesday, I ate lunch with Sam and Serena, a married couple who worked at the ranch resort. They exemplified exactly what I hoped might be my future love story. The two were outdoorsy, spiritually secure, and each other's favorite companions. They seemed to be always on the go and often brought a certain aura of inspiration and life experience to those they shared their time with.

Our conversations were always animated with stories of adventure, but that day, we had talked only about the goings-on at the ranch and the recent fires all around us. That was different, but it wasn't until a lull in the conversation that I caught a certain knowing glance between them.

I leaned forward. "I saw that! You're thinking of something cool to do. Come on, tell me!"

"Well—" Serena grinned. "Would you like to do something wild but wonderful with us?"

"Let's see," I said with pretend contemplation, tapping my finger to my chin, "Um—yes, of course!" We all chuckled before I continued, "The mountains and canyons and moon have been calling me, and I haven't organized anything yet, so what's your plan?"

"That's exactly what we feel too with the moon being full this weekend. Have you ever hiked Angel's Landing in Zion National Park?"

"Not to my knowledge, but I know it's famous. I don't know the park as well as you, but I trust you. I'm totally up for going. So, when are we doing this, and is anyone else coming?"

"Friday night and everyone we've talked to about it, so"—Serena glanced up as she did some brief calculating—"about ten people so far."

"Wow, it's definitely not just me who knows how cool you guys are, and for the record I think hiking any trail under a full moon will be an out-of-this-world experience!"

"You said it!" said Serena.

"We can hardly wait!" Sam added, "Make sure to bring good hiking shoes. It gets steep."

"No worries. My shoes and I can handle steep."

"Also, it's your birthday this weekend, right?"

"Yes, Saturday."

"Then we'll make sure you live to see it."

Wait a minute ... huh?

The puzzle in their words froze me to my seat. They grinned, wordlessly putting their food containers away as they skedaddled back to work. A slight backwards glance from Serena held a mischievous glow, making me wonder what I was getting myself into.

THE ALTITUDES OF ACCEPTANCE

Awesome! A promise of intense adventure without certain death—something I never knew I always wanted for my birthday!

With that thought in mind, I giggled to myself. There was limited computer access and internet at the ranch, so I hadn't taken the time yet to research the trails in the area, but I knew my coworkers and I understood wilderness safety. It was easy to believe any of our adventures would be well organized and worth the risk. Over the next few days, however, I began to hear more and more of my coworkers talk about what was ahead, saying things about how this hike was a rite of passage, that people had died on the hike, and that it wasn't for the faint of heart.

Well, now Serena's words made sense. But I wasn't at all afraid—despite this news, I got another message through the grapevine: This hike was awesome, and people lived to tell the tale.

Friday night at about 8:30 p.m., just as darkness enveloped the resort, we piled into the designated adventure vans and drove into the park. It appeared to be a ghost town since so few tourists engaged in nocturnal hiking. All the world seemed so still along our way, except for our giggles and conversation, which increased as our group absorbed the spike of adrenaline and anticipation!

As we disembarked, bushes and rocks high on the canyon walls began to be more discernable. The long-awaited glowing orb had not yet begun its path across the sky, but in the horizon beyond the cliffs, one could see it was daring the darkness to defy it.

"Watch out for bats!" someone offered. "We like bats. They eat all the mosquitoes!"

"Whatever. I think I'll just watch out for the mosquitoes …"

"What about bears?"

"What about 'em? They aren't going to be on our tails, not with all of us together."

"As reassuring as that may be—don't cougars hunt this late at night?"

"Yeah—they're stealthy but their eyes will reflect from your headlamps in the darkness!"

"Ugh. That sounds like a chilly experience, to be close enough to see a big cat's eyes!"

"Cats don't attack groups either, so if we stick together, we'll be fine."

"Yeah, let's not have anyone get lost or eaten tonight."

"Does anyone know how to tell the difference between glowing animal eyes?"

A hush fell across the group as our shared knowledge deficiency sank in.

We had started hiking, and since the likelihood of running into wild animals on a popular trail was low, I decided we could do without the worry! It was time to change the subject and ask a question. "Will the trail be completely concrete all the way up?"

Sam said, "Just the first mile or so, to help control erosion. Up higher, it's sand and rock."

Ah, right. That makes sense, but it also makes the popular trail seem less "wild".

As we continued, the concrete path was easy to follow in the dark, so I kept my light off. Still, the bouncing shadows from everyone's lights seemed bothersome to my night vision, so I hung back a bit so I could walk with fewer shadows and more moonlight—never too far from the group. Soon, I noticed another friend doing the same.

"Are you okay walking in the dark?" I asked.

She nodded. "Yeah, I actually prefer it."

"Me too. Want to walk together?"

In companionable silence, we enjoyed the glow of the moon, the chatter of our friends ahead of us, and the feel of the path beneath our feet. Soon, the concrete ended, and my feet responded as the terrain upped a notch in difficulty. When the ground changed from rocks to sand it was like walking along an ocean where our shins and ankles burned more and more with each step. Some people slowed down while others, more adapted to the terrain, sped up. My friend and I were among those who were moving quickly, and we reached the cliffside just as the moon rose, encouraging the strange gray shadows and anything available to reflect its light.

THE ALTITUDES OF ACCEPTANCE

Our stretch of sand was ending, and the slabs of rock were beginning. Despite the rock walls ahead of us, headlamps returned to backpacks as the lunar spotlight spilled across the sand, creating a shimmering sea of glitter.

Pointing this out to my friend, I asked, "Are you seeing this? It's gorgeous!"

"Wow! Also, how are we able to see everything so well with just moonlight?"

I saw her point. Looking around, every leaf and tree trunk was shadowy, but distinguishable. Only moments ago, everything had been black, but I now could see every rock and branch I needed to step on—or avoid.

As I gazed upward, I noticed some large-link chains that had been bolted to the rock wall in a few places to provide support for hikers. Each link was cast iron or steel, at least the size of my hand if not bigger. They seemed stable and helpful, but even they bespoke danger. Along each ledge, one wrong step could lead to a steep drop with a short stop and a painful end.

Hand over hand, I took step after steep step, while gradually I sensed the presence of a huge void to my left—and my right. I could see directly in front of me, and a little to the sides, but I could not see the vast open spaces below in the deep darkness that existed just past where the moonlight reached. Not being able to see everything below us felt intriguing as well as terrifying.

How many people had fallen from this cliff trail and died upon impact?

I had heard about the chains, but I had never asked the question.

Why not? Because I didn't think about dying when I thought of adventure.

Maybe I should! If only to learn from the mistakes of others and be more prepared.

These thoughts were disturbing but understandable. I hoped such events were rare. Besides, no statistical values could reveal the key cause of such events. There were accidents, and then there were irresponsible decisions, and I wasn't irresponsible. I had simply long since accepted that being a life-long adventurer came with risks, and I was now operating accordingly. I was confident in my safety and security as assured through my skill and comfort level. I didn't feel the need to give in to fear or shrink away from the challenge of this rare experience.

I turned my focus toward the beauty of the moon's growing celestial presence. Leaving the darkness behind and climbing toward that light felt super motivating. I found that I didn't have to see my feet to know what they were doing, and the moonlight pierced the shadows enough so that I could see where my hands needed to go as I climbed. Finding this path wasn't about being able to see clearly as much as it was about being able to use the light that was already given.

Step after step, we carried on with our climb. Brief pauses at the steep parts gave way to laughter as several people nearly pinched their thumbs in the chains. Finally, the group reached the top. One by one, the demeanor shifted away from slightly anxious to being in awe of the diminishing starlight and how the luminous quality of the moon allowed us to see the far sides of the canyon.

I noted there still appeared to be nothing but darkness below.

The narrow ledge of Angel's Landing was exactly as I imagined it. Its length glowed red and gold in the moonlight, keeping the rocky edges dark and invisible. The long space gave me the surreal sense that I was walking along a runway that floated above the rest of the world.

Someone in our group started talking about how different the trail and canyon were in daylight, and then another person mentioned how you could see straight down into the canyons as though you were flying like a bird!

A shiver ran down my spine all the way to my toes. *The walls are that steep? With all the altitude we'd achieved, no wonder we now could see depth that was hardly penetrated by light.*

I talked about how I had never hiked Angel's Landing in the daytime, but now that I had hiked it at night, under the light of a full moon—I was convinced this was the best way to do it!

Many of us agreed that this was the highlight of our awesome summer.

Looking back, it's a little cheesy to say, but the real *high* light was the moon, and the highest light was God. I'm sure he was there with us. After all, this was Angel's Landing. If he wasn't here, then certainly our guardian angels were!

We all agreed to be very still and turn off our lights for a minute. I sat down, thinking I might fall into the darkness if I didn't, but I also wanted to think and look at the incredible moon. Of all the views in all the world, I had walked through the darkness and into the light of this one.

My meditation faded as someone stood and climbed to the top of a bulbous stack of rocks and struck a pose. That's when we all realized the top of the small rocky outcropping was the actual highest point of the cliff—and that we could have our own photoshoot against the moon!

When my turn came, I found my footing on the tip-top of the rock bulb, bent over, and grabbed my ankle behind me with one hand. I reached the other hand forward, extended my body, and balanced on one leg, fully outstretched like an ice skater. This was a yoga pose, called "the dancer," and as someone took the picture, I turned my head upward into one confident smile.

For just a moment, the moon seemed to brighten, and I felt I was on top of the world.

As I look back on this hike, I wonder how awesome it might have been to find the right romance under the light of a full moon. However, even in those early days of single adulthood and dating, I knew I didn't want a short summer fling—I sought a more real and long-lasting romance!

I should note, however, that I did pursue a love affair for the rest of my life with the moon. After the awesome night hike, I was hooked! As often as I could, I intentionally planned and scheduled hikes, backpacking adventures, and camping trips to happen when the moon was full.

I also researched as much as I could about the moon and learned academic and spiritual things I've valued ever since. For example, the symbol of the moon not only represented the cycle of renewal, but it also pointed to the need for change. In fact, according to W. Jeffrey Marsh (*The Gift of the Atonement*), Roman lunar calendars indicate that the Atonement of Jesus Christ happened underneath a full moon, and this was the night the Savior spent in Gethsemane, praying and pleading with God over the cost of our sins.[4] The Savior's sacrifice made moonlight seem even more special. The light of the full moon in darkness became a monthly reminder for me to stay close to God and be willing to renew my efforts to change, accept, and even appreciate what he was doing with my life—even when I couldn't see or understand.

Looking back, I can appreciate how this deeper realization just wouldn't have been the same experience if I had been super-absorbed in a love story. I wouldn't have taken the time to research and gain the understanding of how God's love and the moon are metaphorically connected, and I wouldn't have had so much interest in helping my friends navigate romance that summer either. It was fun to help with matchmaking and learn about love from a distance.

As it happened, I had no way of knowing how those love lessons would bring new insights into the years I spent working at the high school.

Everywhere around me, young love blossomed.

The young people were discovering each other. Some tiny sparks grew into emotional stirrings. A few of those became simple, sweet romances, while others led to dramatic or even occasionally traumatic love stories. I only got involved when asked since there were still times when it came to love that I felt like I knew nothing. However, helping the young people navigate this part of their lives helped me realize just how much we all have in common when it comes to love.

THE ALTITUDES OF ACCEPTANCE

Young, handsome Brody had a great smile, dark hair, blue eyes, and was a true high school gentleman, always helping the teachers and students. He seemed totally at ease with himself, and his good behavior and amiable personality earned him the admiration of the whole school. In fact, he was so rarely without the capacity to joke in a positive, cheerful manner that it really bothered me one day to see him almost crying.

"Brody, what's going on?"

His voice seemed lost and trapped in the tears he was trying to hold back.

"Ah, Miss D. Something happened with Rosie today. We're not dating anymore but I still really like her. I was sitting here thinking about my dad too—he gives great advice."

Behind his sarcasm, there was a hint of irony. *No teen wants to admit their dad was right!*

"I'm so sorry! Why did you decide to break up? Rosie's also been looking sad, and I noticed you weren't together at lunch. For what it's worth, I thought you two were a good couple."

"Well, yeah, we were—but it's a good thing we broke up—at least for now."

"Why do you say that? You're really okay with breaking up?"

He shrugged, then said. "Well, it's like my dad said—boys like what they see, and girls like what they hear. So, boys lie and girls wear makeup."

At first that line didn't make any sense to me. Neither student was a liar, and I couldn't remember when Rosie last wore makeup, let alone if there had been a time when she'd come to school every day wearing makeup. So … what then?

"So—you're saying, you lied, and she started wearing makeup?"

"Oh, no, sorry—we just weren't real with each other. I didn't mean to lie to her, and she didn't mean to put on a face. Things got so … weird. It happened without us even thinking about it."

"Is the word you're going for *estranged*?"

"Uh, yes, that's right, estranged. We haven't been dating very long, but we just … stopped connecting. She said she felt super self-conscious. It made her worry too much, and she got mad when she was worried because she felt like she couldn't be herself. Then she started blaming me for stuff without talking about it. So she acted differently toward me. Which threw me off because I couldn't tell her what was on my mind anymore. I didn't like that, but I still liked her, so I started saying things she wanted to hear instead of real conversation. When we finally talked about it, we decided we didn't know how to act in relationships, and we didn't want to hurt each other."

He sighed. "So, we decided to stick to being just friends for now. I mean, we can still do things together since we still like each other, but we don't want to be serious."

"Oh. So, what you're getting at is, women like words and want to hear nice things, but men might be more prone to lying with words, curtailing truth to some degree, and avoiding talking about the truth. Also, women try to protect themselves by putting on a face, or cover up the truth about their experience regardless of how it made them feel, instead of facing up to it?"

"Yeah, that's about right. Sad story, but kind of common—don't you think? Like a movie?"

"No kidding. Brody, I hope you know that was a hard choice. In fact, what you just said is one of the most mature things I've ever heard."

"Really, Miss D?" His eyes lit up for a moment.

"Really. It's hard at any age to know whether to call it quits. But it can be healthy to do so."

"Then why am I still sitting here all alone feeling terrible?"

"Healthy, but not always happy. Breaking up is sad and hard even if it's right. But, if ending the relationship was the right thing to do, you will feel better eventually."

I told him a few things from my own experience, about how lying is strangely easy to do in romance. It can be either intentional or unintentional. Lies happen when people don't communicate where they stand when things matter, about how they really feel or the impact of certain behaviors, or by neglecting to share their real opinion about something. Any kind of lying often causes more pain when it snowballs out of control, and lying can prevent hurt in the short term, but it usually hurts a relationship in the long term—if the truth is never spoken.

"Brody, you're a good person, and I think it's good you feel uncomfortable about any lie. It's hard to face mistakes we don't know we were making in the moment. Afterwards, all you can do is learn from it and simply work toward doing the right thing next time."

"Oh. Ah ... okay. Thank you, Miss D." His eyes still hadn't regained that confident twinkle, so I expected he still had some emotional processing to do. Feeling some momentum, I offered him a smile and asked if he had time for a few more thoughts.

His head nodded from side to side as if considering the idea. "Sure, it's still lunchtime."

"Okay—so, you think of lying as not telling the truth or withholding truth, right?"

"Uh, yeah."

"Well, a couple of summers ago, there were a lot of romances happening at the camp where I worked. Sometimes those relationships worked out well, and sometimes they didn't. Even when I thought they were well-matched, some couples dissolved, so I got curious. I noticed the ones that didn't work out got complicated because of what they were *not* finding out about each other, or what they were holding back or hiding. With what you said today, I think their breakups might have often been for the same reasons yours happened. Clarity and candor matter. Maybe the most successful relationships have certain things said or done between the two people."

Brody cocked his head in thought. "Yeah, it doesn't work to not share the truth."

I smiled. "Yeah, so it seems. Here's my idea for why men like what they see and women like what they hear. It's rooted in what drives them—you know, biologically. Both women and men seek closeness, but women reason with emotions and are driven by what they feel, while men reason with facts and are driven by what they see."

In retrospect, I would have added, "Women feel secure emotionally when words align with actions, and men appreciate and seek security in what they see or sense before seeking emotional intimacy." But I hadn't learned that lesson for myself quite yet!

In the moment, Brody responded, "Yeah, I can see that."

"So, at camp, there seemed to be a trend in these relationships—they both wanted something real, but men held truth back from the women because they didn't feel validated, and the women 'put on a fake face' because of what they thought the men wanted. Then, lacking mutual authenticity, neither got what they wanted."

"Hmm. I just realized something, Miss D."

"What's that?"

"People lie to each other to avoid dealing with the truth about how they are feeling, so maybe we lie because we don't know the truth and don't want others to find out. So, we need to know it's okay not to know the answers all the time."

I stayed silent for a moment, thinking, then tilted my head as I spoke.

"Yep. It's not easy to be vulnerable. To expose our emotions and say what we know and don't know. But struggling with emotions and being honest is a good part of a good relationship. We need to be vulnerable without losing ourselves or our standards. But I think we are all capable of lies, and I wish we were less good at justifying them and better at discussing painful truths."

He was nodding, so I asked, "How do you think relationships would change if we more wisely shared the truth and avoided any type of lies?"

Brody looked down and around, then met my eyes with a combination of scrutiny and resolution. "I think a lot of relationships would still end, because the truth can hurt and change things. Like with me and Rosie. But many relationships would become better, because the truth can make things right."

THE ALTITUDES OF ACCEPTANCE

"I agree. And you found out the hard way that at some point we must accept the truth and become alert to effects of our behaviors."

"Yeah—it seems like any type of dishonesty can affect anything we do."

"Sure thing. And you can take the truths you learn into your next relationship. Whether it's with Rosie or another girl, you have a new perspective now. I think you're on the right path, Brody. It's rocky but it'll all work out."

The bell rang. "Speaking of work," I said, and then stood up.

"Yeah, one way or another, Miss D, I think it will."

He gathered his backpack and waved a goodbye.

Was it just me, or did lunch feel a lot longer than thirty minutes!

"Miss Deanna."

Carter's desk was not far from mine, and as I looked up, I took in the scene. Carter's bright eyes were earnestly on me, but all I saw was his phone on his desk—it was free time, but that meant he was supposed to be working on his projects, not on his phone.

I leaned over and whispered, "Might I ask why you have your phone out, Carter?"

He whispered back, "The girl from prom and I have been texting, and it's been a long time since she texted me back. What should I do?"

I cocked my head, curious about the concern in his voice. *So, he's just told me one normal and natural reason he would have his phone out—a desire to stay connected. To a girl! It was a typical teenage boy's situation, and if I made him put away his phone without trying to bring peace to his mind, there was no way I'd get good work out of him.*

Besides, I was too curious to resist. That year prom had been combined with another high school, which meant the "other half" of this quandary was not within my reach. So, I couldn't be a proper ally, but I could still help. And I wanted to help. Besides, it wasn't like he had his phone on his desk all the time. I couldn't remember any other time, in fact.

He's a good kid. I'll allow it. Just this once.

"So, does she still like me?"

"Well, Carter, she might. Opposite genders can be hard to read because guys and girls think so differently. How long has it been since you texted her?"

"A whole day." His face was earnest, but his eyes were dark with disappointment.

My eyes would have glistened with amusement, except I knew this young heart was loaded with expectations. So, I resisted the temptation to quip something about how grateful we could be that this wasn't the 1800s. Back then, paper mail often took several weeks to move between lovers!

Once I could speak without smiling, I asked, "And when you were texting regularly, was it going well? Did you get the impression she really likes you?"

"I think so. We had a great time and laughed a lot at the dance." A spark of joy brightened his gaze. "It's been fun, even though over text it's hard to say for sure."

Having been a longtime admirer of Carter's excellent sense of humor, and the joy he found in telling a story, I grinned and asked, "Really? What did you say in your last text?"

"Hi."

What? No clever banter? Not even an exclamation point? Just a one-word greeting? Who was this kid, and what had he done with Carter?

He had become a man of few words, which was totally out of character for his daily self, but totally in character for an infatuated fellow!

I wanted to grin wide and tease the humor out of him, but the teacher in me figured his teenage friends would do a better job at that after class. This wasn't exactly a private conversation.

"Hmmm ... Well, let me see ... Just a moment ..."

I bent over at my desk as though writing something down, but really I just needed to think because I had never seen his shy side. And yet here it was, enclosed in a case of enamored speechlessness as he sought mature help and perspective.

Frankly, I had seen this movie before. High school romance has a well-known predicament that either wilts in a learning experience or blooms into something dreams are made of.

"So … she hasn't responded for a whole day. How long had it been since you last heard from her, before you texted 'Hi'?"

"A whole day."

Uh-oh. Has Carter misread this girl's signs? Are his feelings his perspective and getting in the way of reality? Do high school girls know how to play hard to get? Is she simply a busy high school girl? After all, some girls have time for prom but not for boys.

"Interesting. Maybe she just needs to be reminded about how awesome you are and the good time you had. What can you say in a text that might make her laugh? I think it's time to tease her a bit, get her attention again, be more assertive, and use some of that charming humor I know you've got in you!"

"I could do that?" His face froze for a moment before he restated the words with gusto. "I can do that!"

I almost giggled as his ocean of gloom substantially drained away, and I felt relieved for his sake. This outburst was evidence of Carter's customary confidence. If there had been a storm, he now had the gift of a rainbow as new vibrant enthusiasm and colorful curiosity took over.

"But what should I say? How should I say it?"

I didn't have the heart to tell him there was a risk of a crashing wave in his future, so I said, "Just be yourself! Think about the night you met. Tease her about how hard it is to find her and then ask an open-ended question to see what she says. Or use a pickup line."

"A pickup line?"

"Yeah, one that invites her to tell you where she stands, like, 'I think you might be a marathon runner because you've been running through my mind all day.' Or 'Hey! Is your nickname Waldo? I keep losing you, but I'd much rather keep finding you! Do you want to be found?' Or if you both like math, you could say, 'If you were a triangle, you'd be *acute* one.' Then if she responds you can invite her to a new level of friendship beyond texting by saying something like, 'Hey, I think there's something wrong with my phone. Could you call it and see if it works? My friends at school don't have phones yet.'"

Now Carter's smile had returned in full. "Miss D, all of those are so clever!"

"Yeah, well, pickup lines and one-liners are easy to find online. But you, Carter, have an uncanny ability to make up your own too! Who knows, maybe you can make up one that's totally personal, one that she'll get because of prom. A little caution though—if you use that last pickup line, make sure you wait until after school. I wouldn't want you to get in trouble with answering your phone in class." I gave him a sideways glance and raised my eyebrows while moving back and forth from his gaze to his phone, to the other students, and to his face again.

With a twinge of sheepish compliance, he threw me a grin to show me he perfectly understood my meaning. Then he picked up his phone and dropped it quietly into his backpack and did his best to turn his attention to his assignment.

I knew he was fighting the temptation to check his phone, but at least he was less distracted and more inclined to work now, which led me to whisper an ounce of encouragement in his direction, "Don't worry, good things come to those who wait."

His smile was full of trust and hope, and that just about made my day.

THE ALTITUDES OF ACCEPTANCE

"She's gonna kill me!"

Danny's scream from halfway down the train station platform brought my head up.

He's going to die? Uh, no way. Time for some death-defying interventions—

As annoying as Danny could be, he still had a long life ahead of him filled with meaningful lessons. Would this be one of those days when a lesson would sink in?

I heard some kind of racket and took my leave of the person I had been discussing the weather with on the train platform. I started walking in the direction of Danny and the girl, Brianna, who was chasing him.

From my distance of about fifty feet or so, I heard Brianna's voice respond to his alarm. "That's right—you're a no-good, rotten, terrible monster! I'll stop you if it's the last thing I do!"

Sassy, socially savvy Brianna was trying to grab his arm or shoulder to slow down his speed. It was not the first time she had displayed vehement disgust for his smooth and impetuous behavior.

As I closed in, I slowed as Kyle, another character of mischief who possessed a pleasant sense of humor, tried to keep pace with Brianna to cut her off and make her stop running. Kyle had a habit of choosing to be a friend or an enemy according to his convenience, and today Kyle seemed to be choosing in favor of Danny.

Eventually he got into her face, scowling at her while Danny hovered behind him. "Now, Brianna, please do not kill Danny. He's my friend, and he's essential to our life on Earth!"

Wow, that's a new one. Danny cursed to death by one person only to be declared essential to life as we know it by another. I guess now I know who his getaway driver will be in the future!

Striking a pose as though she were queen of Egypt, Brianna planted her feet about shoulder-width apart, folded her arms, and stood as tall as she could while staring Kyle down.

I did not expect Kyle to last long under the heat of her glare, but Danny leaned forward and whispered something in his ear.

Whoops! That was a mistake.

Brianna stiffened and scowled.

Then, Kyle mimicked—or mirrored—her behavior, standing straight with feet planted.

"To get to him, you'll have to go through me first."

I imagined Brianna's mind whirling in the silent moment that followed Kyle's bluff. Her face neither revealed admission of defeat nor irrational anger. Her earlier threat and movements toward Danny's pending destruction seemed to pause like an arrow mid-flight. She could make good on it and kill two annoying birds—but then again, what stone did she really have?

This ought to be good!

As I stood there watching, the fierceness in Brianna's face seemed to soften as a sort of smile replaced the fire in her eyes and thinly pressed lips. I could see method to her madness, and as a fellow female I both appreciated her and found myself amused by her in this moment. The girl had these boys right where she wanted them, like a couple of nails set into pre-drilled holes. But what overall situation she was setting them up for, I couldn't be sure—yet. Some kind of snare, no doubt.

Hands went to hips as Brianna claimed a pose of defiance. "He betrayed me. It was annoying. Why are you defending *him*? I seem to recall that he did the same thing to you *yesterday!*"

And there was the hammer coming down on the nail—finishing the door of her cage.

Two little trapped birds. Whatever will the boys do now?

"Because he's my friend. And you are too. But only if you don't kill him."

Wow! For a kid, this was an impressively diplomatic outreach.

The ball was in her court and in return she said, "Okay, okay. I won't kill him. But I have a couple of conditions." She took off her backpack and held it in front of her.

THE ALTITUDES OF ACCEPTANCE

Sensing a victorious de-escalation that wouldn't end in his demise, Danny stepped out from behind to stand at Kyle's side. Then, without speaking, he reached over and tried to stuff something I couldn't see into—

The forest green canvas bag was almost jerked away as he reached over, but just in time, Brianna realized what he was doing, held her ground, and even opened the top of her bag.

That's weird! I couldn't believe they hadn't noticed me standing there observing yet. I thought it best to wait and see how this played out. Despite the mystery, it seemed things were moving in a good direction.

Kyle's glance took in the exchange, then he looked up at Brianna. "Uh, okay."

"First, today, on the train, we will sit near each other, so I can keep my eyes on your troublemaking, and as such Danny must sit on the far side, away from my backpack because he's way too tempted to get into my stuff." With a satisfied expression, she glared at Danny while zipping up her backpack.

"Second, if he gets anywhere close to my backpack today or in the future, he's asking for—*major trouble*. In return, I promise not to … you-know-what." Her eyes narrowed as she emphasized those last words, clearly alluding to her earlier threat. Then, she said something that sounded like, "Oh, and by the way? These terms? Not negotiable!"

The boys just looked at each other.

Danny still hadn't said a word. Even from where I stood, there was an unmistakable innocence in his eyes. I thought it might be true remorse, but knowing Danny, I couldn't be sure.

All I knew was that he'd taken something from her bag and, against Brianna's will, attempted one of his show-and-tell campaigns with the other kids. It must have been something private, something a boy would get curious about—or else she'd never have been so annoyed.

Brianna reached out her hand. "Do we have a deal?"

One by one each boy shook her hand, agreeing to keep their distance.

Ha! I felt proud. Student resolution without teacher involvement was utterly amazing.

The train approached, and as I moved toward the boarding area, my joints were stiff from being rooted in place to the concrete below. Looking around, I used the pause to roll my ankles a bit and ensure all the students got on the train.

In that moment, I caught a glance exchanged between Brianna, who was entering through the doors on one side of the train, and a young man named Stevie, who was climbing onto the same train car through the other set of doors. Stevie's ears turned red, while Brianna's face, all aglow from her victory with the other boys, took on a grin that released words never spoken: "I see you seeing me, and you saw what I just did! You're next!"

I suppressed a giggle as I fully expected to see another laying down of the rules by Brianna once I got on the train.

I sure did love her sassy superpower. She was such a sweet girl when she wasn't being brazen that I figured this was the delightful contradiction all the boys were interested in.

Still, it appeared Stevie was having a hard time. His red ears and irritation seemed like the opposite reaction than one might expect from a boy like him. His natural self-assurance, good humor, and leadership qualities made him successful at almost anything he touched, and I knew he could make it in a neurotypical school if he wanted to. I thought he'd be a great match for the sweet and sassy Brianna, but it was interesting to note as I did my rounds on the train, he was seated about as far from Brianna as he could be.

Today was not the day he wanted to deal with her antics.

Some days later, I was sitting on the train not far from Stevie, Brianna, and Danny, quietly reading but with my ears on alert. The three of them together was a concerning combination.

Today, Brianna sounded assertive and accusing, but kind—a little less than a pure force of nature. "Stevie, you flirt with me all the time. You always come over to where I am at, then you follow me and throw things at me!"

THE ALTITUDES OF ACCEPTANCE

That sounded complicated, but also candid. Secretly, I hoped she would always be the kind of girl who clearly communicated her feelings, observations, concerns, and expectations. I also hoped the right young men would respect her more for this charming quality, and the wrong boys would quickly lose interest and let her alone because of how this trait demanded more of them than they were willing to give. Of course, in my mind, Stevie was one of the right young men—

On that note, I could see Stevie wore a face of determination—and disaster! He looked stuck between a hard place and a woman—Brianna was a rock for sure, but the thought caused me to wonder, was the "hard place" the circumstances or Danny?

Danny's face carried a thrilled expression, as though he didn't mind seeing another person taking what Brianna was dishing out. I couldn't blame him. He was only the wrong kind of boy for Brianna because his mischievous nature went directly against her law and order. Personalities like that might be friends but not lovers. Mischievousness was a better fit for fun-loving responsibility, someone who enjoys light-hearted antics. No doubt Danny would find that girl someday.

"No, I don't! You're always where I am. Also, I chase you because—well, you want to be chased!"

"Do I, Stevie?"

Stevie went quiet and looked down at his lap—not quite embarrassed but now looking rather forlorn and somewhat uncomfortable. Clearly, Brianna was running for other reasons.

"I think you're the one who flirts with HER, Stevie. You totally try to LICK her!" Danny piped in.

Ew! My head came up, no longer hidden behind my book. *What is this about?*

"Um, it's not what you think! I chased her once with a little piece of metal I licked, and she thought it was gross, so now the threat of licking her gets her to run away! And I'm okay with that."

Stevie's face took on the intensity of an honest man being pushed into a corner. Behind that mask, I suspected he had enjoyed her reaction and was simply not happy about this moment—his feelings and vulnerability being displayed in mixed company.

I sighed and smiled.

Young love? Maybe. Had I misjudged the attraction between Stevie's self-assurance and kind nature and Brianna's orderliness and sweetness?

Either way, Stevie was swimming in the deep end of youthful flirting, which I knew from experience could be rather fickle at times. As much as I thought it was good for Stevie to face his feelings, and Brianna too, I considered what I could say that might help smooth things over for all involved. Plus, it seemed like a good time for me to figure out what was really going on.

Standing up, I slid into the seat next to the three heated youngsters. Speaking quietly to try to help bring down the temperature and noise, I gave Brianna a sympathetic glance and offered a little redirection. "You know, Brianna, if you don't run, the boys can't chase you."

"I know, but I don't think about that when he's trying to lick me!"

"That's a good point. A much younger me did the same thing, though without the licking! It can be more fun or make more sense to run ahead of the boys than to figure out words and feelings at your age. So far, you're doing okay, and maybe I can help, but not today—here comes our stop."

We arrived at our train station and commenced disembarking.

I thought about this case of the first crushes while I herded the children off the train and into cars. As usual, the bonding between two people was complex. I still wasn't sure what to say yet, but hoped I would eventually find some adult perspective that would create a great learning experience.

A few days later, another argument began between Stevie and Brianna, so I started out with a question. "Stevie and Brianna, what are you going to do with yourselves? Every time you two are around each other you're either at peace or at war. I can hardly keep up!"

Stevie countered, "She's the one causing all the trouble. She was going to poke me. So, I had to poke her!"

"Stevie, I don't like the idea of you playing poker," I said, deflecting the conflict with humor.

Stevie rolled his eyes and gave me a stare, "Oh, har-dy-ha-ha, Miss D. Very funny."

I grinned and then offered a more practical follow-up question. "So, what was she poking you with?"

Stevie answered, "Well, she was trying to poke me with that thing. I mean the little safety pin on the back of one of those round metal badges."

Brianna's quiet but sassy smile reminded me of what a perfect little actress she made.

Then, it hit me. I started putting two and two together. "Oh. Are you sure that's not just her wanting to give you a kiss? Or to give you that badge? She is playing Wendy in the *Peter Pan* show, you know."

Then, with a pointed look at Brianna, I offered, "Girls try all kinds of things to get a guy's attention."

For once, Brianna was speechless, but her demure smile showed appreciation for my effort in trying to make sense of their situation.

Stevie, on the other hand, looked fierce and decisive. He turned and leaned toward Brianna. Then he defiantly said, "Brianna, I don't want any of your thimbles! I don't want to be kissed either!"

With that, Brianna found an opportunity for compromise, "Okay. I won't give you those things—if you don't pretend to lick me."

I felt enchanted by how hard these two were working to know what was wanted and needed from each other. They were starting to compromise and negotiate, and to resolve their own squabbles! Their current mutual discomfort might be wrapped up in the whole delightfully simple and strange licking and poking issues, but I knew, or at least hoped, that age and experience would bring new relationship opportunities and problems to solve. Meanwhile, I could enjoy how awesome it was to see wisdom growing from young love—even though they would never admit it!

Most people know relationships are essential in life. I've said it before, and I'll say it again—we cannot go through life without touching other people's lives, and vice versa.

Every path we take in life involves other people. Every relationship is an adventure. We never really know what's around the next bend. No relationship is simple or straightforward. People are intricate, messy, and complicated. Some people create obstacles for us, while we create obstacles for other people. When our path is steeper than we wish, if we are willing to receive redirection, our relationship with others can become an adventure of togetherness.

Especially as we grow closer to God.

In fact, it almost seems that if a person is heading in the right direction in a relationship, friendship, or decision where other people are affected, there will always be some kind of uphill climb. I think that's because we need spiritual growth and illumination, and relationships are a great way for God—the master of connection—to give us light while helping us understand love.

Love stories matter to all of us, in one way or another. It takes a lot of work to grow together with someone, including deep conversations, shared observations, and studying each other's ideas and behaviors. When all is said and done, love teaches us more about life than life can teach us about love. Every love story is its own mountain of challenges, and in some cases, love can be lost as quickly as it is found. We don't always get to decide how love stories work out—whether they'll be able to join us for the whole adventure—but then again, what if they do? We never know how another person will beautify our view, or how much we will appreciate what color their love adds to our experience as we climb higher together.

THE ALTITUDES OF ACCEPTANCE

At some point, while working at the school, I realized I was not only recovering from the other sources of pain, but that I was also progressing emotionally after the failed engagement. As I healed, I discovered something new about what I wanted in my future love story.

My life had repeatedly shown me how God and his truths are the ultimate solution, and while romantic love can help quell and manage pain, and provide aid and wisdom for solving problems, the relationship I had with God was always going to be the most important one.

Meanwhile, from a combination of watching the students experience dating and starting a new chapter of dating for myself, I started learning certain lessons I still rely on today.

- Relationships are about honesty and being willing to dive vulnerably into unknown spaces.
- Love is about trusting both the timing and importance of talking through changes.
- Wanting and keeping another person in your life is about resisting the temptation to handle things alone.
- Closeness is about choosing—to invest in, lean into, and give love even when it's hard.
- Being individually strong is as important as being strong together.

Aside from the bits of wisdom mentioned above, framing each of my dating experiences as an opportunity for growth and fun has been a pathway to self-reflection and confidence, and it often creates a good foundation for a desirable future with another person.

The tricky part is becoming mutually secure in each other's love and then aiming together in the right direction. But what is that right direction?

TRUST THE PATH

Last year, I climbed a fourteener at sunrise. As my group claimed the summit, I looked to the west and couldn't believe what I saw! A shadowy but well-defined and transparent isosceles triangle hovering at eye level in the distance, with its highest angle pointed straight to heaven, presented a mystery to us all. Eventually, we realized it was a silhouette created by how the sunlight shined across a pyramid-shaped mountain to the north.

That might have been enough of an explanation, but I wouldn't be an outdoorswoman if I didn't understand how several unrelated but interacting factors had to fall into place for us to be able to see that triangle. In addition to the sun's angle, our location, and the amount of particulate matter in the air, we had to emerge out of the darkness onto the peak at exactly the right time.

Without intending to, my group had done all the things to complicate arriving at the summit in time to see *any* part of sunrise. We started half an hour later than we intended and experienced an additional delay when we began hiking up the wrong ridge! It had been no small feat to get my group there on that specific day—at the precise time—and if God knows his craft the way I think he does, there are no coincidences. That is why, all things considered, I think of this climb as one of the rarest climbs I have ever taken.

The story was particularly illuminating as I wrote this chapter because it occurred to me how this moment on our mountain peak provided a vivid analogy for the point I'm trying to make about love and relationships. In life, we take path after path. Sometimes it feels like we are going in the wrong direction because of our imperfections and choices. Although we see success along the way, what we want most is to make our relationships better and find love through meaningful experiences. Throughout life, God's light can influence the paths we choose, how we experience the journey, and the way we see things, even if we start out in the dark. If God can get everything into position where great things like this moment can happen, he can get us where he wants us at the right time and bring the right relationships forward when it's time.

So, I think the love relationship we want to have forever and the direction we want it to go are well-represented by that giant triangle in the sky—with each lower corner representing two people and the highest one representing God. When two people finally find each other, if they hang onto each other and point their paths upward to God, they end up rising along the sides of their triangle, growing closer to each other and to God than they have ever been. And the more they climb together, the more they can enjoy the great views all around.

In the scriptures, God gives a promise, saying that regardless of what we can or can't see right now, if God is involved, the adventure of life is leading somewhere with a great view.

He's just that good at what he does!

God can also help relationships grow and improve, but it's up to us to do the work.

While it may be impossible to get everything right all the time, we can reach the most desirable altitudes as we get closer to God, the truth, and our best selves. I think accepting who we are is knowing we are enough but not giving up on who we can become with God in the lead.

In fact, gaining this altitude of acceptance can help us appreciate that the great views we get to see are less the result of having everything work out as planned and more related to how God's light is and always has been shining into our lives—and not just through sunlight or moonlight. That is because God's light shows us the amazing people and important lessons we would otherwise miss as we climb through our lifescapes.

Unfortunately, it is too easy to get distracted by lesser views or bogged down in the mud or sand of life's adventure. We can ignore the light or forget we don't need to see everything to keep moving forward and stay on the right path. But if we believe God when he says life is about where we are *going* rather than where we have *been*, then we are more likely to believe it matters whether we are going there with him and whether we are loving other people along the way. We will also be living a life that shows our trust that God will reveal what we need when it's time.

This is what it means to trust the path.

CHAPTER 12

LOVING WHO YOU ARE NOW

*S*lippery, as though you could slide for miles—if at any time you tried to stop.

That is how I would describe driving during snowy, wet, Utah winters. In fact, at one point I thought it might be better to go to work with snowshoes. Or I could ski! That would be fun, but this winter was an exception to some meteorological rule.

I could count the number of times it had snowed on one hand, but the number of freezing cold days required both hands and feet! It didn't bother me that the temperature had dropped below my age, but the snow had missed its cue for outdoor fun.

Sure, it had snowed on Christmas Day in Utah, but I vacationed in Arizona at the time, visiting my sister and escaping the cold for the holiday. Now, on my way to the train station, the ground was as brown and boring as the dull underside of a doormat. I had no way to justify wearing my favorite snow boots, and to make matters worse, my students seemed to be in gloomy moods. There was no making them laugh, and it was all I could do to keep them talking about positive things. After we got to the school, I noticed my coworkers didn't appear much better. Everywhere I looked, I saw symptoms of illness and seasonal depression.

It made me sad. It wasn't fair. My students' worlds were the hardest ones I had ever witnessed. They needed to know their worth and recognize true joy was in who they trusted and how they chose to live.

Why is it so easy for us to not know our own worth when circumstances drag us down?

I thought of other places and circumstances where either weather or worlds were different, such as how people in Florida were happy with year-round summer weather. However, they traded snow for hurricanes. There was no perfect way to find a solution if you simply traded troubles.

I could only conclude that where people are struggling to like themselves, the weather, and the world they must live in, perspective is everything.

There must be something I can do to inspire a little joy.

And that's when I had an idea, having recalled when the prince from the movie Enchanted asked his friend, "Do you like yourself?"

In the movie, the prince responded with, "What's not to like?" I didn't mind that answer. It showed bright confidence in what the prince thought of himself. It's always good for us to think well of ourselves and have reason to do so. Still, I couldn't help but consider how in real life, the most honest, humble response to such a question would be based on who a person is at their core as well as how they feel about themselves. And yet—despite knowing such happiness is a choice, too often we allow our happiness to be purely reflective of how we feel about our circumstances.

So, that is what I will do!

To combat the seasonal depression, I will spend the rest of the year helping students get past their circumstances and focus on deeper reasons to be happy. I'll ask students what they like about themselves. It'll help them be positive, and I can get as specific as I want.

With my plan in place, I soon found my first experiment!

Sam, a high school student with lots of anxieties, had been unfairly teased about his nervous tic and showed all the signs of needing to rise above his circumstances.

"Don't let them get to you, Sam. People often tease about things they don't understand."

Sam looked skeptical, as though he figured he deserved to be teased. He didn't, but believing you deserve something bad is a hard state of mind to escape. This was my chance.

"Sam, what do you like best about who you are?" I asked.

"Hmmm ... "

That was all he said!

As he faded off, it seemed clear that he wasn't interested in talking further. So, I went over to tell the teaser to back off and let Sam be himself. Eventually, I looked back and saw Sam smiling! I hoped it was because he thought of something he liked. If not, at least his mind was in a better place. And if I hadn't made the difference, it was still true that some things, including loving who we are now, just take a little encouragement and time.

That year was Danny's first year of high school varsity basketball, and he was struggling with a severe leg injury that had an impact on his ability to play.

As luck would have it, one day I found him in the hallway nursing his leg. I couldn't help but notice the absence of his usual mirth, and realized it wasn't the weather alone that was getting to him. His eyes looked wistful, and his face looked dismal. This was an opportunity.

"Danny, you're looking like that injury covers your whole body—not just your leg! Mind if I ask what's eating you?"

"I don't know, Miss D. All I want to do is play basketball. I hate being hurt."

"I know what it's like to have something taken away and be right at your fingertips yet inaccessible. But just so I know, are your friends making you feel bad about not being able to play?"

"No, they're cool about it."

"Are your teacher or parents making you feel bad about your injury?"

"No way. Dad got hurt like this once. He gets it. And Mr. Dixon says one game is not a whole season."

"That sounds right to me. So, then—why are *you* making *you* feel bad about your injury?"

"Oh, I—but Miss D—" He squirmed. "It's just my whole life is on that court!"

"Is it really? Let's think about what you do off the court. I mean, I hear how you help teachers every day. Also, you are great at math, you care about others, and you have friends who think they are lucky to know you. Not to mention—"

Danny's brow shifted upwards.

"I happen to know a couple of girls who think you would be a great date to the dance next month."

He blushed.

"The truth is, Danny, much of the great life you lead off the court probably got you onto the court to begin with. So, stop being relentless and impatient with yourself in ways you would never be with others! How about asking yourself what you can still do to find joy in this circumstance?"

There was assurance, a smile, then new light in his eyes. "Tell me more about the girls …"

Yep, still Danny.

As the cold, dry winter progressed, my work assignments changed yet again. At first, I wasn't excited about working in the middle school gym class. Sure, a more active workday sounded nice, but middle schoolers were not as mature as high schoolers.

As someone who deals with anxiety, does it really make sense to keep putting me in with kids who were plagued with identity issues, wild emotions, and unpredictable hormones?

THE ALTITUDES OF ACCEPTANCE

Only time would tell, and God would show.

As I worked to adjust to the emotional excesses, I noticed a girl sitting on her own. She was normally in a super chatty clique. After about a week of this isolation, I found her in the corner of the lunchroom and decided to pry a little further.

"Lillian, I've been watching you sit alone this whole week. Is something wrong?"

"My friends didn't say it, but I can tell they don't like the way I talk. Do I talk too much?"

Ouch! So, the chatty part of this clique is Lillian? I doubt it!

"No. Those other girls are capable of talking just as much as you do."

Her shoulders sagged, her gloom apparent in the mild sniffles and the hint of tears in her watery eyes.

Whoops! As soon as I said it, her reaction told me I had invited the wrong kind of thinking.

I'd have to try a different approach.

I decided that rather than ask her a question, I'd try to offer a vote of confidence and emphasize that despite being talkative, Lillian was a caring person. Surely her friends valued this!

"Come on now, there's still hope! Lillian, you've had these friends for a long time. I'm sure things are not what they seem. If they have abused your emotions with their words, that's not okay. And even if what they say is true, feeling aware of how others respond to you is normal, and I think it shows great maturity. Maybe they need you to talk less about some things, and more about other things. What if you asked them to help you understand?"

Her head raised and she straightened a little, but her eyes were still doubtful.

"If you do, I think you'll figure out what's really going on with them, then you'll realize your friends really do like you, miss you, and value what you have to say."

"And if they don't?"

"Well, if they don't, it's their loss because you are sensitive and kind-hearted. If you weren't, we wouldn't be having this conversation. But I really think you're jumping to conclusions."

Lillian wiped a few more tears on her sleeve. "So ... find out more about what they are actually thinking and stop worrying about what I think they are thinking?"

"Uh, yes. Sometimes we tell stories to our own minds that aren't true. Besides, you won't be able to stop worrying about it until you ask and find out the truth."

That was a solution from my own experience. Navigating anxiety with self-acceptance meant identifying when I believed the wrong stories about myself.

Later, I saw Lillian with her friends, and she looked happy. I'm not certain how things played out, but I do know that discovering and believing true stories is generally a far happier experience.

Speaking of truth and stories, I often ran into Sally, the young, lower-functioning, sweet girl who had ridden the train with me. She was hard to understand sometimes, and she didn't always have her words worked out in a clear way, but beneath her shyness I thought she was super smart.

There was one day in gym class when I could tell Sally was bothered and distracted, so I let my teacher partner know she needed some one-on-one time. Then I drew her aside, sat her down, and tried to listen as her words were coming out in snippets between sobs.

"I ... full of holes ... need to be fixed," she said, among other things.

Who knew. She and I understood each other, and we hadn't even talked yet.

"What do you mean, Sally? Did someone break something that belongs to you?"

THE ALTITUDES OF ACCEPTANCE

Even as I asked her the question anyway, her concept of holes seemed to match exactly how I'd felt during my first years of teaching. I had gotten pretty bent out of shape over my mistakes—my holes—especially ones that affected others.

"No, me. I'm ... broken."

Then she tried to describe something awesome that her friend had done, and then I understood she was self-shaming and struggling with personal flaws. *Yep. Been there, done that!*

However, I knew what Sally didn't know yet—how those flaws would be good stories one day. Also, everyone needs fixing to some degree. But that doesn't mean we're all broken.

She just needs someone to help her see.

Her voice went silent, and her head went down, so I decided it was a good time to ask the question I hoped would lift her head and brighten the light in her eyes.

"Sally, what is one good thing that you did today?"

"Well-ell ..." She cocked her head to her right side. "There was a spider ... Ellie told me ..."—she flinched—"I didn't scream!"

Wait, what? Why is this the first time I've heard of it?

"Sally, uh, way to go—way to not scream about spiders!" My eyes then shifted about as I worked to counter the tingling sensation creeping up my spine. "Also, where was the spider?"

"In the corner."

"Of the gym?"

"Yeah."

"What did it look like?"

"Small and black, with white ... What kind was it?" She looked at me expectantly, but I had no clue. It could have been a harmless garden or jumping spider, but I couldn't be sure. Those little things were always visiting buildings and coming in during the weather changes.

"I'm not sure, can you show me? I'll take it outside if it's still around."

"Okay!" She grabbed my hand and pulled me toward the corner by the door with more enthusiasm than I expected for a girl who didn't like spiders.

Wow, this girl is full of surprises today and doesn't even know it.

Arriving at the gym corner, we scanned the space, our heads bobbing up and down. The walls looked fine until you got that close to them. I could see grime and odd sprays of some mysterious grit and dirt.

Hmm.

Just as I was about to call off the search, Sally said, "Miss D, ... a hole, here."

"Huh, so there is, but not for long. Watch this." I grabbed my backpack, pulled out an old notepad, tore off a piece of paper, rolled it into a tiny ball, and stuffed it into the hole. To me, it looked too tiny to be a spider entry, but if there was a spider on the other side, it would not be coming back any time soon to scare any other children.

"Miss D, the hole is still there, you know. You didn't really fix it."

I almost laughed at how obvious her words were but remembered that would be a rather confusing reaction for her to decipher.

Standing up, I said, "You're totally right. But sometimes plugging the hole is a good enough solution. Although it's only temporary."

"Is plugging up my holes 'good enough' too?"

As my eyes met hers, I realized we weren't talking about the spider anymore. We were talking about people who might see their own holes very clearly, who might measure themselves by how those holes affect them, rather than what they do with them or in spite of them.

I smiled. Drawing parallels really worked for some of these kids.

"Well—it might help, although, the holes you're talking about are much more complex than holes in a wall or the ground."

"Really? So no plugs ... I will always be holey?"

"'Always' isn't the right word, but it's okay. Believe it or not, everyone has holes."

"Even God?"

"Oh, he's the holiest."

THE ALTITUDES OF ACCEPTANCE

We both giggled and I knew she had been teasing me. We had figured out we were a part of the same church while riding the train, so I wasn't surprised she mentioned God around me.

As Sally's smile met mine, I noticed a tremble in the corner of her lips, her doubt dragging her back down. "Sally, no one is as perfect as they seem. Except God, of course. I think you feel holey and we are all holey because God made us that way."

My mind raced ahead, and I wanted to tell her how I believe there is a purpose for our imperfect holey-ness. The reason we are the way we are has a lot to do with how God made us, and he made us with holes to help us become the other kind of holy he wants us to be.

"Um ... I don't know what that means."

"Right, uh ... What I mean is, God gave us holes to help us become better."

"So ... the holes in us are a good thing?"

"Depends."

"On what?"

"What we do when we notice them. The holes make us feel broken, so we can feel bad about them. Or we can use them to teach us what we are missing so that we can work on becoming better. No matter how we choose to deal with our holes, they can help us understand other people's holes. I think it's important in this life to have reminders that we aren't perfect."

My eyes glistened with tears as I spoke—there was truth in what I was trying to explain.

Now I was the one feeling emotion, and she was the one with all the questions!

The voice in my mind added, *God understands our holes because he put them there and because he knows what it's like to experience and endure every single one of our holes.* I would have said that out loud, but Sally asked, "But ... we do need to fix our holes, right?"

Thinking back on all the holes I had discovered since the year I had started working at the school, I said, "Well, yes, we do, some or most of them—with God's help. Sometimes it's okay to plug or work around our holes until we can figure out how to fix them, or if we really need to. Sometimes our holes cause pain or heartache for other people, and I think those holes do need to be fixed. In some cases, fixing just takes one decision to change a behavior. In other cases, we need a whole lifetime of changes!"

I thought of my worth in God's eyes even with all my own imperfections and struggles to understand them. This time, I spoke all the thoughts. "Then again, some holes don't need to be fixed. Sometimes our holes exist so that the wind can blow through us like tree branches without knocking us down, or they were put there on purpose so that we know where we are supposed to plant something that will grow in us until we become God's kind of holy."

"But which holes need to be fixed? And which ones don't?"

She was calmer, talking more clearly now. We were back to her current reality.

I wanted to talk about prayer, but there was another tool I knew I could recommend. "Well, I think that's something that is between you and God, but for now, I think when you feel like people have been poking at your holes, or like you're so broken you need fixing, it's time to ask yourself, 'What have I done today that makes me feel proud of *me*?' If you do that, I think you will feel more connected to what's great about you, instead of focusing only on your holes. And if you find yourself feeling broken all the time, you might need to talk to your parents for help."

Sally nodded. "Okay, I can do that. 'What have I done today—" She paused and hesitated, looking at me.

"—that makes me proud of me?'" I said, helping her fill the gap.

"Thanks, Miss D."

The bell rang and away she went with her head up and a little more bounce in her step.

"Sally!" She turned. "You really should be proud of how you handled that spider today!"

She smiled and went along her way while I was left to consider whether I had a spider incident to report. In the end, I decided it wasn't necessary. I hadn't actually seen a spider! And sure, holes exist, but the truth is, some just aren't big enough to hold anything truly threatening.

We just don't get to know that for sure until after we've thoroughly investigated them.

A month later, the gym class transitioned to outdoor baseball. I was no ace at the game, but I had been able to catch and throw a ball since third grade, so I felt well prepared for at least that part of the sport. What I was not prepared for was how one of the tallest students, Dillan, refused to play.

"Miss D, I can't play. Last year I was hit seven times with the ball. In the head!"

While the other teacher taught, I dealt with this nearly unbelievable report, by asking a few more revealing questions. "Dillan, do you remember anything that was happening when you were hit? Like, where you were, who you were with, and what you were doing?"

As if he'd been tracking my thoughts, he said, "Miss D, you can't *do* anything about it. I'm not going to play."

"I hear you, Dillan, but could you still give me some examples of when you were hit?"

"Well, one time I got hit and I wasn't even playing the game! I was just sitting there tying my shoes. Another time I was standing behind home base. I was supposed to be catching but my friend said something, so I looked back and got smacked in the side of my head. I also remember minding my own business, walking around at lunch, and someone hit me with the ball."

Interesting. Wrong place doing the wrong thing at too many of the wrong times—

I tried to assuage the situation and persuade him gently to try, but he would have none of it. He became quite vocal about not participating, and while I tried not to show it, I became irritated, carving a downward spiral for my thoughts.

Finally, I dragged myself out of those depths and reminded myself to take a deep breath.

It doesn't matter what I think. It just matters what I teach.

He had a reality and a wall, and I would prefer to see him face it and tear it down.

So, I made a deal with Dillan—if he would give it two days and accept lesson one—which was to watch the ball, know where it was at all times, and use arms to block if necessary—I would make sure he could pick a team when we got through the practice rounds and played a real game in class. The students didn't always get to pick their own teams and always wanted to, so if they had to play for a grade, selecting a team was appropriate motivation.

A few arm blocks later, I encouraged him to test his skills out—while warming the bench, "Dillan, please sit right here, don't do anything else—just keep an eye on that ball. Okay?"

He looked at me, nodded, and appeared slightly surprised that I hadn't tried to persuade him to go stand out in the field or man a base. About two minutes after he sat down, and much to my surprise, a ball came fast, aiming straight for his head like an apple in a lunchtime food fight.

I held my breath, but he noticed it and ducked, while blocking the ball with his hands, successfully saving his head from another hit.

"Yes! Great job, Dillan!" His reaction looked so natural that I couldn't help but feel proud!

However, a short time later my ears started to pick up words I didn't like.

"That guy who let the ball fly in my direction did that on purpose!" Dillan said to his friends.

"That's so true, I totally saw him throw it this way."

"Yeah, that guy has a really good throw but really bad aim. Home base is over there!"

Humph! Folding my arms, I continued to listen without looking. Neither his friends nor that pitcher had been there for the conversation I'd had with

Dillan, but it was clearly a waste of time to try to prove either side of that story, which meant time for lesson two.

Except the next day, lesson two never happened because Dillan skipped class.

Or so it seemed.

No other students or teachers seemed to know where he was during class, yet all agreed that until gym class started, he'd been present throughout the day, so he wasn't absent.

I started to feel a little bad about the lecture inside my head.

Did I put too much pressure on him yesterday?

Then, at the end of class, I saw him while I was helping another student. Even though I stood angled away from the stage, I was able to take note of how he crept out from behind the curtains, oblivious to my watchful eye.

Phew, found him.

Although, it was neither the right time to put him in his place by calling him out, nor did I feel like I should. Besides it wasn't like he had ever skipped class before, so it wouldn't hurt to let it slide—this time.

The next day he came to class but there were zero complaints against baseball and he didn't mention his worries about getting hurt. In fact, not only did he *not* speak out about his insecurities, he acted confident about getting out on the field, stayed with his team, and even caught and threw a few balls while manning a base.

However, on numerous occasions, it was clear he was steering out of my path, and I never wanted to make a mountain out of a molehill. But in this case, what was the mountain, and what was the molehill? Did lesson two even matter now? How had he changed so much in just forty-eight hours?

Sure, I thought he might change a little here, ask me a question there—but never had I suspected he would overcome his fears so quickly.

Unless his fears had nothing to do with his skill level or experience within the sport.

Observing all this, I said very little; finally, during a brief discussion, I took advantage of the chance for positive reinforcement.

After our conversation, even though I made sure to comment with supportive gratitude on how he contributed to his team, the old anxiety crept in. This had been a complex exercise in situational awareness for me as a teacher, and I was not sure at all what exercise it had been for him, other than physical.

How did I miss so much about him? My mind wandered as it tried to process this young man's behavior.

Again, just wait. Stop. Breathe. You need more information and you need to remain calm until you get the full story, or as much of it as you can get—and then you need to be okay with it.

My mind went through the events of the last couple of days. Despite my original frustration, I had stopped myself from giving him the obvious *duh* lesson and felt I could be proud of myself for that. Also, I had chosen to come from a calm, loving place, which was better than any other option I could have tried.

Not to mention, I had refrained from embarrassing him in front of his friends, even when he deserved it. Maybe he knew I had heard them and had felt bad about that, knowing it was all an effort on his side to feel good about not participating. *Did he need time to determine how to change his response to his fears and be more honest with our class—especially me—about his abilities?* After all, without saying a word, he had unjustified his prior behavior by performing beyond expectation.

Or, is this all a game to him?

Nah. He doesn't seem the type.

But he showed me I could figure out how to motivate students toward personal success!

Or maybe the success was already there. I might have had very little to do with it.

I sighed as the reminder sank in. Self-mastery in any moment could be significant to the success of the student, and the student's success is often not the same as the teacher's success.

At the end of the day, all I could really hope for was that Dillan knew I was on his side. If I had done that, then it was enough. It was good to meet students where they were, give them the tools they needed, and allow them to rise on their own. Or with a power of their own.

Or God's power.

Or all the above.

How children think does not always make sense to adults, but it makes sense to God.

Throughout the following days, Dillan seemed to have forgotten the incident and acted genuinely interested and stayed consistently alert and active in class. Then one sunny and slightly blustery autumn day, the students were lined up with partners about ten yards away from them. I kept thinking how the field was far too small for all the action happening, but it happened anyway.

Standing to the side, I found myself talking with a few female students, trying to help them practice throwing the ball at progressively longer distances. As I finally got them on board with my plan, a ball flew into our circle and pounded my right temple.

I crumpled to the ground in pain, not quite blacking out—at least I think I stayed conscious.

So, my right side is not always spared from injury after all! Good to know ...

Seconds later, the girls were reaching for my arms and asking if I was okay.

Dillan and his partner ran over. It turned out he had not caught Dillan's ball, and the next thing to stop it happened to be my head.

Poor Dillan. He never admitted out loud it had been he who had thrown the ball, but his face said it all as his partner displayed none of his quiet hesitancy. Dillan was embarrassed and scared, and yet we were both completely aware of the irony.

Looking like he had climbed his own mountain, I did not want to give him a reason to turn around and give up by punishing him for my injury. So, as we locked eyes, I smiled a weak smile and tried to wink at him.

Ouch, that hurt!

When the other teacher arrived at the scene, he saw my hands still holding my face and invited me to go inside and get some ice. While inside, I also saw the school nurse who said I should watch for signs of a concussion. Given how much it hurt, I believed her!

When I went back outside, I felt dizzy, so I lay down on the bench. At first, I tried to keep offering tips to the students but giving instructions while laying down just didn't have the same effect as standing! They'd listen for a second, and then they'd be off, chasing their ball. As it happened, the fog in my head kept growing until all I could do was watch out for the balls flying around me. When a few came too close, I was touched when some of the girls formed a line around me and voiced their plan to catch and throw any balls that came at me.

Ha! Well, way to be, that's one way to use your new knowledge!

One of the most fascinating takeaways I gleaned from working with the teenagers at the school was because of *how* they learned. They picked up on things I had actively taught them—they learned things I didn't know I was teaching them—and they learned things because of who they were, and how their natural inclinations aligned with the lessons.

Overall, they were like sponges, with a lot of intelligent capacity that craved autonomy.

On reflection, it seems like teaching required diligent effort from me, but success in teaching was always less about what I—the teacher—was doing, and more about how the information was getting through to what God already created. To that end, most days I had to trust that God could use me to educate those little sponges beyond my ability and training. In fact, I might never understand all the ways he used me on their behalf.

For the record, Dillan and I eventually reached good terms again, and Dillan's story is just one example of how these young people had to deal with individual challenges every day—how they had good days and bad days as they faced emotional battles or transitioned between medications. I came to understand how they often couldn't convey or explain what was going on with them. But I was always amazed by how, in the end, they recovered and surprised me!

Now, I think every person has their own little map of the world in their minds—maps formed by character, decisions, problems, and many interrelating factors. Each map holds all of the person's lifescapes, including the things that connect their personal mountains and valleys. They use their maps to make sense of the world they live in.

As we interact with each other, we never see someone else's entire map.

But we can rest assured—God knows every inch.

In 2014, I met a student, Spencer, who loved the new *Les Miserables* movie starring Hugh Jackman. He was undeniably his happiest when he was singing, and when I met him, I had just finishing memorizing this melody from the movie, "Can you hear the people sing, singing the song of angry men ..." to prevent classroom interruptions. But when I was caught humming it in the school hallway, he started waving and directing my song like a conductor. I had to laugh at his genuine enjoyment, his big smile, and happiness over the song. It was contagious, and after that we were fast friends.

Whenever he saw me, he would begin singing the song, and if it was appropriate, I would sing it with him. Almost every day for weeks, we had this moment of fun. It became tradition, something to make his harder days happier, and because of this I worked to keep his favorite song in the hallways by raising my volume or lowering it as needed to be polite to others.

One day, Spencer and another teacher were talking and when I walked into the classroom, he said to me, "Gorgeous, you make me crazy!"

Well, this is new and not our song.

I cocked my head at him. What did he mean by it?

"Spencer, are you quoting a movie at me?"

He just shook his head and again said, "Gorgeous, you make me crazy!"

The other teacher, a male jokester, ogled around Spencer, sending me an amused smirk.

Uh-oh. I'm in trouble!

"Yeah, no kidding, Spencer. She has a certain crazy effect on people."

I had to giggle at that. People could be crazy about me, crazy with me, crazy because of me, tell me crazy stories … but *making* people crazy might—at times—be a gift. And as much as this staff member teased me, if he had felt the impact of my 'crazy' a time or two, he deserved it!

But it was anyone's guess where Spencer was coming from.

I didn't want to assume anything, and hoped Spencer was coming from a place of harmless, genuine admiration and fun. I looked at my coworker again out of curiosity, to see if his behavior could help me identify what he thought about Spencer's behavior.

As it turned out, my colleague's behavior was a joke, as usual.

I could take a joke and dish it back too, and I might as well own an allegation if it's harmless and comes from a good place. So, I struck a contemplative pose while saying, "Hmmm … I could do worse!" We all laughed, and Spencer made a plan.

I found out about it the next day when he started giving me a daily salutation of "Gorgeous!"

Every time he saw me coming down the hall, he said the word. In return, I smiled and gave him a high five. Usually, he continued with our previously established tradition of conducting and singing "Do you hear the people sing?"

And I never hesitated to join him. His playful salutation grew on all of us, and I didn't mind when he started using "Gorgeous!" for a few of his other favorite teachers. We knew he was happy to see us and to be alive, that this was simply Spencer's way of making sure we felt as special as he believed we were.

At the end of that school year, the celebratory field trip for our students was to attend a *Les Miserables* musical at another high school. I still had not seen the movie by then, and the students were giving me all kinds of nonsense about how I sang all the songs but hadn't seen the movie. I suppose turnabout was fair play in this case, but I couldn't help but occasionally feel like saying, "Honestly, if some people could just learn to *Let it Go*, they might realize their own answers to *Who Am I?*" Which is one of the songs from the movie, of course.

Anyway, as circumstances would have it, there seemed to be an unspoken agreement among the authorities that I would be Spencer's buddy on this trip. It made sense—after all, we had been singing together for months and as a member of staff, I was tasked to keep the students together and safe—and that included Spencer.

In the eyes of his class teacher, Spencer's attachment to me would help reduce his inevitable wanderlust tendencies. It also seemed he and I had unknowingly developed a kind of call-and-response system. If he got lost, he could sing a rather appropriate song for the venue and performance, and I would know exactly where he was.

Of course, I managed to convince him to leave off the "Gorgeous" part in public!

The end of that delightful, moving performance marked the end of the school year for us, and that summer went by too quickly before another year began, making Spencer a senior in the school-to-work program, which would prepare him for life as an adult.

As it happens, becoming an adult is when the "University of Hard Knocks" begins.

For Spencer, it started with his homeroom teachers encouraging him to address individuals with proper titles. On the other side of the conversation, I was advised to be more judicious about encouraging his singing, and—sadly—to put an end to the much-loved salutation "Gorgeous!"

Such pressure to change was real for him, and I really missed his personality and smiles. There was no resulting tension over the things that had been forced into the past, but I could see and sense a loss of connection. It broke my heart, even though I understood the reasons. It was important for Spencer to prepare for professional relationships in the workplace after graduation, but I couldn't help feeling like the bright light of his big positive energy was shrinking into the distance like a falling star, never to return.

The more Spencer worked, the less I saw him. The few times we did cross paths, all we had time for was "hello," plus a few words of encouragement or a quick supportive parting, like—*keep going, you got this*! Or—*who's making it a great day? This guy!*

It didn't help. With each passing, poor Spencer seemed closer and closer to tears.

I struggled as only a teacher does—I felt torn, knowing what was best for him yet seeing how hard it was for him. Gloomy students didn't perform, yet it was right for him to have this training, even if it stressed him out and made him sad. Sometimes life's adventure required us to endure the kind of pain that would make us better in the end.

Besides, despite his sadness, Spencer seemed convinced to try no matter how he felt.

As graduation speedily approached like a long-awaited day of decision, I knew some seniors could stay a little longer in school if they needed more time, but for all I knew, more time was not what Spencer needed. If he needed to get out into the world, I wouldn't see him again.

One stormy day in April, Spencer didn't go to work for road safety reasons. The streets were flooded, and the threat of hail was real. I was moving down the hall when he waved me over with his familiar headshake and hand wave. The strangeness of this greeting between us seemed tangible.

In a tone of voice that rivaled any man in a pinstripe suit, he uttered, "Hello, Miss D."

It was the first time he had called me by my professional title since the day we first met.

I loved the name the students had given me, but I didn't like it when he said it! I missed his more cheerful greeting too much. *Would he ever get his larger-than-life cheerfulness back?*

Shaking off my melancholy, I tuned in to how proud I was of him over the last few months.

"Hello to you, Spencer!" I hoped my far brighter greeting would let him know I was happy to see him. There was a certain new concentration in his eyes as he continued the conversation.

"How are you?"

"I'm good, how about you? Ready for graduation? You deserve to be congratulated, way to go. That's such an achievement!"

Trading some of my energy to inspire a little of his usual good cheer didn't work.

I looked closer and saw how his eyes spoke volumes about his trepidation for the future. His broad shoulders caved in, his bottom lip gave way to a little quiver, and the words got stuck. He seemed not to know what to say next, and I repented of my misplaced enthusiasm.

"Hey, hey, Spencer. It's okay to feel anxious about graduation. It's totally normal."

"I know, Miss D. But life is going to be—different."

"It will, but different isn't always bad."

He gave one of those nods that said, "Well, yeah, although I hadn't thought about it like that yet." Sensing Spencer's vulnerability, I felt nervous about his emotional state, but then concluded it had been a long time since he'd thrown a tantrum. In front of me was a much calmer and more mature version of Spencer, one who could manage himself with care.

So, I figured it was time to ask a question that might lead to positive discussion.

"Do you know what you will do after you graduate?"

His head came up in slow motion. Tears were welling up in his eyes—the opposite of what I was going for. *Wow, I'm really doing good here. Stop trying to make him cry, Deanna!*

As fate would have it, seeing his tears triggered a mini waterfall of my own!

But it was not in me to cry! Not when this moment was about helping Spencer.

So, taking a deep breath, I dammed up those tears just in time to hear, "Oh, Miss Deanna. Change is hard. Change is—so—very—very—hard!"

I paused, able to only look at him as the simple truth he had just stated sank in. He'd just said my full first name. That so rarely happened, it stood out like a pillar of rock in a flat valley.

Did children with autism experience change the same way I experienced change?

Does their brain structure affect their response to change differently?

In that moment, I wasn't sure.

An eight-year-old me would have said the same thing. The memory of younger me sitting in my bedroom crept in. I held that book with mountains on the cover, deciding whether to let go or hang on to the past. I had chosen to let go, to let change be hard but not let it overwhelm me.

Then my mind breezed through all the moments change had been hard for me since then.

There was a younger me trying to figure out how to be an adult and climb mountains in several new lifescapes—Oh! There had been more than one place I hadn't been sure I could love, and in the end, with a little help from God, I loved each one and learned from them anyway!

Then, an older me on a rooftop, gazing at mountains and valleys, contemplating how lifescapes could change so drastically and wondering why things in life had to feel so severe.

The hallway was eerily silent for a moment, and I realized I would never see the extent of Spencer's tears, fears, and sorrows. I had, however, seen evidence of Spencer's character as he took on uncomfortable parts of his lifescape. His authenticity in facing change was based on trust in the judgment of those who wanted the best for him, and this seemed to motivate him to reach out to connect with others. With me, he was not seeking attention but rather seeking to fulfill greater things than himself—to enter the life that waited beyond his comfort zone and accept who he became because of that decision.

As the stormy weather gave way to a glow that began pouring in through the windows, I felt at a loss for words. But the sunlight felt hopeful, and I wanted to help him resist the brink of despair. "Spencer, I am so proud of you! Those tears are not a flood of 'I can't.' They are a torrent of 'Life might be rough water going downhill right now, but I'm not going to drown!' You're saying, 'I'm going to flow along and fight the currents, face the truth, fall flat if I have to, find flexibility to finish what I start, and figure the rest out as I go.' That is what I'm hearing when you recognize that 'change is hard.' Also, you're not alone. I cried a river about moving into the world after high school too. We are the same in that way, you and me."

He gave me one of those happy Spencer smiles, then lifted his head just a little more.

There was hope in his eyes, and he could use that to his advantage if he knew about it.

"I know it feels hard now, but it won't always feel so hard. Not every change is hard like this, but when it is, hang on to hope. Hope is the ounce of courage in you right now that says—eventually, everything is going to be all right. If you keep a perspective of hope, and always love yourself and other people, you'll be able to do the things you've learned to do *and* be your best cheerful self too."

I could see his mind working as his tears subsided. Then the smile he gave me matched the sunshine coming through the clouds outside. I smiled back, feeling relieved and encouraged to see a little of the old Spencer breaking through. Then, he put out his hand in a way that he used to, and it felt so reassuring to be able to see Spencer's old self mix in with his new self.

"A high five hand-hug, Miss D?"

Aww, a gesture worth a hundred words, if not more.

As I reached out to squeeze his hand with mine, I knew nothing was really lost, and Spencer had everything to gain. It was a moment that brought back the happy feeling I had enjoyed when his voice had rung through the hallways.

Sadly, that was the last conversation I ever had with Spencer, but I've never forgotten the way he said *change is hard* with such acute awareness, emotion, and acceptance of the impending greater complications. The way he said those words made me think Spencer had, in his own way, understood change was also important. Eventually, it also seemed clear to me how differences in brain structure and issues with emotional control did not of necessity eliminate common human needs or reduce the impact of life experiences.

When I look back at how I initially believed Spencer's upset and confusion would rattle mine, the way I have learned from his emotions becomes even more interesting. Now I realize it would have been a mistake not to extend love to Spencer simply due to fear and anxiety. I would have missed out on a very special person who surprised me and taught me more than I imagined.

I now see how Spencer needed someone to help him believe in a better world, just as his world was about to change. In the same way, I needed many "someones" like Spencer to come into my world and help me become a better me.

THE ALTITUDES OF ACCEPTANCE

In hindsight, I used to not be aware of missing out on other people, but now I know better. We never can predict, based on our feelings, whose experiences or troubles will touch us, and from Spencer's perspective, we never know whose life lessons might need the person we are.

But given the evidence in my life's adventure, I trust that God does.

In telling these stories, I'm reminded that real change feels like we are going against the grain of our natural selves, and that can hurt. Sometimes we must even set aside lesser habits to get over the big humps and challenges of personal improvement. We have to make that consistent choice to go beyond the comfort zone, to be willing to do what's best rather than what's comfortable. In my experience, personal improvement tends to be imperceptible—we don't notice our own changes as easily as others might. This often makes the rewards of change feel too small.

The scriptures talk about change in terms of choosing God and our connection to him over all the draws life has upon us and the twists and turns it has in store for us. When open ourselves to personal improvement, God promises to help. He guides our very character, tolerance, and skills toward change by sending small and simple personalized invitations. Some come without words, some ignite a much-needed perspective shift, but some come through angels and other people.

When it comes to other people, life's adventure is fraught with complicated emotions, situations, and the people who come with them. However, building connections can be a short journey instead of an everlasting quest when we are willing to make changes. Such changes can be fueled by connections while also creating them, so it would seem the power to truly change lies in how we wish to conduct ourselves with others and how we turn to God when it really matters.

I used to think feeling knotty and full of holes was wrong, but now I know there is nothing more normal and natural that also deserves to be viewed through the lens of change. In fact, the defects of our lives, from knots, splits, cracks, warping, and so on—also known as internal battles and infirmities—can be very distracting, but there is a far stronger force at work here.

Who we are is largely originated in God, who might be looked upon as a master carpenter and project coordinator. He intends for us to experience all that we are, holes and all, so that he might motivate change in us as God's divine design unfolds. He aims to create something beautiful with us—never to limit us.

To use a different analogy, learning how to manage our holes and our lifescapes is like what someone once told me about the climate and the weather. The climate tells us what clothes to own, but the weather tells us what clothes to wear. Correspondingly, who we are, including our holes, tells us our long view of change, but the current lifescape tells us what we can do each day.

We have seen beautiful artwork come from gnarly old things, and we are all inspired by stories where the most unlikely people with small, unprepossessing lives have the most awesome adventures. And just as beauty is in the eye of the beholder, hope is the deep fire of change. Hope tells us to believe that life is less the way it is and more the result of who we are and will become.

CHAPTER 13

THE ADVENTURE OF PEOPLE

Sometimes I wonder about the people we meet throughout every lifescape who fade away or who we lose for various reasons. This occurs when life encourages us to look back at the faces and voices attached to our memories, especially those that belong to people who influenced us. However, sometimes we get so far ahead that we can't see those people anymore. If that happens, do we still know how lucky we are that we got to walk with them for a little while?

One person I still feel very lucky to know—who taught me so much in some very remarkable and dynamic ways—is Brent.

We met during my first year at the school when I worked in the middle school science class. For age thirteen, Brent was tall and stood at about my height. He was low-functioning, and his sweet, gentle spirit was often disturbed when other students had meltdowns. It wasn't long before I learned his anxiety skyrocketed when things became unstructured or unfamiliar.

One day, early in the school year, I was late getting to the science class after lunch. As I rushed up the stairs, I found him red-faced, pacing, and in tears by the elevator in the hallway.

His head was pressed into the wall he was leaning against, so I placed my hand on his shoulder. "Brent, you're crying! What is wrong?"

"Miss Deanna! I-I'm crying b-because—I didn't know I-I was in the right place—b-b-because y-you weren't there!"

Wait—I'm his landmark? I'm the reason for his tears?

Then I recalled how I usually stood at the doorway when the kids came in, how I always said hi to Brent and his friends as they filed in, and how I was often the one assigned to help him throughout the class period.

No wonder he sets his clock by me.

"Oh, Brent, I'm so sorry. I didn't know you needed me like that. Can I show you a couple of other ways to know you are in the right classroom after lunch?"

"Okay, Miss Deanna."

I pointed to the number on a plate tacked onto the granite wall next to the door. "See these numbers—two, two, six? 226. Two hundred means second floor. Twenty-six is the classroom."

"Can we put a yellow bird sticker on it?"

I smiled at his random but excellent solution. "That's a good idea—I'll ask the other teacher later. Oh, and by the way, you can also know you're in the right classroom by knowing who the other teacher is." I pointed out the man walking around inside the room. "He's really nice. Remember, he's the one who helped you finish the DNA project with gummy candies and marshmallows yesterday. Also, this is the only classroom right next to the stairs. Does that help?"

"Sure, Miss Deanna." He wiped at his tears and that angry red hue began to fade from his cheeks.

"Good—are you ready to go inside and do some learning?"

"Will you be there too?"

"Of course. I'm not leaving for the rest of the class period."

With a sigh of relief, he took his seat.

The rest of the class went about as might be expected, lesson and all, except I kept thinking about how remarkable it was to have people in life who help us know without a doubt that we are in the right place. From parents to friends and leaders, these are the people who truly care, support us as we figure out where we belong, and always help us feel at home.

THE ALTITUDES OF ACCEPTANCE

These are the people we want to keep close, the ones we need to surround ourselves with—the ones we need to accept aren't perfect—but then, neither are we. And they love us anyway.

From that day on, Brent did find his way to class more easily, but his connection to me became more and more obvious. I became his go-to person—any time he experienced an involuntary reaction to a nervous system overload, this is pretty much how it went down:

A sweeping shriek like that of a banshee flew down the corridor and into my classroom, sounding something like, "Miss Deanna!" but with multiple *n*'s and *a*'s lasting beyond a full minute. Door open or not, the voice was unmistakable.

After feeling a little embarrassed to have my name raised to the rafters, I'd smile a bit sheepishly while the students and teachers would say, "Time to go, Miss D."

So, I would go into the hallway and do what I could to talk Brent out of his meltdown.

Initially, I was used as a reward when he was able to calm himself down after being triggered by other people's behavior. However, if he was responsible for causing trouble and set himself off, I would be waved away upon my arrival. Then as the year progressed, they had him adopt other more tangible rewards, and I would respond to his "Miss Deanna" with discretion. Occasionally I would be encouraged to wait five minutes, and they'd bring him to me instead. Eventually, another go-to reward became his iPad. I wasn't sure about the benefits of that iPad overall, but I knew everyone was grateful it put a stop to the screaming and tantrums.

When I began leading the train transportation program, I met Brent's parents. I realized very quickly how dedicated they were to ensuring Brent's quality of life. They learned about his connection to me and concluded that Brent could ride the train with his brothers and sit with me because my presence helped him feel safe. Brent loved trains, and I believe riding the train every day helped him thrive. That's just what happens when we find a level of adventure we can cherish.

A couple of years later, in late April, Brent's father dropped off Brent and his brothers and approached me with a proposal.

"Good morning, Miss Deanna."

"Good morning," I said with a smile.

"Look, I was wondering, well—we are going to have all three of our sons attend the local high school closer to our home next year instead of the charter school, and we want Brent to feel ready. We think he needs an exercise coach and mentoring for high school classes, particularly math. Would you be willing to work for us this summer? Help him get off his iPad and get healthy? I mean, there are things you can get him to do that no one else can! We'll be sure to make it worth your while."

I couldn't believe it. After all this time, the forest I'd been lost in was opening into a meadow and the view was getting wider. It sounded like I was being offered a job in which I could use my bachelor's degree to plan recreational activities and manage a youth program, even if only for one youth. I felt ready for a new opportunity, and I knew I could help Brent do hard things, like transition into adolescence, but could I help him expand his interests beyond his tablet and into the outdoors? There was only one way to find out!

Still, I felt cautious. After all, I had to make ends meet. Then Brent's dad quoted an hourly wage that was far better than my other summer job and told me workdays would be only six hours long. That seemed auspicious—I could work fewer hours and still make enough to live on.

Also, I cared. I couldn't allow an iPad to take over Brent's health!

THE ALTITUDES OF ACCEPTANCE

Choosing this job meant I would have extra time and more control over my summer schedule because I would no longer need to work at the summer camp. It also meant I could explore some of the free community environmental education courses held in the late afternoons for teachers.

There were a few reasons I had gained interest in their courses about water. First, I had seen algae growing in lakes and areas where it shouldn't. Next, I had recently witnessed mold and plumbing issues in my home. Finally, when I heard that clean, safe water was threatened in a weather crisis, the hunger to know more was real. Now, I wouldn't have to put it off any longer!

So, I made my choice and began working daily with Brent.

Starting with day one, my first task involved helping Brent earn high school credit for physical education over the summer. He and his two triplet brothers had signed up for a summer course that lasted three weeks, and I was Brent's partner with a large group of students. We spent hours every day doing lunges, push-ups, stretching, and indoor and outdoor sports.

At the end of week three and as with every curriculum, the teacher threw in a big test …

"Class, today you are going to run a mile. That's about sixteen laps on the concrete sidewalk around the soccer field. Your time today will be your personal time to beat at the end of the summer. Get a drink of water, walk out to the starting line, and let's see fast footwork."

Uh-huh. Brent—running? We shall see, together.

As our run started, I worked to give him words of encouragement, not just instruction. "You got this, Brent! Breathe in through your mouth and out through your nose, keep your arms in, shoulders back, head up. I'm right here with you!"

He ran *very* slowly, making the first quarter mile rather painful. Arms flailing, he finally said, "Miss D, my heart hurts—this is going to be the cause of my death!"

I pointed out, "You don't look about to die to me, in fact you look like you're very much alive—you're still running. Besides, the more you exercise, the less your heart will hurt. So, just keep going. It'll be okay."

"Okay, Miss D."

That day, sixteen laps didn't happen. In fact, we only managed eight laps—half a mile. I had to keep explaining to him about keeping his arms in and his head up. A few such improvements turned out to be enough to please the teacher who saw Brent's effort. For my part, I knew Brent would be asked questions about his day, so I decided to check in on what he would say.

"What will you tell your mother when she asked what you learned today?"

"I might have died if I did not stop running."

Uh-oh! My work was clearly cut out for me as fear was still the stronger influence.

After the PE class was over, my plan was to learn and apply ways to help Brent run, walk, stretch, exercise, and otherwise work on muscular development. When we weren't exercising, I planned to set up our schedule based on library learning resources, online materials for improving math skills, field trips to educational places, and my favorite—hiking.

However, since Brent was not accustomed to his beating heart while using the two legs God gifted him, but was good at staying upright on his bike, we ended up doing a lot of biking before we could do a lot of hiking. One day I challenged him to handle some hills with his wheels to strengthen his leg muscles and encourage mental mastery of appropriately shifting gears.

Having mapped out a distance with a few hills of varying gradients, I felt the distance was doable. We biked two miles through the park and beyond the cemetery, halfway to the mall, and then circled back to the park. The reward—the longest, steepest downhill—would be last, right ahead of a picnic in the park. What great bike ride didn't include the chance to fly?

But when I led the way down the big hill, the distance between Brent's bike and my bike increased. How had I missed that the faster I went on hills, the slower he rode?

Finally, we came to the park, and I turned my bike off the bumpy sidewalk into the grass and aimed toward a table. Although some distance away, I could hear Brent coming down the hill behind me.

Mission accomp—

—skidding, brakes squealing, wheels clattering, a young boy—

"Ah! Miss Deanna!"

Well, pride does go before a fall.

"Miss D, help!"

I set my bike against the table and turned to go assist Brent, who was trying to crawl into a sitting position in the grass. I thought how falling off a bike happens because there is distance between you and the ground—because you failed to do something right or took a risk beyond your skill level—because all other supports give out—and because the law of gravity takes over.

Failed to do something right?

Oh no! I never prepared Brent to navigate falling from a bike! Also, maybe he needed more practice with hills before this one? One thing's for sure, I got way too far ahead of him, and I bet he felt like he had to keep up, so he went too fast and got nervous about the speed, and then he fell.

Although the intent of my plan had been to strengthen and interest Brent in longer bike rides, I had failed to factor in his fatigue. I had failed to thoroughly assess his skill level related to hills, and now I had failed to keep him safe for the whole bike ride.

Now, Brent was hurting.

"Uh-oh, Brent, how did you end up falling?" I asked as I headed over to him.

"The ground was wobbling. And so I had to jump off."

I wanted to giggle at his way of sharing the details, but I noticed the sidewalk where he'd fallen was indeed bumpy and uneven. I also noticed he didn't use his left arm when I helped him stand up and put his backpack onto his back.

I could have assessed the injury more fully in the park, but his wrist was already swelling. I was certain it was broken, and the park was not the place to find an ice pack or an arm wrap. So, I prioritized getting Brent to a more comfortable location first. Then I would call his mother. No doubt he'd be taken to the hospital, and then—it was hard to think of what else might come from this.

Brent was able to walk despite his injuries, but I didn't want him riding or walking his bike home, so I grabbed his bike by its handlebar neck. That's when I noticed how he'd landed on the grass away from his bike as though he had jumped away from the fall. That was impressive, but jumping off a bike could have led to worse injuries. Still, it seemed only his arm was in pain.

Next, I collected my bike similarly in my other hand and aimed both in the direction of my home. Brent and I took a slow walking pace all the way to my house, and I tried to stay cheerful on the outside to help reduce Brent's tears and worries about his arm. But inside, I was sad that neither the bike ride nor the picnic in the park had become the fun rewards I thought they would be.

Although the same ride that tested his skills also broke him and didn't make me look good, it was the fall that showed me what Brent and I could learn from the experience.

For example, there are always consequences of failing or a hard fall that must be endured, and as his mom took him off to the emergency room, I was left to rethink our activities for the rest of the summer. At very least, biking would be off schedule for a while—Brent would be wearing a cast.

As it happened, he actually ended up with two or three different casts that summer.

He often complained about his itching arm after we went swimming. Even when I rinsed his arm and taught him to use pencils to relieve the itching, he took matters into his own hands at night. Two different times, he slipped his arm right out of the cast! It was so strange—I had never heard about a kid doing that before. All I could figure was that he somehow couldn't understand that being uncomfortable was part of the healing process, and that his arm needed to be protected for a while, no matter what.

On review of Brent's situation, I think of several scripture verses where God says we should be perfect and come unto him, allow him to protect us, and to try not to fall away from him. However, there are also pages and pages on what to do if we fall.

Apparently, God knows that we will fall, and he's prepared for it. Therefore, he wants us to accept what is in our best interest, even when the solution feels itchy and uncomfortable. That is to say, even if we can take off the cast God makes for us as we heal from the injuries of our fall, it would be wiser to endure its discomfort.

When people fall and experience distance from God, that distance might have been created by failing to do something that would have brought them closer to him. However, we must remember that flawed people make good choices all the time too. So, knowing that, I believe this is one of God's mysterious methods for teaching us that failure and flawed are not the same thing, that both are an intended part of life's adventure for everyone.

As for my part in instigating Brent's situation, I used to think the best plans would allow God to protect me from failure and make me perfect sooner, but now, I know that's not completely true. Effort can neither prevent failure nor ensure perfection.

The good news is that in life's adventure, even though we are great at blaming ourselves, it's not always our fault that we fail. There are many external circumstances we can't control. Too many factors, from genetics, upbringing, and the effects of other people's choices, tend to directly impact how we switch from standing upright to falling flat on our faces.

I think God has it all worked out so that failures are attached to our successes to help us be less likely to forget the lessons of failure. In fact, failure is often a prelude to our successes. Even more importantly, failure can play a key role in the process of self-realization and self-acceptance.

We learn a lot from mistakes—if we're willing to accept the lessons. Yet perfection is not a matter of becoming a collection of everything we've learned from mistakes. It's also so much more than becoming everything we think we should be or are supposed to be.

I think perfection is a personal experience that will come as we figure out how to appreciate all that God made us to be. It's a journey with many steep steps and perilous heights. Just as a mountain requires us to work out the steps needed to reach the top, God expects us to take every step necessary to reach him and achieve an individual kind of magnificence.

Five months and a healed arm later, I was aching for adventure, and I thought trying something completely new and out of Brent's comfort zone would help him discover new lessons to learn. So, I took Brent for his first snowshoeing adventure over the holiday break.

When we arrived, fresh snow had fallen, and the sky was slightly overcast. *Great!* In the first mile of snowshoeing, each footstep sank into the four top inches of fluffy whiteness. Everything seemed easy for Brent after I taught him about coordination between his hands and feet and three ways to get back up onto his feet when he fell. If this had been a ski trip, I would have teased him about it being all downhill from there!

THE ALTITUDES OF ACCEPTANCE

Or so I thought.

"Miss Deanna, where's my home?"

"It's in the valley."

"And where are we right now?"

"Well, we are in the mountains, in the snow, above the valley." Deciding the practical approach to his questions was not enough for the purpose of our adventure, I added a comment to help him focus on the present. "And it's beautiful!"

It really was! In this winter wonderland, a three-inch layer of perfectly white icing covered every branch. Some limbs drooping under the weight of so much snow caused the formation of delightful arches we could pass through. The green spruces, firs, and pines. The blue sky above. The likelihood of more storm clouds bringing snow. It was absolutely invigorating—at least for me!

"I'd much rather be in the valley, Miss Deanna."

Smiling, I supported his use of clear communication, preference, and tolerance of the activity with encouragement. "But you're safe and we're having fun!"

"But I'm so tired, Miss Deanna. Can I take a nap in the snow?"

Thump!

I turned around to see he had fallen back in the mound of snow before I could stop him.

Are we about to make snow angels in snowshoes?

I nodded a *no* answer, so he tried to stand.

"I can't get up! Also my heart hurts."

We'll see about that.

Under all that protesting bluster and the act of stopping in his tracks, there was still a willing heart, and I was not willing to let him give up. Plus, it was cold—and we were a good distance from the car.

"Brent, remember what I taught you about moving around when your heart hurts?"

"Yes. It means exercise. And it's good for me."

So proud!

"You're correct, way to go! Now, do you trust me?"

"Yes, Miss D. But I am so tired, and I can't get up!"

"I get it and that's okay! But I still need you to get up. We need to walk back to the car and to do that we need to keep moving. Also, you might get too cold if you do sit down too long. So, up you get! I know you can do it! Come on, you've fallen so many times since we started, only to rise up every single one of those other times!"

I took off my glove so that I could grasp Brent's gloved fingers more firmly. I had nearly fallen a few times myself while helping him, but this time I had some solid snow packed beneath me and good leverage.

In no time at all, Brent staked his pole into the snow, putting most of his weight on it, and let my arm guide him to his feet. Then I used my glove to brush the snow from his head, shoulders, and arms that were sticking out like tree branches.

"Did you know you have been doing physical activities with me for over a year?"

"Really?"

"Yes, and your muscles are much stronger than you think they are. If you can handle long bike rides and two-mile hikes, I know you can handle this. Trust me!"

Perhaps Brent needs a job.

"Do you think you could find the prettiest spot on the way back to the car? We need a great picture to send your mother. She'll be happy to know you're doing great!"

That seemed to encourage him, and he stayed on his feet, using his trekking poles the way I had taught him to navigate the snowy terrain behind me.

I pointed out a place where an elk or moose had rubbed an aspen tree, then showed him a ponderosa pine that was so tall and wide it could have been a Christmas tree—a long time ago. The fact that its lowest branches

THE ALTITUDES OF ACCEPTANCE

held their positions above our heads, creating a ceiling scented with glorious pine and fresh snow, told us such a fate would never apply to this tree.

Like magic, as we stood beneath the tree, it started to snow thick, big flakes.

Mesmerized, I took a few steps through the untouched snow beyond the tree, but Brent stopped me.

"Miss D—right here. This is the best place in the snow forest."

Interesting choice of words!

But I agreed—this was a snow forest!

I turned to look at him, and the blanket of snow covering the tall ponderosa and a few nearby, much smaller Douglas fir trees made it look like Brent was in a Bob Ross painting. He posed perfectly with his arms extended forward, holding his poles with relaxed gloved hands. His head tilted toward the sky, while his eyes remained on me, glittery and glowing. But the best part was Brent's smile. It was the best, most peaceful smile I had ever seen.

Sometimes, God does allow us to have these little perfect moments. Moments that are meant to be photographed, cherished, and remembered—the best moments any lifescape has to offer.

As I snapped the photo, I didn't have to ask my traditional question of what he would tell his mother when we sent it to her. I knew what he would say: *I made it to this spot because I fell down but kept getting up.*

That's what awesome people do—they fall—but they also get back up because deep inside, they know the best secret of all. The secret of being continuously in pursuit of higher ground, the quest of spiritual elevation, is that the best of them is found in how they respond to the fall. Choosing to take the higher ground and see the best in ourselves means we value the journey, the mountain, the valley, and the view of ourselves through God's eyes, not the eyes of the world.

THE ADVENTURE OF PEOPLE

Several months into the next year, it was summer again, and Brent was ready for longer hikes. This time I chose a waterfall destination. I had been taking water classes for two seasons now, so to enhance Brent's experience in the days leading up to the hike, I organized a few scientific practical lessons about how important water was to life. I demonstrated how water filters worked, and talked with him about how waterfalls had inspired modern hydroelectric power to create resources that led to clean and safe water for entire communities.

When the day arrived, it was all blue skies and sunshine—the best of circumstances.

Brent didn't start exhibiting tired behaviors until we had hiked about three miles, and even then it was several minutes of slower trekking before he said, "Miss Deanna, can we please turn around? This is really hard, and it's hot."

"You are right, this is hard work, and this is a good spot to turn around." I paused. "However, we have already hiked three miles, and this trail was only four miles long. Do you really want to miss out on seeing that waterfall, given we are so close?"

Brent's eyes went wide with the expectation of what waited. "Okay, okay, we can keep going!"

So, we did.

Twenty minutes later, we had reached the waterfall and walked over to stand in the refreshing spray wafting off the walls as the water crashed down from above. It felt so good, and I taught Brent about wetting a bandana and tying it around his neck to help him cool on the way back.

We sat on two large rocks to eat our lunches. Unfortunately, the stone was well populated with ants, and rather than keep fighting to keep our seats clean of ants, we only ate about half our food before we began hiking back.

Once the cars were visible in the distance, I asked Brent my usual question: "What are you going to tell your mother about what you learned today?"

"I am going to tell her that I am glad we didn't turn around, and that we saw a waterfall because we kept going!"

THE ALTITUDES OF ACCEPTANCE

Victory!

After a year of outdoor experiences and education, Brent was finally remembering the benefits of hard work and exercise. If it took a waterfall to help him master this mentality—well, thank God for water!

Stepping into the mentalities of another student, Oscar was a student with an eager smile and what seemed to be a great burden: He rarely seemed to remember his assignments long enough to complete them. However, why this was his story was a mystery because comparatively his memory was excellent with other things.

I realized this when he asked a simple question: "Miss D, do you remember my birthday?"

It wasn't common for teachers to memorize personal information of students, so I said, "Um, no. Sorry, I don't! But I could look it up if you want me to." For a split second, I thought he had forgotten his own birthday, and that maybe he wanted to write it down on some important document I didn't know about. However, that thought was short-lived.

"But I remember yours!"

"You do?"

Now I saw the tease in his gaze and wondered where this was going. Staff birthdays were known at this school because of how we would celebrate each other, or because the teachers found ways to celebrate their birthdays with the students. The side effect was that students picked up and retained such information easily, so I wasn't surprised Oscar could know this information.

"Yep." He proceeded to state my entire birthday correctly—month, day, and year. Then he shared, "I went for a long walk to the store on your birthday this year."

Given that my birthday was almost six months ago at this point, I felt intrigued, amused, and slightly confused. I stopped grading the papers on my desk and turned toward him with a grin. "Wow, what did you do, wake up and say to yourself, 'Today is Miss D's birthday. I think I'll go on a walk to celebrate!'?"

Oscar's demeanor brightened with a slight red hue as he returned the tease. "No! I just—I just remember what I did. I had to buy myself something that day."

I was so tempted to object about his remembering to buy *himself* a gift on *my* birthday, but instead I decided to keep the conversation centered on him. "Do you remember what you have done on other days this year?"

"Yeah. Mostly birthdays. And holidays. And three-day weekends. But why do I remember your birthday and you don't remember mine, Miss D?!"

He got me there. But two could play this game.

"Give me a break, mister! I mean, you've known your birthday all your life, and I've only known yours since last year. Also, there are far fewer teachers than students—I couldn't possibly remember all your birthdays much less pass a test about them!"

Oscar grinned. "Haha, Miss D. I guess that just means I have a better memory than you!"

My jaw shifted as my lips pursed in resistance to the truth of his statement. In the end, I conceded, with an exception. "I guess you do, Oscar, I guess you do, But say, Oscar—maybe one day you will remember your work and assignments better than my birthday?"

"Not a chance!"

This kid is awesome. Such flattery will get him—everywhere!

At first, I simply appreciated how Oscar exercised his memory in a meaningful manner. But then I understood something that ran much deeper—Oscar was authentic about making the most of his abilities, and in this matter, he wasn't interested in what he couldn't do. Oscar knew himself, and he knew he could remember things about other people better than anything else. No doubt the adult version of Oscar would be able to make good use of memorizing dates and activities!

Oscar wasn't alone with such capabilities. There was a younger student who could reveal the day of the week for any date someone told him on any calendar year—past, present, or future. It only took him five seconds to tell me I was born on a Monday!

Clearly, the children I worked with could do amazing things. The truth is, despite expectations, brains with autism work; they just work differently.

I had been waiting forever—or at least four years—for my name to appear on the list.

Ever since I had learned teachers could accompany students on the end-of-year student trip to Lagoon, an outdoor amusement park, I had watched for this list with anticipation, curious whether it was my turn or if I would forever be bereft of such enjoyment.

Inwardly, I knew it was a trivial matter, but my excitement was undeniably uncontained when I found out I was a member of the in-crowd that year. Being numbered among the teacher chaperones gave rise to a splendid sense of belonging. However, on the outside, I maintained a calm demeanor, which a soldier or security officer would be proud of.

The day of the trip was what the child in me dreamed of—while in reality, I was attached to a small herd of students. I jumped onto gravity-defying roller coasters, got soaked on water rides, and wandered to every open ride possible. Sweets I hadn't seen since I was a kid emerged out of the woodwork—giant jawbreakers and candy rock crystals. I don't know how I managed to limit my sugar intake to just cotton candy.

As might be expected, the bus ride away from the park was filled with many sleepyheads, me included. By the time we returned, the last bell had rung, and most students were leaving. But the next day, what I didn't expect was to be accosted in the hallway by a middle school student from gym class as soon as I walked back into the building!

"Miss D, I heard you were having the time of your life yesterday," said Arden.

His eyes were clear with his intent, but he kept the reason for his statement wrapped in mystery. I could think of a few better ways to spend my free time that my adult self would qualify as *the time of my life*, yet in all honesty, he was not wrong.

My curiosity led me to question him. "Oh really? Where'd you hear that?"

"From Mr. Denshaw. I asked him where you were, and he said, 'She's having the time of her life at Lagoon, and I'm stuck here with you …'"

Trying not to laugh, I couldn't help but wonder if Mr. Denshaw really said he was *stuck* or if this was just Abe's version of a busy gym teacher's response? Or maybe something terrible had made the day feel like a genuine burden?

Yikes, what had I missed? Was Mr. Denshaw jealous, or was it simply a rough day for him?

Before I knew it, *my* imagination got stuck in the worst-case scenario, and every mental conjecture seemed to snuff my feelings of fun and excitement. Half distracted by my own thoughts, all I could say was, "Well, that sounds horrible!"

"Yep, it was." Then he turned around and walked away.

That's it?

I raised my hand to stop him, hoping to get more information, but there I was, left standing in a mental muddle as I stared at his back disappearing down the hallway.

And then, it hit me.

Arden was using the teacher's words, if indeed the teacher had spoken them, to get a message to me. He was saying, "I noticed you were gone, and I just want to say, don't stay away. I missed *you* yesterday, and I don't want to miss you more!"

I had been on Arden's mind.

I mattered.

I belonged.

I was more than just a void, or a space, or a speck filling a gap.

This was a very rare occasion. I hardly ever understood what others did or felt about me when I was absent, but here I was, face to face with it.

For the first time, I understood that when we are missing from our usual places, our absence can have an impact on the people left behind for better or worse, whether we are still living or have passed on. A wise man once told me how important it is to live life well while paying attention to the lessons of death because the two are invaluably intertwined. The lessons of death are in the lives of the loved people left behind. And if we are the people left behind, we never really know the true impact of a person until they are gone, when the voices of people who knew them come together to share what they know.

I used to think belonging anywhere was achieved by making my presence known and succeeding in everything I set out to do, but now I know the most awesome way to fall into a better future and to belong in the world is to fail.

That is, fail to go the distance alone.

Filling the time in our lives with rewarding relationships and *life-centered* choices, allowing opportunities to help each other, and giving our time and believing we matter, even to just one person, and especially to God—these create a sense of belonging.

Recognizing I mattered to others—especially a child—and letting others know they mattered to me, prompted me to stop underestimating the impact of my presence or absence, and to think differently of others with greater love and appreciation for what they brought to my life when they were gone too.

THE ADVENTURE OF PEOPLE

Some months later on a bright summer day, I found myself again working one-on-one with Brent. I don't quite recall how we got there—maybe we were just taking a walk or on a field trip—but we ended up in a cemetery surrounded by headstones. For whatever reason, we were looking around at the headstones and thinking of these people's lives even when they were gone.

After observing ten or so stones, Brent spoke up. "I don't have a date of death yet."

I choked back a laugh as I looked at him to see if he was serious.

With all the solemn respect I could muster for those who were six feet under, I finally nodded, swallowed, and replied, "I can see why you would observe that fact—in a crowd of people who do."

A slight pause, then came another of Brent's unusual thoughts with a detached sigh: "I'm tired of not being dead."

My eyes jerked in his direction, searching for any telltale signs of risk. It was not my place to talk with him familiarly about death or loss, but another thought came to me—*Did Brent understand death to be a rest from the rigors of this life? Or was he saying something else?*

A friend passing our spot by the tree overheard Brent and started to sing and dance to the rhythm of "Uh-oh, uh-oh, staying alive, staying alive!"

I glanced at my friend, wanting to join in, but after finishing my assessment of Brent, I decided to stay with him in his moment.

Brent wasn't the kind of kid who read books about death. He felt certain things deeply and often displayed genuine empathy and concern, so sometimes he brought up family members who had passed away, but he generally preferred to talk about math, clouds, planes, and trains.

But as one of those absorbent little autistic sponges, Brent had a certain quirk. He didn't know how *not* to get emotionally involved when other living things around him were struggling. So, a cemetery must have represented a thousand various life struggles to him, and that caused him to fall into a personal reflection about the rigors of life.

What can I say? I felt kind of proud, amused, and concerned all at the same time!

"Brent, that's so profound. I must say, I have also felt that way from time to time, and I'm sad to say this will likely not be the last time you feel that way."

As we continued to wander through the cemetery, my mind kept returning to the words *staying alive* and *not being dead*. As far as I could tell, *being alive* and *staying alive* were two different things. In between, there was something else—*being lively*—but *being lively* was a matter of character and choice.

Based on what I knew from experience, *being alive* meant I could feel things, bleed, and die. Because of my faith, I saw *being alive* as a gift from God—a gift that can be given without being fully received, which is evidence that *being alive* can be tiring. However, when we die, it needs to be when it's our time to join God in the greater causes he has on the other side.

So, just as God prioritizes our lives, we should too.

Hmm, so what does that perspective say about staying alive?

Given how many ways there are to leave this world, *staying alive* is all about what happens before we get that second date on a headstone. It's more than simply not dying or living in an eat-drink-and-be-merry sort of way.

As I look back on this story, something a friend once said in passing comes to mind as an answer—*As long as I am on this side of the grass still buying green bananas, I know I'm alive.* It made sense to me—green bananas are chalky and bitter, but after they ripen a few days later, they taste amazing. Being willing to pay for green bananas means we expect to live to see another day. If we intend to stay alive, we plan. We also seek good things in abundance.

Spiritually speaking, *staying alive* also means intentionally following a sense of right and wrong in the direction of fulfilling our purpose and understanding our potential. It means engaging persistently in courageous quests that serve God but could cost something on a worldly standard.

THE ADVENTURE OF PEOPLE

Staying alive is finding motivation to do hard, uncomfortable, and important things that we have never done before. It is knowing God leads us through every hardship and adventure. It is believing God can move mountains on our behalf.

It is also realizing that if God decides to let us climb instead, or to move us up, around, over, or through those mountains, then we still trust him and his promises to get us where we need to go.

As my fourth year at the school entered the halfway point, a high school student with jet black hair named Jason started riding the train from the same station as I did.

Jason actually helped me understand what it meant to stay alive on a whole new level.

Although my job as a chaperone had ended, I still kept an eye on the students as needed. I tried to board with them so that they would know I was there, and one overcast winter morning, I stood right behind Jason as the train pulled up. As usual, there was a giant soda in Jason's hand—it was one of those large gas station drink cups with a lid and straw.

Like all the other train doorways, there was a metal grate below the sliding door. They usually offered good traction for those hopping onto the train. However, a storm had just finished blowing through, and ice was building along the side of the train and accumulating onto the grate. Most people were stepping over it, but not Jason.

Jason wore Vans with zero traction, and he stepped squarely onto the ice. Just like in a mystery movie when the viewer sees an event unfold but doesn't comprehend time passing, the clock slowed down for a fraction of a second as Jason's leg skidded off the grate and his whole body gave in to gravity, lodging his leg in the narrow space between the train and the platform!

"*AH!*" Jason's scream was so loud, so clear, and so high-pitched that everyone on the train platform and inside the train had likely heard it.

Around him, men were reaching for his arms and shoulders, while I stood there feeling a few notches below hysterical, frozen in place, and terrified I would see the train move.

Thirty seconds passed and the men were still struggling to pull him out; the ice was as slick as oil. I wanted to turn and run fifty yards to the front of the train, to wave down the conductor, to stop the train, to—but I couldn't move.

Jason's arms waved about in irritation with the fumbling rescuers, inviting them to back off. When they got the message, he carefully set his drink on the platform, making sure to keep it out of the footpath of any other people around him.

A few persistent people were waiting to use the entry he was blocking.

Move along to the next door. Can't you see this is a situation, folks?

Finally, Jason used the dry sleeves of his coat to gain traction and managed to pull himself up. Once he stood on the concrete again, he brushed off the snowy ice chunks his clothes had accumulated, quickly studying each clump the way a war general studies the enemy.

When he finally looked up, his face wore a remarkably serious expression.

His first words matched the fire in his eyes. "I did *not* just scream like a girl!"

Then, pulling off what looked like a boy-band dance move, he leaned down on one foot to snatch up his soda, locked eyes with me on his way back to a standing position, and returned to business as usual, marching with purpose onto the train as if nothing had happened.

And that big cup of red soda? Never spilt a drop.

The teacher in me was disappointed in his lack of gratitude to the men who had tried to assist him, so I expressed a thank you to both who were still watching with me before I entered the train and caught up with Jason.

"Jason, are you okay? What just happened out there?" We were climbing the stairs, so I could see he wasn't limping, but I caught a bewildered look beneath his fiery eyes.

His response—a shrug of his shoulders. He was just as shocked as anyone else but was totally playing it off like he could have planned the whole thing.

His wordlessness and dazed eyes triggered a giggle that stayed with me all day. To the point that during math class, a few students gave me odd looks, no doubt wondering what was so funny about trigonometric values and formulas.

During lunch, I finally had a chance to record the story and write down the part I loved most—how Jason's fall had not kept him down in any way. It was like he had the gift of both physical and mental resilience.

A couple of months later as I rode the train, I discovered the school's bus transportation was out of commission. It figured—at 11°F, it was freezing cold!

I took responsibility and called the school, thankfully discovering that the schoolteachers who did not have a first block class were on their way, driving the vehicles that I had driven as the train monitor. It was the only way to collect as many students as possible on the first trip. With the wind blowing, it took about twenty minutes before the first car pulled up, and there were more than thirty students waiting to be picked up.

At this point, the students had lost interest in jumping jacks and counting the number of snowflakes they could catch on their tongues, so they were ice cold and quickly climbed into cars.

When there were no more seat belts left, three students and I remained.

Shivering, I mentally prepared myself for a longer time in the cold. This level of exposure to the cold in addition to the somewhat sedentary situation

THE ALTITUDES OF ACCEPTANCE

felt extreme. If I had ever been out in such temperatures for this long before, it was for snowshoeing or cross-country skiing. Without constant high level physical activity, my blood circulation was struggling, and despite doing everything I could to try and stay warm, I must have had purple lips by the time another car arrived.

Wait—is that who I think it is?

The window rolled down and the driver said, "My dear girl, I insist you take my place in this car and take the students with you to the school. I'll wait here at the station. Just don't forget to come back for me, would you?"

Oh wow, it's one of my former train program partners, the school counselor, rescuing me again!

Usually, he rode the train on snowy days, but for some reason, he had driven that day.

"What are you doing here?"

As he parked his car and left the ignition on, he stepped out of the driver's side and held the door open for me. "I got to school and heard about the transportation, or lack thereof. Thought I could offer some help. Not like I have any classes to worry about this morning, being the school counselor. Come on, get out of here and take those kids with you!"

I was too cold for words, and hearing his resolve, I had no desire to retort. Staying in the cold and letting me drive his car was one of the most selfless acts of service I had ever been given. So, I nodded and mouthed, "Thank you," before sliding into the driver's seat.

Welcoming the already warm environment and feeling my cold fingers fumble with the mirror as I adjusted it, I noticed the students already piled in the back.

"Everyone strapped in?"

"Yes, Miss D!" They answered in unison.

While I didn't want to leave the school counselor behind, I didn't see any other way. As we pulled out of the parking lot, I saw my friend starting to walk in laps around the parking lot and train platform.

Good, with that kind of exercise he should be able to stay warm.

THE ADVENTURE OF PEOPLE

Once the students warmed up, their chatter ensued, but I stayed quiet. It was all I could do to drive and defrost. As soon as we got to the school, I asked one of the students to tell the front desk and my classroom partner what I needed to do, and then drove back to get the counselor.

He was easy to find, still pacing across the platform. Parking his car and climbing out as he approached, I gave him the warmest smile I could, and said, "You might be a hero today!"

"Sometimes a little hero goes a long way. You look much better," he said, settling into the driver's seat, while I walked around to the passenger's side.

"Thanks to you! I feel much better!" I felt genuinely cheerful and relieved.

Little did I know this wasn't the end of what I would feel grateful for that day.

During lunchtime, I was assigned to monitor the student kitchen classroom. Students who could neither handle the noisy lunchroom nor go outside or to other classrooms ate in the kitchen when it was too cold outside. I usually preferred the chance to monitor outside activity during the day, but I had had plenty of outdoor time that morning.

The best part of being inside the kitchen during lunch was that I could eat while hanging with the students instead of waiting until lunchtime was over. As I unscrewed my soup container to reheat it in the microwave and began walking across the room, my shoes encountered something oily on the ground. They were clog-style platforms without much tread, so despite being warm for the outdoor weather, they were no match for an oily kitchen floor.

In an instant, I found myself upended, with one leg sprawled to the side and the other one bent under me.

THE ALTITUDES OF ACCEPTANCE

I probably looked like I had broken my femur or my tailbone because I held my position on the ground for a full minute after I stopped. The students watched silently with breathless, wide-eyed expressions as I lay there, my back on the ground, and my head lifted for protection. When I finally did move, I relaxed my head, forgetting about the oily floor, and directed my eyes toward my arm, which was somehow reaching for the ceiling.

I might have been a wax figure inspired by the Statue of Liberty!

A halo of light seemed to surround my container of soup that perched on the end of my arm. Somehow, I had managed to not spill a single drop.

Just like Jason.

Unbelievable. And so weirdly awesome!

After making sure I wasn't injured, I heated my soup and seated myself to eat. I started telling stories to the other students while pretending nothing weird had happened.

Huh. Jason did that too.

In the early spring, the school began midterm testing, and as a result I was assigned to be a test proctor in the classroom I normally worked in. This meant I had to ensure the students left the room only for necessary reasons, ate their snacks, and shared responsibility to keep the space quiet for best results. It was a teacher's dream, to have everyone hard at work doing what they were supposed to be doing without being told.

Everyone, that is, except Jason, who had finished earlier, caused a ruckus, and been encouraged to leave the room, and Tara, one who had been working diligently since the start of class. Tara was waving me over so I could look over her test.

Peering over her shoulder, I saw one, then five, then ten correct answers. I had known the neurodivergent could mentally zone in on things, but Tara had somehow tapped into a brain-based ability to shut out all of Jason's noise and focus 120 percent on her work. Would most neurotypicals be able to understand why she could do this? Nope. But maybe they should try!

Because one day Tara might finish her thesis on a noisy subway or make a life-altering discovery in a busy lab full of competitive scientists. I wouldn't put it past her.

In fact, if I didn't know any better, I would suspect I had just discovered a superhero in the making. All the stories I knew about superheroes started with awkward traits or problematic challenges that set them apart from their peers and acquaintances. Because of this they are perceived as being unable to experience life in a normal fashion and become the target of exclusionary tactics. However, despite this the hero always found the motivation to take steps that led to becoming an incredible person.

Besides, why wouldn't its heroes be among the growing population of people with autism?

It's about time the world saw that those who are less likely to do the expected are usually the most likely to do the unexpected. That could apply for better or worse in some cases, but whether the world can see or not, those who face an inability to do the expected need to know and comprehend the truth. Those with neurodivergent minds are in a unique position have individual gifts and capacities that might not make them popular or perfect—yet—but they do make them who they are.

In the Book of John, chapter nine, we come across a man who has been blind since birth. One day the disciples asked Jesus if the blind man deserved to be blind due to some sin, or if the blindness was a result of parental behavior.

Jesus's response—The man had been made blind, so that the power of God might be displayed. Then Jesus declared he is the light of the world, which can be taken into context when we consider the pending changes to the darkness the blind man had been experiencing all his life.

He then proceeds to heal the man's sight. Jesus made mud with spit and plastered it across the man's eyes. Finally, he instructed the blind man to wash in a specific pool some distance away.

Nothing is mentioned about anyone going along to make sure the blind man reached the destination, but then he was used to being blind and obedient and was probably willing to try anything, with or without help. I like to think he also knew that if he received his sight, he wouldn't need extra eyes on the return trip.

After washing, the man received his sight, and, for better or worse, so much more.

Upon his return, his friends hardly recognized him, and others denied it was him. They stopped him in the street, demanded an explanation, and then took him to the authorities—not to celebrate the fact that he could see, but to convince him the way he got his sight back was against the law and a sin.

To his credit, the man didn't deny the miracle he had received, even while under pressure to throw Jesus to the wolves. He stuck to what he knew had happened and even declared Jesus to be more than a prophet because he had healed him when nothing and no one else had been able to help him.

Hearing this, the authorities went to his parents and tried to get them to deny that this man who could now see was their son. None of the family succumbed to the pressure to tell a different story.

In fact, the man testified how this miracle was unprecedented and declared that if Jesus was not of God, he could do nothing like this. He knew the authorities wanted a reason to take down Jesus, but the man knew the truth. He honored God until he was set free—literally. He was thrown out of the room because the authorities could do nothing else with him, or his story.

Jesus heard of this and went to the man, and having told the man who he was, Jesus rewarded him for his belief by helping him understand that his small role played a critical part in why Jesus was there.

Years of dealing patiently with his unresolvable challenge had made the blind man honest, resilient, and unfettered by the need to fit in. This man, who spent years being unable to see as others could see, and who had spent his entire life as an underdog, had been conditioned all along to humbly recognize the workings and dealings of God. He had gained perspective and was empowered to do something that seemed strange to others. He took the higher ground while under pressure, displayed true courage, and most importantly did the right thing while fulfilling God's purpose. No longer hidden from the world by blindness, the best of what was in the man became a way for Jesus to share his light with the world, a way to provide powerful evidence and proof that God could do what he said he would do.

It is also important to note that his story might have been recorded to help us heal the rifts and great divides that exist in society today.

Although his story filled only one chapter, and though we never know his name, this man has been read about and talked about by Bible readers and church leaders for centuries. It's a story of healing, yet it also shows how important to God it was for one man to live a certain life and become who and what he was so that he could accomplish his purpose.

If this was important for one nameless, blind person, it is important for everyone.

I used to think the person God could use to bring about great things would be a prophet or leader, but now I know God intends to accomplish his purposes in life's great adventure with me and those great people around me, when we are ready. That includes awesome people like Brent, Oscar, Tara, Jason, and the school counselor—all of whom belong in my lifescape and taught me things about myself and others.

From them, I learned that being great is not about being recognized by the world, which is less important than having the right people around. Those who hold on tight to the truth about themselves and what God thinks of them don't have to tell the stories the world wants to hear. I respect those people who outwardly seem to take up only one chapter in a book, yet they possess an entire volume's worth of personal growth and acceptance.

This is the kind of quiet humility we often don't see in ourselves or others until after it's already been there for a long time. As we engage in and exemplify the actions that help us come closer to God, step by step through our lifescapes, we will find this defining purpose and wisdom—and we will reach the altitudes God intends for us to reach.

CHAPTER 14

TAKE THE RIDE

"*I* want to get off!"

The piercing shriek came as I was standing in line for the biggest white, rickety roller coaster at Denver's Six Flags. Anywhere else such a shrill scream would have curdled my blood, but today, of course, there was nothing more normal.

Looking around, it didn't take long for me to find its source. A young girl with long hair in two braids, wearing overall jeans, a pink shirt—and a panicked expression—was sitting in the roller coaster car slowly making its way forward.

I was only ten yards away. As the machine click-clacked slowly toward its first ascent, I heard a concerned voice say, "We talked about this … you said you were ready …" And then, "It's okay, you can do this."

Although I overheard only snippets of sentences, the man's voice had to be her father. It seemed her squirming under the grab bar stressed him out. His face looked tart and confused, like someone had just tossed a pickle in his apple cider. Still, he desperately tried to console her as he reached out to keep her from slipping beneath the bar.

I felt bad for him, knowing he was probably dealing with his daughter's emotional state as well as he could. I bet he had even looked forward to sharing the experience of her first roller coaster ride. And yet, here she was, completely discouraged and afraid.

My gaze swept to the coaster crew. The young men were giving each other sideways glances.

No one made a move.

The meaning couldn't be clearer if it were written on the walls—there was no stopping this ride unless it was a real emergency. And they believed this was no emergency.

Figures. I imagine hearing screaming passengers is quite normal for them too.

As the screams continued, so did the public level of discomfort. The girl's distress floated through the air, eliciting a response from everyone in earshot as if it was a contagion. Conversations paused, laughing stopped, and all eyes were on the ride. The roller coaster was about the only thing that didn't respond to the screams.

When the girl was brought back under the grab bar, a few people around me released their white-knuckled fists.

No one fell out. *Whew!*

I had to give the father credit, even if he had his work cut out for him in an unexpected way. I'll never know how he got her to sit in the middle of the seat with her legs pressed into the footboard and arms on the bar just in time, but I could see the resolve on the girl's face as the car slid up the track. There were tears, but it was clear to all of us that something had changed.

As the car careened around the curves, the onlookers released a collective sigh as the daughter's screams of terror transformed into high-pitched squeals of laughter.

I'm not sure what happened, but by the time they got back, the little girl looked happy—and a few years older than I expected.

I cocked my head in confusion.

How—what the …? Maybe without her pigtails …?

Her scrunchies had fallen out, and she didn't seem to notice or care about them.

Heh, she had really let her hair down.

In fact, she was a new person, laughing and leaning into her dad's shoulder as they climbed out of the car.

As I climbed in, I couldn't help but notice the dad's satisfied 'I'm a rad dad' expression. Well earned, given it was a *mission accomplished*. However, there was also a hint of seriousness, enough that I imagined their entire post-roller coaster conversation going something like this:

"So, that was totally awesome! Did you love it or what?" the dad would ask.

"Dad, it was great. I can't believe I did that!"

"You did it and I'm your witness! Also—remember how you wanted to get off?"

"Yeah. I am so sorry. I don't know why I freaked out."

The daughter would hesitate to meet his eyes but seeing this he would direct her firmly by the shoulders to look at him.

"That scared me too much! I was terrified of how I wasn't going to be able to help you. You could have fallen out, you know, by giving in to the fear right when you felt the roller coaster going up." He would then take a calming breath before continuing. "What made you finally grab the bars and be still?"

She would look away, display a new kind of squirmy, but the need to talk to her dad about hard things would already be a good habit, so despite her discomfort she would turn to face him and say, "I thought I was ready—I really did. You told me a lot of things to get me ready, but I never *felt* what a roller coaster was like. When I saw the steep uphill and the drop on the other side, I just forgot it might be fun. I didn't know it was going to feel so scary. I promise! I swear!"

"Oh, I see. Some things in life, I guess I can't fully prepare you for. But it's over now."

"Yeah," the girl would say, looking down at her feet, wondering if he was disappointed in her.

Trying to ease her discomfort, Dad would say, "So, you grabbed the bar when you realized you had no other choice?"

"Kind of. It was more like—well, I realized I had already made my choice. But in the moment, I found I knew only one thing—you were right there with me, and because of that I could handle anything!"

"And you did. Just as I knew you would."

His arm would go around her shoulders and give her a squeeze as they turned toward the path, onto the next ride. Or so my imagination told me. For all I knew, they were just putting on a show for the rest of us!

Still, like the smell of cotton candy on my clothes, the apparent trepidations of this first-time rider stayed with me all the way home. I was no stranger to the thrills of a roller coaster, so I was not exactly in the girl's position. I knew what to expect on these wild rides, but if I was honest, there were times when hardship or fear made me scream to my Father, "I want to get off!"

However, the truth is as cold and hard as the metal poles, cogs, and chains. We not only need life's roller coaster, but we are also built to handle it. It seems like God doesn't want us to know everything about how the ride will feel or to comprehend every rise and fall before it happens. What he really wants is for us to choose to get on and ride it out. God wants us to trust in him like this girl trusted her dad. As with the "University of Hard Knocks," regardless of whether you think you're ready for the roller coaster ride, the best way *out* is *in*. And like it or not, we often don't get to know when it's over until it's over because the ride is on his timing, not ours.

Speaking of God's timing, as I was compiling stories for this book, I reconnected with a childhood friend, Megan. Although we had fallen apart for years, it appeared our lifescapes carried perspectives and lessons sourced from similar roots—navigating the world of autism. My perspective was that of a teacher, while hers came as a parent because one of her two daughters had autism.

Talking with Megan, I sensed love, selflessness, and self-awareness as she spoke in a way that showed consistent involvement with her child's engagement at school. I knew raising a child with autism was hard for even the most loving of people. Collecting stories from a parent far outside my school environment seemed equally worthwhile, and our conversation went as follows:

Me: Megan, your challenges—from sometimes feeling stuck or robbed of experiences in life to feeling positive about raising someone with autism. Can you tell me a few things you've learned from raising your daughter, like the mountains you've had to climb?

Megan: Well, at first, I didn't like Reece having to deal with a challenge she didn't choose. No parent dealing with the hardships of autism would wish that on their child, but now I can't deny that learning how to live with autism has sometimes been a blessing.

From raising Reece, I've learned life is just a journey when you do it alone, but it becomes an adventure when you include others. From the beginning, Reece seemed to get that and understood the rest of her family were a part of it. She loved involving us in her life, and I love witnessing how God works with her too.

Reece is a natural at seeing purpose in pain. It's almost funny the way she deals with it. The other day, she scraped her toe against the sidewalk, and instead of crying, even though I knew it hurt, she said, "Mom, it's not a good idea to walk there!"

Me: Aww. She didn't assign fault to the sidewalk? That's precocious! I mean, some adults I know don't know how to *not* blame everything else including God for their hurting.

Megan: No kidding! I think she arrived with a different way of seeing the world. I am not sure how much of it is autism, or how much of it is just her special little self.

Me: Reece sounds like the sweetest! Maybe it's both. Do you have any other stories like that?

THE ALTITUDES OF ACCEPTANCE

Megan: Well, one week at a church activity Reece was given a yellow balloon. I had never seen her more thrilled or excited. Afterward, she skipped beside me down the sidewalk to the car, but she looked like she was floating!

Then the balloon met a tree limb above her head. There was nothing I could do to prevent it in the dark.

Pop!

Reece was devastated. I've never seen her so upset. She cried every day the next week. I think she'd had such great plans for that balloon that it was like a family member—a part of her life's adventure—and it was hard for her to let go of its memory. I had to comfort her and help her understand why sometimes things we are happy about sometimes go away.

A few days later we went to our favorite restaurant for her birthday dinner. They were very kind and gave Reece and her sister, Lily, two big colorful balloons.

Neither balloon was yellow, but with a big grin, Reece cheered. "Oh! I finally got my balloon back!"

I grinned—I knew Reece knew balloons didn't get resurrected, but the thought was so like her! The way she hugged the new red balloon all the way to the car like it was a long-lost friend just melted my heart.

Of course, just as we reached the car, Lily lost hold on her pink balloon's string.

It blew into the grass and exploded into pink rubber pieces. Spotlighted by the nearby lamppost, I saw Lily gasping, and then a silent heartbreak crept all over her face. It wasn't her fault—it could have happened to anyone—but she seemed to think it was. I offered her a hug and tried to comfort her as I tucked her into her car seat, hoping the drive might calm her spirits.

As I slid into the driver's seat and reversed out of the parking spot, I glanced in the rearview mirror. Lily's eyes were still wet.

I wish I had looked over at Reece to see her reaction as she watched her sister sorrowing. I am sure I would have seen Reece's most compassionate expression—her earnest, concerned eyes staring, trying to figure out the other person, because the next thing I heard was, "It's okay, Lily, you can have mine."

Reece held out her red balloon for her sister and Lily hesitated for just a moment, then took the balloon in one hand while wiping her eyes dry with the other.

For me, all the red roses in the world had never done more to symbolize love to a person than this red balloon had just done in the hands of my beautiful Reece. She had given everything she had to her sister. She was among the poor herself yet was still willing to give.

God loved to see love like this.

From the front, I said, "Reece, I am so proud of you for being so kind and doing that."

Reece said, "Mom, remember when my balloon popped last week, and it was like, the worst feeling in the world? I don't want Lily to feel like I did. I don't want her to cry."

It's easy to get caught up with the challenges of raising a neurodivergent. When people realize I'm raising an autistic child, most people say, "I don't know how you do it."

But it's glowing moments like this, that are the "how" for me. Sure, sometimes it can be too much, especially when it's early in the morning or all day long. But when I get to witness this kind of spiritual maturity, strength, and compassion, it blows me away.

And it's not just Reece. It's Lily too. The two of them growing up together, under the same roof, have given me quite an adventure. Lily is neurotypical, yet she is so loving and patient with her sister. I have no doubt this helps her earn such love and devotion from Reece, but I also know Lily feels the brunt of getting significantly less attention. Yet she bears it with more grace than most adults.

I am so incredibly honored to be the mother of these amazing little people and can't believe that God saw fit to lend them to me.

THE ALTITUDES OF ACCEPTANCE

My friend's story reminded me how children might sometimes increase our lives' complexities and chaos, but at the same time, they are precious gifts from God. Amidst all the ups and downs, children remind us to cherish our past, present, and future moments, especially inspiration that arises from people, experiences, and even the most unexpected sources.

If I am honest, over the time I worked at the school, I had grown comfortable with life as it was. Over the five years, my face had finally healed completely, all my implants had been installed without complications, and I felt recovered from the disappointment and emotional and physical trauma of my twenties. Now, I was simply used to the structure of my life, to things as they were.

I was finally commuting by bike and train almost all year round, driving only as needed to work, making enough money to live on, and enjoying the activities and responsibilities of my work environment. I also enjoyed plenty of mountain adventures. I knew I had something good. I wanted to keep my lifestyle. I had no reason to make changes in my life.

Or so it seemed.

Now that I was comfortable, I was at risk of being somewhat complacent! I was nearly twenty-eight and still had no idea what I wanted to be when I grew up. Working at a school with kids, I happened to be in good company, yet there were some students who had big dreams for themselves. Certain feelings came to the surface when I heard about their plans, poking me with the idea that I could pursue bigger things again too. There was more to come and more that I wanted, more that I could do, more that I could become.

It turns out not needing to change anything might be a good reason to make or allow a change. I think God likes what change does to us. He likes stretching us, exposing cracks in our worldviews, or causing a path to appear, one we never noticed or sought before that leads in a direction we've never gone. Such directions could be good for us, if only we would choose them; in fact, we might find it best to bend our autonomy to what God is directing our attention to, simply because we trust a new direction is best for us, even when it seems hard.

The obstacle? I knew no matter what altitude I reached, leaving behind the current lifescape and letting it become a memory was almost always required before I could accept and take on a new one. I think sometimes it takes a lot of work—including several divinely orchestrated exchanges with other people—for God to get us to start moving in a positive new direction.

I have also found that often, even before we are ready, God might decorate the distant view of a new lifescape by pouring in a little light and comfort or inspiration. Then, something in us yearns to respond, to go to it, to be there with it, whatever it might be.

In my case, it was 2015 before the hint of a new lifescape dropped into my view.

I hadn't been able to change my life trajectory in a long time, and it wasn't for lack of trying. But when an administrator asked me point-blank—"Hey, are you interested in taking evening and summer education courses at the college and getting your teaching license?"—her question jolted that subconscious concern about where I was going in my life.

I knew the administrator had lots of reasons to ask such a question of me. She knew I had worked at the school for four years. I had demonstrated self-awareness and become popular with these kids, and becoming a teacher was trending among several of my fellow paraprofessionals. Several had already taken on teaching roles that best suited their interests, just as I had with the dance class, and I really loved what I was doing with the students.

THE ALTITUDES OF ACCEPTANCE

Maybe this trajectory wasn't such a bad idea.

I asked her, "Do you know which course I would be most needed to teach?"

"That depends on your interests and whether you get a general or specialized certificate."

With my lips pursed in thought, I realized that wasn't a direct answer, but a general one. The administration had to already know my interests—environmental science, recreation, water education, and dancing—but those subjects weren't full-time standard curriculum topics. I raised my eyes to meet hers and see if I could tell what she was thinking. All I could see was that she was kind, and she knew this was a hard question to answer.

"I don't know exactly what I might be interested in—yet—but I'll think about it!"

"Best of luck with your decision! Let me know which way you decide to go," she patiently encouraged.

It didn't take me long that day to conclude that my current paraprofessional income felt like a ceiling and a trap. *I couldn't be paid more for what I was doing at this level of teaching, but what is holding me here besides the children? What could I do that the school would value and pay me for?*

And so it began. I could see the roller coaster in the distance, but before I could take the ride, I needed to do some research and preparation.

I stood in the classroom that was used for the environmental science course that the school had added a year ago. As I turned in a slow circle, I saw the themes and personalization on all four walls, showing a little world that had been confidently crafted with learning in mind.

But when I envisioned myself as a teacher and pondered my own four-walled world, nothing filled the blanks.

When I learned the environmental science teacher shared walls, space, and time with the high school physical science teacher, I was reminded about how the school had to do certain things that wouldn't be up to me much of the time. My voice might be heard but other factors could easily supersede my opinions and preferences, including funding, space, teacher seniority, and so forth. I knew me, and I was already very hard on myself. I wasn't sure I could rise above the political aspects of being a teacher enough to earn value as a teacher at a school.

The truth was, I appreciated the freedom of being a paraprofessional and how I rarely felt the need to take any work home. Evenings were generally personal time. And how had I been using that time? Hiking, being active, enjoying music and dancing, sharing meaningful experiences with others through recreation, taking environmental education courses, and, most recently, figuring out how to help increase general understanding of and interest in scientific truths about water. And I was healthier for it. Maybe this way of living couldn't last forever, but it couldn't be denied either.

Hence the reason I ended up in this classroom, asking as many questions as I could to know whether that last subject of interest fit into the course curriculum. The hydrologic cycle was taught in the environmental science class, but it sounded like a very short section compared to what might be needed to really understand the role of water resources. Then when I learned the course's inclusion was subject to annual curriculum changes and financial support, I inquired further and verified that the person teaching it might be asked to teach something else next year.

Hearing that, I felt dubious that I'd have job security if I didn't teach core curriculum too. Then, upon further consideration, I realized I had a huge question that was left unanswered.

Why would a school leave out or let go of such an important subject?

After teaching in the gym and dance classes, I knew the better versions of these young people came forward when they were making healthy food choices, being active, or getting outside, yet they knew so little about how the daily quality of their lives was connected to the natural world and good

THE ALTITUDES OF ACCEPTANCE

health practices. In fact, it seemed like they needed connections to the outdoors as much or more than I did.

That's when I concluded that education was important to me, but I was more *mystified* by these missing components of education than I was *interested* in having my own classroom.

I thought about several environmental topics— water, climate, ecology ... and investigated how these fields were tied to public health, nutrition, mental health, and outdoor education. Next, I noted how people in general, including my students, struggled to commit themselves to physical health and weren't as connected to nature as they could be—which led to another question.

Were specific mental conditions, including autism, triggered or worsened by certain behavior patterns, such as not going outside or investing time in physical exercise?

The answer seemed obvious. Most of the students succumbed to the lure of phones, texting, social media, and computer games like mice to cheese, while a few of the students were pretty consistent about getting outdoors or doing something active during their free time, and these students were usually the ones who had fewer emotional challenges.

However, others aimed for the nearest technological device ... and how healthy was that, as a habit? Looking closer, I decided this was a dilemma with the rest of the world too.

I come from the generation that knows what childhood and adult life was like before technology changed everything, and I believe mine might be the first and last generation that can understand—from personal experience— the blessings *and* predicaments that technological advancements have created.

It was easy to see why young people were becoming more and more centered around their devices. There were apps for everything now, and the internet made it so easy to speedily access anything. Under this trend, how could people, much less students, have any idea of the impact that technology had on their day-to-day or on the environment? Not enabling children with sufficient knowledge of technology in our modern age would be a disservice, but could we do that without centering their lives around it?

This was a cost-benefit analysis I didn't have enough information to make—yet.

Eventually, a few pieces of this puzzle fell into my lap.

A couple of years prior, the school had received newly donated Chromebooks. It was exciting, but I heard whispered concerns. Getting a bulk gift of technology was like being given a whole new world of opportunities for students—but it was a packaged deal with unseen, incredible costs. The school would have to absorb expenses for computer-based curriculum, general upkeep, and consider the capacity of the school's small IT department.

In a grant and donation-based environment, where would the money come from? Would this reduce budgets for other loved programs until they were no longer affordable due to expensive tech-related investments? Would such a cost be worthwhile for the sake of adapting education to the habits and abilities of the present population of children?

I also heard concerns about the rising accessibility and equity issues. Many of our students were skilled and disciplined with computers, but others were not. This was a truth all parents, teachers, and kids had to confront as the student's life centered around technology. Many projects would need to be completed on computers, and good student behavior earned extra computer time for those who wanted it. Therefore, knowing how to use computers was an advantage and relying on technology could easily become a habit with negative side effects, like an addiction.

Technological dependence could even preclude students from learning other skills they really needed. I noticed how some students with limited social skills tended to hide behind their technology, even when they might benefit from something social. I didn't know whether they could be motivated to choose better balance in their lives, but if they could be sucked in, something needed to be done to pull them back out.

Where was environmental education to help the children understand how they both benefited from and impacted the world they lived in? Why had this been left out of education?

The mystery of the situation both appalled and attracted me, yet it was all I had so far.

One bright and cheerful Saturday that same spring, I invited two friends on a hike who had never met each other. Ellen was tall, deeply kind, and had been a microbiologist for years. Mindy had studied social sciences, and her engaging personality had led to her success in social work. As the hike began, we realized that although our workplaces were worlds apart, several global issues affected all our fields and interests. Before too long, it felt like we'd all been friends forever.

As we rounded a lake and headed back down the mountain, the conversation shifted.

"Hey Deanna, have you thought about going back to school?" Ellen asked.

Uh—wait a minute, how did she know? I hadn't yet mentioned my current dilemma to her!

"I—well, actually, yes. Staying with my current job isn't right for me for the long term, and so far, I've tried everything to upgrade my life except get a higher degree, so I'm thinking about going that route. Maybe sooner rather than later!"

"It's good to keep your options open and explore," said Ellen. "What about you, Mindy?"

"I have, but I already have a Master of Science, and a PhD is a bit out of my price range."

"Me too. About both things. I've been thinking about going back for my PhD, but I'm not sure I'm ready to invest that kind of time or money."

"Wait, guys, when did you get your master's degrees?"

Ellen shared, "My undergraduate had a direct shot into a master's program. I just paid tuition for two more years using a small loan and scholarships and got it done. It was so worth it."

Then Mindy said, "When I was in my undergrad, all my professors said I would need an advanced degree eventually to do really well in social work. I didn't have a huge job prospect yet, so I figured it would be much more effective to get it all done at once. So, I applied to a few programs and got into a more prestigious university in another state."

"Simple as that?" I was doubtful as going back to school was a lot of extra work and money.

"Not really. I spent a lot of time in my last year of undergrad filling out applications."

I knew it! Paperwork is the necessary evil of going back to school. And I should know by now that anything I do to grow will feel uncomfortable.

"That was smart. Once you get off the education track, it's hard to get back on," said Ellen.

"I'll tell you one thing—additional school was expensive but totally upgraded my skills, income potential, and career."

Ah, yep, not only uncomfortable but also expensive. But who couldn't use a boost like that? We do have to pay for things. Living to work is not ideal, but working to live and live well means hard work. I could work hard. I really could. But money—that I didn't have.

I cringed a little, thinking of the kind of money they were talking about and considered how one was thinking about buying a condo, while the other was about to get married. There was no argument—they were doing well enough for themselves.

But was the big expense worth it?

I had to ask.

"Hey, Mindy, how did you afford another degree right after you finished your first one?"

"Well, when I applied and got in, the university offered me a job in my department and to cover my tuition. That required taking a minimum number of credits each semester."

"Nice! No debt. That's my favorite kind. Did you have to work forty hours a week?"

"Sometimes I had to work a lot, but they usually cap student job hours at certain salaries. Students can be program managers, research assistants, or even teaching assistants."

"Wow, that could work for me. Money is the one thing I don't have a lot of these days, but I don't think I'm the kind of person who can work full-time while going to school."

I had had a cousin whose type of brilliance could get four hours of sleep every night, work forty hours a week, and still end up with top grades—but that wasn't me. My kind of brilliance needed seven hours of sleep and although I could memorize anything I learned when I devoted at least an hour per day to reviewing notes per class, my methods were time consuming. Even though I usually received the grades I wanted, in my undergrad, I had often felt like I was working harder rather than smarter.

If I went back to school, I really needed to enhance my own productivity.

"I earned a few certificates this year and took a few trips to explore some career aspects, but so far those haven't worked out. Seriously, if I could find an affordable, meaningful degree, I might go back to school. Even after ten years!"

How difficult would it really be?

"So ... time for the big question then. What were your master's programs like?"

As they dove into the details, I stayed quiet, listening to them discuss experiences that had strengthened their careers and self-confidence. I liked what I heard about the courage they had to make changes in their lives to make space for their degrees. And this is when it occurred to me: Like the roller coaster, if I took the ride, once I got started, the only way out would be the way in, but God would be right there with me—even if I freaked out. And I probably would, knowing me.

Still, the benefits of going back to school seemed clear. It was less of a mystery now, and although it had never been plan A, B, or C, and even though more research was needed, I began to feel how a change like this could be the right choice.

I thought school was behind me in a different lifescape, not in front of me. But as a few fourteener trails suggest, sometimes the highest elevation in life is only attainable by those willing to trade a little altitude for a new approach—one that takes you down the valley and up a ridge you've never been on before.

To get there, I first had to decide what field to study, and I only had general ideas so far.

In the water courses, I had learned about water testing and treatment and exactly why it was so important for people to understand where fresh potable water came from. I was interested in learning about drinking water and contamination and how humans interacted with Earth's natural resources. That was one idea.

However, I also learned how human ingenuity and innovation had solved many of the problems created by our use of those natural resources. So, human dimensions and interactions with the environment were clearly important—there was no quality of life without them—but today's world provided conveniences that separated the public from environmental connections and stewardship. What degree would allow me to investigate more about that topic?

Most humans use computers every day. I had learned that building a computer requires four hundred gallons of water—that's more than the average American household uses per day, so it is no trivial matter to make a computer, and computers exist because of the combination of human ingenuity, resourcefulness, and water. But no one thinks about owning a computer in terms of water! In fact, most people don't think about most of life in terms of water.

Why? Because it's not taught in schools. For some reason I couldn't comprehend.

So, what about studying conservation, sustainability, and education?

Eventually, I decided I could try out an experiment. I could teach one of the water course group lessons to the students, just to see how they responded. My thought was, *What if knowing how water is present in their daily lives beyond the drinking fountain could convince tech-savvy, autistic kids to think about and conserve water in their lives?*

With this plan in mind, I worked to get permission to teach one hour of the hydrological cycle to the high school students in the early autumn of that year. Once I made it through all the bureaucratic red tape, I used the teacher training course stipend to help purchase and create my own educational equipment. Soon I had a lesson about the journey of a drop of water and was ready to present the lesson to the students.

I started by asking a question to connect the student's present knowledge with the lesson.

"What are the places we find water on earth?"

A chorus of responses came from all the listeners.

"Oceans!"

"Rivers!"

"Rain!"

"Excellent answers!" Then I noticed one young man at the back of the group sat looking off into the distance. I wanted a full class of learners, so I tried to draw him in.

"Hey, do you have an answer? I'd love to hear your thoughts!"

"Well ..."

As his voice faded into the space-filling word, it only took me a second to realize something awesome and unexpected.

"That's correct too!"

Stunned, the student looked blank for a moment, staring at me until he became aware of his own inadvertent humor and a sheepish, smiling expression filled his face. A well was another accurate place water could be found.

And with that, he took it upon himself to focus on the lesson with all his energy.

As I continued, some students were more into the information than others, but overall, the students laughed and caught on to the concepts of how water flowed through their lives. It really surprised them to find out how much water was in their technology! In fact, I don't think everyone believed me, but a little thought like that can resurface later and go a long way toward the truth.

However, it was a one-day deal. I taught the course only twice, and I knew it would cost more time, money, and space than the school could afford to try again.

But what if environmental education became the norm in school curriculums? Wouldn't it benefit all people to be more connected to the natural world, allowing whatever choices they made to help both current and future generations?

I believed the world needed good education and clean water, and if I could help with one or the other—or both—I might make a difference and find a future for myself. This got me thinking about how I could expand my horizons and focus on the benefits of environmental education for everyone, including people with and without autism.

But how?

It wasn't long before I was talking with college and university department representatives who agreed that children with autism could benefit from environmental education, and frankly, all children needed more access to and opportunities to be outdoors. However, because of state standards and funding restrictions the education system couldn't hit the mark. So, one thing led to another, and before I knew it, I had applied for and scheduled tours at two universities with two different but related master's programs—one was local, the other required travel and relocation.

But only one offered a position that allowed me to work for an income and pay my tuition.

The future seemed to hold a thousand mysteries, but in the end, I was thrilled when the University of Arizona accepted my application and offered me the job.

When it was time to leave the school in May for the last time, my friends and colleagues sent me off with an encouraging but bittersweet speech of thanks and a wreath as a gift. Once I reached my car, I paused to look back as I turned the key, realizing what driving away implied. Part of me was eager for the new adventure, but there was a growing part of me that would forever miss the time I had served the students and teachers. I was grateful and satisfied with my experiences and memories, but it was hard to believe the life I had known here was over.

And yet, this was the way of change—something lost, and something gained.

Although I had chosen my path and said my goodbyes, I still had all summer to earn money and figure out low-cost ways to move to Arizona.

I couldn't afford a moving truck, and my stuff needed to be transported to several places. The stuff I couldn't take to grad school had to be delivered to my parents' home while the rest needed to be transported to Arizona, one way or another.

So, I sold what I didn't need and then packed boxes for everything else. I marked them for Arizona or Colorado, and in due time, my parents and I arranged to meet halfway between Utah and Colorado for a campout, but when it came time to move my stuff to Arizona, an awesome thing happened. People showed up to help me and clear my path, almost as though they were chess pieces moving right into place for my big win.

First, I discovered a favorite roommate from college was living in Phoenix and had room in her garage to store things until I was ready to move into my Tucson apartment. A member of my church with an empty van, who was headed back to Phoenix from Utah in July, offered to deliver all my things to her home. At first, it seemed sketchy, but I felt trust for the man with the empty van!

By the end of July, everything I couldn't fit in my car was waiting for me in Arizona.

The timing was perfect because my Utah apartment lease ended on August 1st, and graduate school started on August 21st. It's odd to say, but I became homeless when my apartment lease ended. I simply packed my car to the windows and borrowed one friend's couch for the first week, and another friend's air mattress for the second week as I kept working.

Finally, it was time.

My parents joined me on my way to Arizona, and we camped near the Grand Canyon. It turns out few experiences are more perfect for starting new life adventures than a chance to see the Grand Canyon glow orange at sunset! It wasn't a mountain, but the view was incomparable.

That first day in Tucson proved to be nothing like I expected. Moving into my apartment came with surprises—the bathroom was as dirty as a jail cell, and there was no open space in the kitchen. My roommates hadn't prepared to welcome me with open arms, and after carrying all my stuff up three flights of stairs with my dad, the pressure mounted until I felt like crying.

I had come all this way for—this?

THE ALTITUDES OF ACCEPTANCE

My mother ended up cleaning that bathroom all by herself. She couldn't carry boxes due to having had recent arm surgery, and to her credit, she was still telling me optimistic ideas as we headed to the hotel for that first night. I wasn't willing to stay with strangers while people I loved were still close by.

As we fell asleep, a summer monsoon sailed in. At first, I wasn't sure if God was crying out of pride or if he was showing me something to hope for because Arizona storms are really something, and I love feeling thrilled by the electricity in the air and knowing the earth was being replenished. The next morning, the air was full of the adventurous, enchanting smell of creosote bushes, and all the ocotillos had sprouted green leaves. They were pokey, but they were beautiful!

The second day started out well, but all the emotions of the day before returned as I watched a lot of money leave my bank account, thanks to the first semester. Things were getting real! When I had a panic attack and had to explain to my parents what I was feeling, I sorrowfully asked my mother if it would be so terrible to end the chaos and just go home with them—even though everything had been going so well, I was no longer sure if it would all be worth it.

But mom said what she had always known, "You have it in you to handle this. If you don't stay, will you be okay that you didn't complete this adventure?"

It was the right question, so after taking a few breathers and taking some time to figure out how to fit my things in my new bedroom, and realizing that if I didn't unpack all my boxes, I could move to a better place when I found one, I stepped outside on the porch at the top of the three flights of stairs to pray. In the distance, I could barely see the tallest buildings on campus reflecting the warm glow of orange on the horizon, and I realized I had been in this exact spot before.

Well, not exactly three stories up standing on a staircase, but almost exactly twenty-two years ago, I had faced a new adventure and a new home. I remembered I had looked up at the mountains and knew I was there to gain a little altitude. I could accept that truth again. This was a new lifescape and a new adventure, and the roller coaster ride had already begun.

I knew I was here for the right reasons, and the best way *out* was *in*.

It seems tempting to think when God prepares the way and removes some obstacles, the path will just get easier, but God loves us enough to get us so far down the right path and then let us choose to stay and show up even when unexpected obstacles arise. He knows even when we make the right choice, there are still hard issues to resolve. He'll help us, but he won't do it all for us—we have to give him material to work—we have to make plans and put forth the effort so that he can help turn any sad or bittersweet situations into beneficial opportunities.

It starts with recognizing the need to grow, then making necessary changes and choices.

Even when the crazy ride through life doesn't feel awesome, there are usually a lot of awesome, experienced people who have believed in us and brought us to where we are. We can also rely on past experiences for guiding perspectives, and as we remember and apply what we have learned from each lifescape, we find out how to make the most of life's adventure.

I believe the choice to take the ride through life with God is a choice to trust that when all is said and done, we will have found joy in the ride and become all that we were meant to become.

The original plan was for fifteen people to go on this hike, but in the end, only two people joined me. First there was Stacie, my dark-haired hiking companion who had backpacked up the opposite side with her father. She hadn't been able to hike down due to serious hail and sleet arriving at the peak earlier than expected, so she wanted a redo.

Stacie and I had been eager to enjoy one last camping opportunity this summer, so we backpacked early the night before and set up camp about

THE ALTITUDES OF ACCEPTANCE

seven miles from the top. We then told stories and went to bed with the sun. I lay there under the calming blue light of the moon, hardly able to sleep for the anticipation building in my system for this hike. I couldn't be sure how much sleep I had gotten, if any, but adrenaline combined with awesome plans and people tends to be a good alarm clock, so we awoke quickly and prepared to join Brandon on the trail with our daypacks.

Brandon, a friend of mine from church, had come because he wanted to get stronger for an international trek he was preparing for later in the year. He parked at the trailhead that morning so that he could take the whole mountain in a single day.

Once we got together, we all agreed that we were hiking right into a perfect day.

As the path got steeper, the trail became nearly vertical in some places. At this altitude, I would classify myself as a good adventurer—been there, done that. However, in my mind, truly great hikers are those who seem unaffected by altitude. Such hikers pass me as though I'm standing still, have the advantage of long athletic legs, or even body compositions with greater lung capacity. Not quite there in my short frame, I tend to work very hard to keep my breath in check.

The glimmering horizon had only just turned to a glowing bright blue as our steep climb began to relax at around 12,700 feet. So far, I had moved through this multi-mile stretch as though it was a giant staircase, keeping one eye toward the top and the other on the beauty of the early morning glow, teasing out a glorious spectrum of colors among the disappearing shadows. Trees and flowers exchanged dazzling effects in every direction. There was hardly a cloud interrupting the sky, and a sea made of mountain ridges decorated the view to our backs.

About half a mile ahead, I could see where the trail finally leveled out. Watching as another hiker crested the ridge above, perfectly backdropped against the early morning sun, I thought about the sun on her face, and I craved the same! Then I saw something else.

"Brandon, I need a silhouette picture. Would you take it for me if I run ahead of you to the crest, when I get to that same point?"

"You're going to *run* up—*this*? After all of *that*?" He playfully waved his arm over 180 degrees of the slightly less-than-vertical trail as though he was showing off a talented musician at the theater.

"Well, yeah. Why not? I may never have this moment again. I don't want to miss it!"

Brandon grinned. "If you don't already know the answer to that question, you never will!"

He was right—finishing that steep stretch of a quarter mile with that kind of gusto would be a real challenge after the last seven miles, but if I could get there before the sun was too high—mere minutes away—then I would really deserve to have that picture.

With that motivating thought, a fresh endorphin spike fueled me into my uphill charge.

The sun caught my face as I crested the ridge. I turned, struck a pose, and hoped I had been still long enough for Brandon to get the picture. The perfect picture. The perfect day. The perfect warmth of the sun on Pikes Peak. Miles to go, but the hard part was over.

I closed my eyes for a moment, and tipped my head upward, soaking up the moment of rest in the sun's golden glow. Then I opened my eyes and gazed at my surroundings while moving slowly in a circle. The west was layered in ranges and basins. The north and south hosted a line of mountains. The eastern plains made me think I could see all the way to Oklahoma.

I found myself uncharacteristically stuck on the view of the valley to the east. It was hard not to notice the hundreds of homes and businesses that dotted the valley below, and the thousands of people down there who shared the same incredible light of a new day. The fact that there might be so many people looking up at Pikes Peak right now under the effect of a sunrise became nearly tangible as I considered so much *awesomeness* existing in the valley below.

I mused to myself, "All of those people have their own story—"

My story had taken me here today. Where would their stories take them?

THE ALTITUDES OF ACCEPTANCE

Even those who stood with me on this peak had joined me for a portion of my lifescape, but beyond these mountain paths, they were climbing different mountains in their own lifescapes. Like the people below, they were no doubt experiencing things I could never understand, yet altogether, and in our own way, we all had a role in filling this landscape with diversity and awesomeness.

As I observed my thoughts, I was just grateful God knew I was capable of, that I had finally ascended to this altitude and taken this path. There are so many paths to take in life, each path represents a decision, and every decision for better or worse influences who we become and what we believe, especially about God. As we each contemplate all the paths of our lives, I encourage us to adopt John Muir's overall sentiment about the value of experiencing the natural world—to make sure that some of those paths are made of dirt.

I used to think life was all about learning to see God's greatness, but now I know it's all that and so much more. It's about accepting God is in charge and is leading us closer to him. It's about getting to know him and identifying the greatness in ourselves too. It's up to us to find and follow every new opportunity to do what God needs us to do, to awaken to the best we have to give, and accept the package we've been given. It can be hard, but God promises we are also worth it.

As we make the most of the potential we have, we realize God doesn't see any of us as small. In fact, he knows exactly what we can do. And it's big.

We might be climbing the mountains God sends to us—or sends us to—but we are also beloved mountains to God. He doesn't shy away from his adventures.

Neither do I. And neither should you!

We all have a lot of work to do.

And when we take the ride with God, the greatest adventures are always yet to come.

ACKNOWLEDGEMENTS

They say it takes an entire village to raise a child, and if that's true, then it takes a fellowship of friends and family to build a life. This book wouldn't exist without the students and teachers who inspired the stories, or all the people throughout my life who are represented in these pages.

Thanks to the teachers I've known who have shown me by their examples what it means to love learning and teaching, and whose lives and experiences helped to guide my life's adventure. Thanks to the students whose lives and experiences inspired and uplifted me on a daily basis and have stayed in my memories through the years. You helped me find healing through humor, and your shared stories shaped how I now view myself and my relationship with God. Even though I haven't included your names here or throughout the book, I hope you know who you are!

A special thanks to countless friends and loved ones whose insights, encouragement, and input provided the much-needed support that has brought this book and its stories into the world. Since starting to write this book, we've enjoyed many hikes and conversations where I felt the value of the wholesome, hilarious, and true messages in my stories. I will be forever grateful to you for helping me find the right words in my heart and mind—for pushing me past the points of doubt and back into the conviction I needed to believe that these stories and experiences are worth sharing.

Thanks to my editor, Emma Tyler, whose attention to detail and ability to call me out kindly when I was holding back helped me learn how to show rather than just tell my stories. I know you know your craft because your capacity to talk about and value what my stories bring to the world has often been better than my own. Also, your insights and improvements to my writing have been pure intelligence at work. Your patience and understanding of your role in the writing process helped me survive through mistakes and necessary perspective shifts as well as find my writing voice. With you, I found the endurance to bring my manuscript to the finish line. Without you, I couldn't have pushed past the academic in my mind to find the storyteller in my heart.

Thanks to my proofreader, Liz Hanley, whose honest and kind feedback sent my mind soaring with confidence and creativity, right when and where I needed it. Thank you for the momentum and motivation you provided during those last hours of final tweaks and improvements. Thank you for sharing with me what my stories have done for you, for empowering me with a vision of what my book might do for others whose lives it hasn't touched yet.

Thanks to my cover artist, Dwayne Gayle. Your talent, attention to detail, and enthusiasm transformed the photographic evidence of my adventures into a striking design that captures the message of my book. It's exactly what I envisioned and more!

Thank you to the scriptorians of the past, the writers I have met along the way, and those who have written more contemporary writings about God. You have inspired me, and your influence revealed ideas that transformed my thinking and helped me discover the writing style for this book. Thank you for teaching me that writing is an imperfect experience, and for reminding me God has a way of guiding imperfect writers as well as paving the way for good books to find the people who need them and are ready for them.

Thanks to my excellent beta readers and all those who have read portions of my manuscript along the way! I have different relationships with all of you, and I will always be amazed by how your feedback was what kept me honest and helped me maximize the impact of my stories. I hope you know how much I value the time it took for you to navigate the long-winded portions, pull out the key points, and then smooth out the rough parts with new vision and understanding.

Thanks to my family, whose love and support has been patient and kind. You have walked with me throughout every lifescape. Thank you for showing interest in me and in our shared experiences. Though I have not mentioned all of you in my book, I appreciate how you've played key roles in my writing journey and helped me refine the spiritual wisdom I share within these pages. You understand my quirks, weaknesses, and strengths as your sister and daughter—and now you'll see them in my writing too! Thank you for loving me anyway, and for all you do to help me thrive—you keep me grounded and grateful.

To all my readers, as you interact with my stories or have questions, I would love to know your thoughts and what this book means to you. Email me at **altitudesofacceptance@gmail.com**.

REQUESTING READER REVIEW

Thank you for reading my book!

New writers and their books grow best when readers share their ideas. I need your input to make my stories and future writing better!

If you found this book helpful, please take two minutes to leave your honest review on Amazon. I appreciate your feedback. Let me know what you thought of the book and tell me a little of your story!

Thanks so much,

Deanna Kulbeth

SHARE THIS BOOK!

You probably didn't stumble on this book by mistake.

Thank you so much for reading this paperback footage of a writer's journey. No writer journeys alone, and I am grateful to all my readers who came along. I hope you find greater altitudes of self-acceptance and strength as you climb your mountains and follow your adventures. Remember to take God with you! His intent is not to leave us as we are, but rather to guide us to become a more perfect version of who already resides within us.

If you feel inspired to share this book with others who might benefit the way you have, or who have inspired you the way this book inspires you, please send them this book's Amazon link or find me on Facebook and Instagram under **@altitudesofacceptance**. The best hashtags to use when you post about your experience with this book on social media are **#lifescape** and **#altitudesofacceptance**.

Enjoy the natural world and every altitude you gain. You are awesome!

NOW IT'S YOUR TURN

Discover the EXACT 3-step blueprint you need to become a bestselling author in as little as 3 months.

Self-Publishing School helped me, and now I want them to help you!

Even if you're busy, bad at writing, or don't know where to start, you CAN write a great book.

With tools and experience across a variety of niches and professions, Self-Publishing School is the only resource you need to take your book to the finish line!

DON'T WAIT

https://self-publishingschool.com/friend/

Follow the steps on the page to get a FREE resource to get started on your book and unlock a discount to get started with Self-Publishing School.

CITATIONS

[1] Lewis, C.S. "The Problem of Pain." *The Complete C.S. Lewis Signature Classics*, Harper One, San Francisco, California, 2002, p. 549.

[2] Lonczak, Heather S. "Humor in Psychology: Coping and Laughing Your Woes Away." *PositivePsychology.Com*, 12 Nov. 2024, positivepsychology.com/humor-psychology/.

[3] We Are Sowing. In *Hymns of the Church of Jesus Christ of Latter-Day Saints*, Deseret Book Company, Salt Lake City, UT, 1985, pp. 216.

[4] Marsh, W. Jeffrey. "The Olive Press." *The Gift of the Atonement*, Deseret Book Company, Salt Lake City, UT, 2002, pp. 34–35.

www.ingramcontent.com/pod-product-compliance
Lightning Source LLC
Chambersburg PA
CBHW050849160426
43194CB00011B/2092